JOURNEY
ON THE CREST

WALKING 2600 MILES
FROM MEXICO TO CANADA

CINDY ROSS

THE MOUNTAINEERS
SEATTLE

THE MOUNTAINEERS: Organized 1906
" . . . to encourage a spirit of good fellowship
among all lovers of outdoor life."

Published by The Mountaineers
306 Second Avenue West, Seattle, Washington 98119

Published simultaneously in Canada by Douglas & McIntyre, Ltd.
1615 Venables Street, Vancouver, British Columbia V5L 2H1

Drawings by Cindy Ross
Cover photo by Todd Gladfelter

Manufactured in the United States of America

Library of Congress Cataloging-in-Publication Data

Ross, Cindy.
    Journey on the Crest : walking 2,600 miles from Mexico to Canada
by Cindy Ross.
        p.   cm.
    ISBN 0-89886-146-2 (pbk.)
    1. Hiking—Pacific Crest Trail.   2. Pacific Crest Trail—
Description and travel.   I. Title.
GV199.42.P3R67 1987
917.9—dc19   87-28160
                                                         CIP

2   1   0   9
5   4   3   2

In Memory of my Daddy
who took me on my first walks in the woods

The soul of man
was made to walk the skies
so that he may be freed
to grasp at something great
—Edward Young

Table of Contents

Introduction

Full moon at the bar. Some derelict grabs my leg. I shove him into the pole by the waitress station. "Knock it off!" He's ordered to leave. Last week someone grabbed my breast. He got the same treatment.

I play waitress at night. It puts food on the table and gas in the car. Pays the bills.

The looks, the lines. It gets old so fast. Anyone over twenty-one is usually divorced, drinking nonstop, pouring it down their throats. "Get everyone a round on me!"

I ask each one individually. "Do you want another one?"

"Don't ask! Just get it!"

I glare at him and continue asking. Drunks want everyone to get drunk with them.

"Sorry, pal. You're cut off. You're not leaving here in a car, on the road killing people. Not with my help."

I love the momentary power. I love the intimidation. The management hates it. Too bad. I make plenty of money. They make plenty of money.

The cook, the busboy, the manager, all say "Fuck you!" to us waitresses. Last night I reached my limit.

"Don't ever speak to me like that again!" I screamed in the full dining room. Later, a lecture was delivered. We were reminded that as waitresses, we are low on the totem pole and must respect all others, no matter how they treat us. Fuming inside, I kept my mouth shut.

Leftover Fettuccine Alfredo and Veal Marsala sit back on the ice maker. Customer leftovers. We zip by, grab a bite at the pig trough. Nine hours on our feet, not even a five-minute break. Waitresses aren't allowed desserts. I sell them to dainty women, knowing that they'll take only a few bites. The rest is mine.

Reciting the specials of the day, ordering pitchers of beer, buzzing around to the beat of the jukebox. I've got two pitchers in my hands when an inconsiderate customer sticks an empty bowl in my face. "More pretzels!"

I flash him a look that clearly says, "Shove it!" Mary, another waitress, says I'm not the same girl that I was when I came to the bar. I can feel myself hardening.

It's two in the morning. Two sweeties in the corner are dying over melting ice. They stare into each other's inebriated eyes. Don't they have homes? I take everything off their table, ask them to lift their hands while I wipe. They pretend not to notice.

"Straighten the forks when you leave, please." I skip out early before my boss sees me. Home. With a wad of greenbacks in my pocket.

Driving home, I grip the steering wheel. Tears fill my eyes. Is this what I'm reduced to? I've walked from Georgia to Maine on the Appalachian Trail. I've stood on the noblest peaks in the East.

Every accomplishment I've had is another support beam for my soul. So much majesty inside and no one can see it. I'm expected to get more pretzels. At home I slump on my bed and pull the cash from my smoke-saturated pockets. Escape money. Another long-distance hike.

"Why not settle down and marry?" they ask.

I dream of a rustic home in the mountains, a loving husband. They aren't found in bars. Neither is adventure or freedom. To walk in the wilderness is freedom. To work a routine, in a subservient situation, is death. In this environment, people merely maintain their existence. I want to live deeper.

They ask me: "Why hike the Pacific Crest Trail, Mexico to Canada, for two thousand, six hundred miles?"

All I can say is: "How can I not?"

PART I

1

On the Verge

March 1982

Early season running. Upper thighs rubbing, chafed legs, double chin. Hiding in sweat pants and shirt until I'm far from the road and down where the river flows and no one can lay eyes upon me.

I dive into the garden. Hair piled on my head, clothes drenched with river water, head dripping with sweat. I'm harvesting tea. Hanging it to dry in the root cellar. Later, I'll separate

Cindy exercising

the leaves from the stems, iron them into individual bags for those cold Sierra nights.

A little Dan Doan's "Exercises for Backpackers and Cross-country Skiers." I lift my legs higher. Twenty on each side. This one's for Mount Whitney.

I race to the stove. Twenty-five pounds of kidney beans are boiling over. Skimming off foam, baking soda foam, to prevent gas, a common ailment for long distance hikers. Together with the beans, there are packages of dried green pepper, chopped onions, ground venison, and tomato powder: High Sierra chili.

The dehydrator hums. The heater turns on and off drying twenty heads of cut up cauliflower. Tomorrow I'll slice fifty pounds of carrots. Earlier this week, hundreds of grapes were cut in half.

I grab my inner tube, throw on my stretched-out bathing suit, shove a copy of Edward Abbey's *Desert Solitaire* down my suit against my oil-soaked chest, and go down to the river. To learn, to dream, to plan.

In my farmhouse there are three different beds, in three different rooms. I take turns sleeping in them all—it depends on where the mice have decided to spend the night. From out of the walls they come for my marinated mackerel and chopped schnitzel. They are competing for my dried food, piled high to the ceiling in plastic garbage bags.

All this for dried food.

All this for the PCT.

Last night I had dinner with my parents. Afterward, Mom washed, I dried. I steered the conversation toward the trail and ran up against her usual negative reaction.

"Mom, you don't ever listen."

"I always listen to you, but you talk about the trail *all the time*. And I told you, I don't want you to go, and I don't want to hear about it. Period."

Well, who am I supposed to talk to? Who am I supposed to share my excitement, joys, fears, and anxieties with? Who understands? I am afraid. There are so many questions and more keep coming.

I'm not so proud that I'll pretend I'm not nervous or scared or apprehensive. I'm not a wonder woman. I have very strong desires and goals. But it's this fear of the unknown, the uncontrollable. I am going into a strange land and feel very much alone.

Appalachian Trailway News *(Sept./Oct. 1981)*
Looking for a partner to hike the Pacific Crest Trail.
Leaving late April '82. Will be going slower than usual to write and illustrate a book. Will get as much completed as possible before bad weather sets in. Cindy Ross.

Four individuals write and appear to be possible partners. Three live close by, so we manage to meet and discuss our goals. All will plug into the hike at convenient times. Only T.P., a fifty-seven-year-old man from Miami Beach, whom I haven't met, plans on going the entire stretch. His enthusiasm for the trek and for being my partner seems extreme. Still, I don't want to be alone. I look to our meeting in San Diego with a tinge of anxiety.

JFK Airport, New York City

"You can't take that stick on the plane," the stewardess informs me, five minutes to takeoff. I rush for a box and conceal my "weapon." I ask for a window seat and hope for a companion to share my enthusiasm. A white-haired senior citizen sits down. Shocking pink rouge blotches her cheeks, brilliant turquoise eye shadow collects in her wrinkled lids. The same blue in her suit. The same blue in her gaudy costume jewelry. She stares ahead.

My own face, scrubbed clean, free of makeup, hair in a braid, gazes out the window. The Appalachian ridge glides by and I whisper farewell.

Across the Midwest, my eyes strain for the first peak of the Rockies. My heart quickens. I study the buried range. Snow, everywhere snow. Half hour later, another snowy backbone passes under us.

"Those must be the Sierra Nevada!" I exclaim to my seat mate. "I'll be walking through them soon!"

Tasha (left) and Cathy

"That's nice."

When we didn't land for hours, I realized that I never saw the Sierra, just scattered ridges of the Rockies. My seat mate never noticed.

The Pacific Crest Trail lies waiting. So does T.P., my enthusiastic responder. Cathy and Tasha, two old AT (Appalachian Trail) friends, are driving me from Los Angeles to the Mexican border, and we'll pick up T.P. en route. Another AT friend, Matt, will meet us at the border, to see me off on my first weeks. T.P., however, plans on staying by my side the entire trip.

"What if he's a weirdo?" I ask the girls, staring, depressed, at the California coast whizzing by.

"Just try it for a week or two. Maybe one of your other partners will come out early if it doesn't work."

T.P. and I corresponded for six months prior to the trip. In his letters he sounded competent and acceptable. When we began having telephone conversations, however, I grew increasingly wary. He was awfully chummy and suggestive for an older man, especially for a stranger. Still, his dedication and laborious preparations impressed me and I was willing to give him a try.

He rises from the chair as we enter the restaurant in downtown San Diego. "Oh no!" is all I can say to myself. He has close-cropped white hair, a remnant of his Navy days. Wears powder blue, double knit "hiking" pants, a polo shirt pulled taut over his pot belly, new boots with "only forty miles on the tread," he says happily. "Want to save the soles."

As we talk at the coffee counter, he sticks his face close to mine. It makes me nauseous. His eyes bulge out of his head. His teeth are rotten. I slump on my stool, not even able to look at him while he speaks nonstop.

This is strictly gut intuition. That's all I'm going on, but it's loud and clear. The girls pull me into the bathroom.

"We've never seen you like this. You'd better say something."

"I can't! I can't hike with him. I can't even look at him. You tell him." We file out of the ladies' room.

"T.P." Cathy starts. "I think there's been some serious misconceptions here."

"Five months is a long time to be together out there." Tasha adds.

Frantically, he turns to me and says, "Let's try it for a week! Oh, I know it can work! I know it! Just give me a chance. Trust me."

"I'm sorry," is all I can mutter, as I stare down at the dirty linoleum squares.

We're driving T.P. to the county bus station. The bus can take him to the border. I climb in the back with Tasha. She puts her arm around me, clutches my clammy hand. My stomach's in knots.

Up front T.P.'s face is in Cathy's for a change, jabbering aimlessly about mindless things.

The question of partners is not pursued again. We lift his ninety-pound pack, complete with rope, hatchet, shovel, and saw, out of the car, shake hands and race to the border for a head start, arriving twenty minutes before the bus.

I later heard T.P. got off the trail after only two days. He told a hiker it wasn't what he expected. So much for partners through the mail.

2

Break Down, Shake Down Period

April 30—Mexican Border

A shot-up, defaced sign sticks on the barbed wire fence, marking the border of Mexico and the beginning of the Pacific Crest Trail. It separates the two worlds. Mine begins here. A lone, white shack stands in the background—it's probably in every PCT hiker's starting photograph.

It's a strange land. Dusty, sandy soil, sagebrush, mountains lie in the distance with no trees growing on them. Did someone drop me on another planet? This is so different from rural Pennsylvania, with its winding streams, moist air, and deciduous trees. I feel numb and dazed, like an alien.

With stiff new gym shorts, spongy muscles, a cheesecake for celebration, and a bottle of champagne, the lone PCT hiker and her send-off crew meander down the earthen road. I fix my eyes on the distant Laguna Mountains and try to visualize the future. Impossible!

The first day's walk from the border is on roads. After that, we hit a most remarkable, well-made trail. This section of the Pacific Crest Trail is light years ahead of our Eastern footpaths.

Back home, we toil manually with mattocks, shovels, and scythes. Here, they take miniature bulldozers and move the earth, carving a perfectly level, uniform tread, which wraps and contours up and down the mountain, with never more than a ten percent grade, leaving me barely aware of an elevation change. "Wrap-around-trail," we hikers call it.

However, much of the Pacific Crest Trail in southern California is incomplete. When we hit a section where the trail has yet to be built, we have a choice of an alternate trail, a road, or a cross-country adventure. So the chances of running into other through-hikers are slim. So much for camaraderie! Having Tasha, Cathy, and Matt for company is a complete joy, but their days with me are numbered.

Water sources are few and far between. Normally, in this kind

Cindy at the Mexican border

"Wrap-around-trail"

of heat, I cannot function without soaking my entire body in the cool liquid. The only water for miles is the two gallons on my back (a burro! I feel like a damn burro!) and I'm certainly not going to use it on my head!

The sun is trying to break me. There is no release. I drop behind the others to rest. No sense getting sunstroke my second day out. Already I feel dizzy and light-headed.

The body is not doing so well. My feet are not cooperating. Yes, the boots are broken in. This is the sixth set of blisters I received from these marvelous boots. My feet are swollen an entire size larger, from the five pounds of menstrual water weight I gained. At camp I peel back the moleskin. Three-layer-deep blisters! Pretty soon I'll be striking bone.

I devise a new way to walk. Sliding my feet along, barely

picking them up, certainly cuts down on heel friction. The draw-backs are that I don't move very quickly and I choke on the dust that I stir up.

Then there's the problem of the rash between my legs, caused by chafing. I walk like a duck, trying to keep my legs apart. At night I sleep with a sock sandwiched between my thighs, to prevent further irritation.

And sunburn! Nothing like sleeping in a down bag rated to zero with a toasted body. While hiking, even my hands fry from clutching the top of my hiking stick. Matt looks over worriedly, thinking of the weeks ahead together. Cathy and Tasha chuckle. They'll be home shortly. "Poor Cindy," they say. "Does Cindy know what she's getting herself into?"

Cindy's not into all this trail nonsense yet. I'd better get myself psyched though. It's a long, hard road ahead. I'm miserable, but I've had enough experience to know that it's going to pass.

The Laguna Mountains are a tease. Up here, trees thrive. Big, gorgeous Jeffrey pines sway in the breeze. Huge cones lie scattered on the ground and the temperature drops. Wonderful, comfortable, cool. This is what I came to see. But it only lasts a day. Soon we are back in the arid, dry land, with push-up lizards and rattlesnakes.

We heard that PCT through-hikers cross the left arm of the Mojave Desert. That is hundreds of miles from here. What I am finding out is that all five hundred miles of the PCT in southern California are predominantly desert. Even the mountains are desert! (High desert, low desert. What's the difference? asked the Pennsylvanian.)

At Mount Laguna, Tasha and Cathy exit. They pick the right place. Nurse Cathy prepares the first-aid bandage for my laceration before departing. I had moved away from a rattlesnake, quickly, and right over a small cliff.

My heart is heavy. These two women are so wonderful to be with. They understand. They have the same discomforts. But I still have Matt's company for the next week or two. He is faring very well. He worked heavy construction before coming west and doesn't even use his hip belt to carry his weight. I hope he can stand me alone, when there are not others to share the troubles and complaints.

A postcard from my AT friend Todd, who was here two weeks ago, arrives at the Mount Laguna post office. "Get ready," he says, "A twenty-seven-mile dry stretch. Then an eighteen, a twenty-two, and a nineteen. Bone dry."

We carry collapsible bladder bags that hold two and a half gallons of water. Each quart weighs two pounds, adding twenty extra pounds. Certainly a joy to throw on my already overburdened body.

Dehydration is a very real danger out here. The air is exceedingly dry. We're from the humid East, used to sweat sticking to our bodies for days. Out here, we're barely conscious of perspiring because the air evaporates perspiration as fast as it forms. So we don't take in enough fluids and become dehydrated. A person must be aware of what is going on out here.

Gains in personal hygiene from the instant whisking away of sweat — and body odor — are offset by the pervasiveness of desert dust. It covers our bodies and forms very artistic swirls down our legs and arms, as though it were flowing. "The disease," we dub this condition, and it usually arrives two to three days after leaving town. As a result, conversations are held at least ten yards between hikers — otherwise, you eat trail.

"Can you walk any faster?" Matt inquires.

"Nope!"

Our mileage picks up to fourteen or fifteen miles per day. That's pretty good for a total cripple with a sixty-pound pack.

The Desert Divide Trail. Matt and I walk north along a backbone of high desert mountains. Below is the Colorado Desert and the Salton Sea, a massive catch basin, most of which is dry this time of year. These mountains block moist air coming from the ocean. It rarely gets to the low desert. With few clouds to block the sun's rays and very little water to evaporate, the land cannot cool itself off during the day. The temperature can only go up. Next to

The Desert Divide

Death Valley, the Colorado Desert is the lowest, hottest desert in California. Happily, we just look on.

Up here, only drought-resistant shrubs grow: manzanita, tobacco brush, and holly oak. They reach only chest high, rarely taller. I try to compact my body and crawl under one for a bit of relief. The sage smells wonderfully fragrant as it cooks in the hot sun. I crush its velvety leaves in my hand, holding it to my nose, hoping it intoxicates me and numbs my pain.

Why am I here? Just why am I doing this trail? I have asked myself that question many times this week. Frequently during the day, I contemplate quitting. But I want new things in this life of mine. I want to experience, change, grow. Growth is ofttimes painful. When pain and discomfort are this great, my reasons for being here become foggy and that inescapable "WHY?" screams in my ears.

"Chariot Canyon is gold country," Matt says, reading the torn-off guide book pages in his hand, as he walks. A dozen times a day we must check direction. He guides me; I just try to keep my body moving forward.

He identifies each mine as we pass the broken-down claims: Cold Beef Mine, Golden Chariot Mine, Lucky Strike Mine. How utterly romantic. Coal mining, which has scarred my home state, doesn't even *sound* romantic.

I envision bearded mountain men wearing sweat-stained leather hats, high boots, clothes that haven't been washed in weeks, smelling like the earth, like dirt. Pans in hand, hunched over a stream, sifting for precious nuggets.

But here, the mines look like oil rigs—large, steel contraptions built on top of the earth's surface. And there are no streams.

"KEEP OUT. BEWAIR. NO TRESPASIN"

It's late. The sun's rays have long since crept up the valley walls, and we frantically look for a place to sleep. I spot a mountain man on his front porch, staring down, just watching.

"How ya doing?" I yell. "Any place to camp around here?"

"Six miles down the road, same direction you're going."

"Right!" I mutter under my breath. As I grow increasingly thirsty, I remember a piped-in spring, a half mile back, near an overgrown field, with tremendous dried cow chips lying about, and the same "NO TRESPASIN" signs.

It's tough, but I talk Matt into going back. I can't hike any farther. He's angry and doesn't want to do anything illegal.

"You're delirious!" he yells, "You didn't eat or drink enough today." That night he is no longer mad, just indifferent to me. Up to now, we have shared a ground cloth and slept side by side.

Up to now we have given each other back rubs every night, just like we did years ago on the AT. Tonight, he sleeps on his own separate tarp, fifteen yards away, and speaks of getting off the trail earlier than originally planned.

I had no expectations of this long-ago friend. We had kept in touch over the years and when he heard I was going hiking, he asked if he could join me for a bit. We didn't know one another well, but it didn't concern me. I was just hoping that we could get along.

The defunct village of Warner Springs lies a day or so away. He'll make up his mind by then—to stay another week or go home. I have a strong feeling he's had enough.

Down to the San Felipe Valley and the long dirt-road walk between the two mountain walls. Open range here, with cattle grazing everywhere. They watch us, looking real cocky and arrogant, until we're nearly on top of them. Then they trot off swiftly, kicking up a cloud of dust.

Matt is waiting for me under the only tree in the entire valley. I throw my pack off, glad to have it away from my body for a while. I lift the filthy water bottle to my lips, checking out the bottom to see how much crud I am disturbing. I gulp the tepid liquid

San Felipe Valley

a bit precariously, so it spills down the sides of my mouth and into my cleavage, cooling my breasts.

"Do you ever share with folks how you feel about the Lord?" Matt asks. I glance at the noonday sun blazing overhead.

"What?" I ask, a little delirious.

"Do you ever share with folks how you feel about the Lord?" Matt reads the Bible every night before retiring.

We walk along the San Felipe highway. Huge, dark red splotches mark the road every quarter mile—cattle that were too inquisitive. Cars speed by, providing some sort of breeze, however sickening. Like the blast of heat from an opened oven door.

"I prefer to live my faith quietly, Matt. I don't like shoving my beliefs down people's throats."

"I'm not shoving anything down your throat!" he snaps, surprising me. I don't understand his outburst, but argue my point in defense. The debate turns into heated battle over who is "saved" and who is "damned." He vents his frustration like a steam geyser going off, and my feelings of alienation increase. We finally call a cease-fire and Matt takes off down the highway, heading for Warner Springs. His sun-bleached, hairy legs move swiftly toward the horizon. That was it, it's all over, I thought. Second partner down the tubes. I slow down my pace, feeling relieved and unburdened, yet nervous about what lies ahead: solo hiking.

I stop for some peanut butter and contemplate life, lean back against a rusty highway marker and sit down in the gravel. It won't be long before the gang joins me from back East, I think to myself. I'll only have a few days to get through alone. I can manage with a map and compass. Bob, another old AT friend who answered my ad, is due to come out soon. Maybe I can convince him to join me earlier.

In bygone days, Warner Springs was a high-class resort, then it went bankrupt. Cottages of concrete painted to look like adobe line the four quaint streets—all deserted, all boarded up. Only the post office is open.

Rain pelts the asphalt, bouncing off the steaming ground. (I

Matt

never thought it rained in southern California.) Matt is there when I arrive in town, but he barely looks at me and says as little as possible. He does inform me, however, that two male hikers are on the other side of the building. I jump up quickly to go greet them. Hikers! The first I've encountered since the border!

The two men look young and thin, with skinny underdeveloped legs, but they are carrying equipment that tells me they know what they're doing.

"Where are you going?" I ask.

"Canada," replies the older of the two.

I persist. "Where are you guys from?"

"Massachusetts," says the same hiker. His voice has a heavy New England accent; its tone says that he is not nearly as interested in me as I am in them. They continue packing their supplies and I sadly move back to Matt. We huddle in a corner on the cold concrete porch of the once-hopping hotel.

Wool shirt wrapped around my legs, I tenderly open each of my twenty-five letters, reading round after round of cheering words from family and friends. They must know I'm having a tough time.

The lady in the post office said she never saw so many letters for a hiker, said I must be a celebrity. No, just loved.

I put the mail aside. "Is everything all right, Matt? Do you feel distant or close to me?"

"I don't feel like your husband!" he yells.

Huh? What does that mean? His outbursts are making me wonder if we're even friends any more.

A dilapidated pickup pulls up and ends the strange conversation. I wonder if we'll get chased for loitering. A big, burly Mexican comes walking over to us. "Need a place to stay?" he asks the four of us. "Pile in!"

The man's name is Jes. He takes us to a tacky orangey-pink cottage, with no glass in the windows, the insides stripped down, a fireplace jammed with cardboard boxes, and old hiker paraphernalia and cast-outs lying about. The floor needs a good sweeping, but the toilet works, the faucet runs, and we're right next to the hot springs that once made the town famous.

Jes says to be careful of the hot springs. "Don't stay in too long or the warmth of the water will make you fall asleep and drown. Hang onto a rock maybe."

Palm trees line the perimeter of the pool. Steam rises all around, giving the air a misty, surrealistic look. We dive in, not bothering to take our clothes off. The filthy garments need a washing too. Dog-paddling to keep our heads up high, we breathe some fresh air away from the sickening sulfur. The mineral turns my silver bracelets a copper color and makes my blisters tough.

Matt says that he's returning to Maryland. I'm not surprised. I ask why he came, why he sold nearly everything he owned to buy a motorcycle and ride four thousand miles to hike with me. I was the reason, he says. Somewhere, something went wrong. I am doing my best. For Matt, it isn't enough.

I ask the two from Massachusetts if I can tag along to Anza, my next town stop. There I'll meet Bob, who has kindly agreed by phone to come out earlier. To me, traveling with two strangers, even if they are uninterested in me, is better than hiking alone.

"Doesn't matter" is Dan's answer. He's the older and more outspoken of the two. Dale, the other, is silent. His unemotional eyes, framed by a red bandanna and brown curls, stare ahead. I know the boys from Massachusetts will move along at a good clip, will really motor. So I get smart. To go along with my new set of tough feet, I throw out half the stuff in my pack, and mail it ahead. If I'm going to keep up with these boys at all, I have to lighten my pack. "We usually take a break every five miles, every two hours," leader Dan says briskly, as we move out over Lost Canyon Road, totally ignoring the exposed, blazing sun. I push up my glacier goggles, mop my sopping brow and think, "Like clockwork. What happens if I die between those two stupid hours? Keep dragging?"

On one ascent I start to die. "At the top we'll rest," Dan says. It turns out to be one of those famous Pacific Crest Trail ascents that go on for hours, wrapping around mountains that, I swear, continue forever. I go around one and there, stretched out in front of me, is another half mile of trail.

My body can't seem to take this heat. I get so fatigued, dizzy, queasy in my stomach. I do not feel like eating, which is very strange for me. I just can't get out of the sun. I like my plush mountains back home, ferns, moss, sunlight filtering through the pines. God, what I wouldn't do to get out of this sun!

I can no longer keep up with the guys. I accept this fact and slip into my own pace. I know I have to watch myself so I don't get too far behind. I yell to them, "Don't cross an intersection if it looks shaky, without waiting for me."

Dan yells back not to worry. "We usually stop around five, five-thirty. That's a full eight-hour workday."

I look for Dan's bright yellow bandanna on the upcoming stretch. We wave across the gorge. I time myself to see how far behind I am, how long it takes me to arrive at that particular point. I look for their little pack bodies winding around the mountains, for where I have to go next. In the curve there, in the crease of the mountain, before I wrap around the other side, there may be a bit of shade. I live for that hope.

We are all looking for a spring, calculating that we'll hit it about four-thirty. But they descend into a canyon and climb out of it, totally unaware of what they're doing. I see where the spring probably was and yell to them. No answer. So I continue to walk and walk. Four-thirty, five-thirty, six-thirty. I'm trailing behind. I see their little figures way off in the distance, far off, continuing to

Dale (left) and Dan

ascend. The mountain never quits and neither do they. Are they trying to lose me, trying to get rid of me? I finally catch up with them at a slow-moving algae spring. They act cool to me.

"You won't hike much past seven-thirty, will you?" I ask.

"Probably not," Dan says. "It won't be light enough." Little did I know what another hour would do to me. We soon cross a dirt road, a perfect place to camp.

"Where are you going?" I yell. "I have two gallons of water for us!"

"Just seeing what is on the other side of the mountain."

Didn't they learn that there is just more ridge and more ridge and more ridge? I have everything I need to camp alone, but don't even consider it. The fear of traveling alone on this obscure trail is more unsettling than the thought of following these two men like a fool. It's getting later, and I'm really beginning to die. I sit down and sob, I can't seem to stop. They march around these mountains like troopers!

I need some diversion. Something to keep my mind off this misery, so I think of old lovers and why they didn't work out and which ones there's still hope for. My mind drifts. Always back to the pain, and then the tears start again.

The full moon is high in the sky. The sun is long down. As we climb higher, a breeze picks up and I feel more vulnerable to exhaustion and hypothermia. In the desert, your sweaty, hot body becomes cooled and chilled as soon as the sun goes down. During the day, when you need wind, it's not there. In the chilly evening, when you need it least, it comes. Soon I hear a whistle.

"Where are you?"

"Up here!" Relief!

I can barely talk or look at them when I come into sight. All choked up, I say, "I didn't think I was going to make it, guys."

"Oh really?"

My legs ache tonight and burn from the sun. Two hours into the night, my right eye really begins hurting like hell. My contacts should have come out long before I quit, but I thought I'd be stopping soon. As soon as the plastic lens is removed and contact is made with the lid, the pain begins. Salty tears make it unbearable.

It feels like broken glass in my eye! I dump my iodized algae water over a wool sock, trying to make a cold compress. It doesn't work, too absorbent. Groping, trying to feel where things are: my flashlight, my bandanna, my open water bottle, the lid nowhere to be found. The tent fly rises and falls from the night wind.

I sleep little and suffer like hell all night. I'm looking forward to Anza. Once I'm in town, I can let Dan and Dale go on. Bob will be there. It will be splendid to hike with an old AT friend. Slow and easy. I sure need the rest.

It's been a week. My God, a week! I am in another world, a world hard to imagine before I left. I read of what I would hear and see, feel and smell, but something so foreign can never be imagined.

The trail to this point has been difficult. It is not as enjoyable as I had hoped, at least not yet, but I have no plans for quitting. The blisters are getting tough. The first layer of burned skin is peeling off. My body is getting hard. And the trail has given me some pleasure. It hardly ever rains here, and there are clear, star-filled

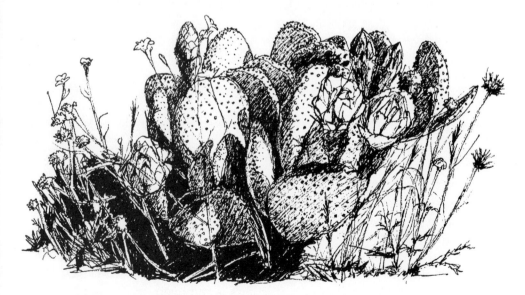

Cactus

nights, with breezes blowing constantly. The high desert is in full bloom, so many new wildflowers, new bird songs. But I can't see them joyously through my suffering. An opaque window of pain blocks out the joy. Folks said, "Oh, once you get out to California, to the West, you'll never want to come home."

Well, it's been one hundred miles so far. I've been in mountains higher than my beloved New Hampshire Whites, I swam in a hot springs, I ate Mexican food, but so far, my heart still belongs to the East!

Bob

3

Life With Bob

May 7

Bobby is coming! Salvation! Security! I'll never be alone on this crazy trail again!

Just forty-eight hours ago, Bob, a grad student in geology at the University of Maryland, was taking exams. Then he dropped out of the sky and raced to the trail. With geology still fresh in his mind, he teaches me all sorts of interesting facts about landforms, as we truck up Penrod Canyon.

He is twenty-four years old, blonde, with incredibly light blue eyes. He wears a Scottish wool cap and speaks in a ridiculous, phony Scottish accent. He's trying to be cute and almost succeeds.

His pale, skinny body is either covered with cotton cloth or sunscreen #15. Now we take our breaks in the shade. The desert sun is merciless.

He follows me closely, getting accustomed to looking for snakes. Four today, mostly rattlers. None warn us. They have a tendency not to rattle in this part of the world. I can feel Bob flinch every time a lizard scurries into the brush. It takes some getting used to, keeping your eyes and ears alert, yet staying relaxed and not jumping every time you hear motion.

I feel good today, the best I've felt all week, both in mind and spirit. Bob is such a pleasure to hike with. Living in a hiking environment again, memories of the Appalachian Trail come flooding back. These early weeks I compare the two trails and it's comforting to know that Bob hiked that trail also and shares these feelings.

Mount San Jacinto is two miles high. It is snow-covered all winter and spring. Right next to it is Palm Springs, in the low desert, with an altitude of about four hundred feet. Palm Springs gets seven inches of rain annually; San Jacinto gets five times that. All the moisture from the ocean is dumped right here on the mountain, leaving practically nothing for the land to the east.

It will take two days of nearly continuous upgrade to reach Mount San Jacinto's ridge. From desert shrubs and scorching heat to alpine firs and snowdrifts and then back down to desert again.

At six thousand feet, the wind is ferocious. We walk into it, fighting with all our energy, Gore-tex glued to our limbs, voices barely audible over the roar. After what seems like hours of struggling, we arrive at a side trail and race down the three-quarters of a mile to a campsite and sheltered safety. Good-bye ridge!

Winds shook my flimsy tent last night. It rose and fell like a great sleeping monster. Twice I had to crawl out and snap down the fly. We were hit by fog in the night. When warm, moist air that is forced up a mountain hits cold temperatures up above, it can condense into fog that whips over the mountain tops. Water vapor may freeze right to the tree limbs, as the saturated air blows through the branches.

Sounds of frantic activity from other campers nearby tell us they're moving out, getting off the mountain fast. And we're going back up there? Glory be! In the warmth and safety of my tent and bag, I dread the coming day.

We finally pull out at eleven. Mist and fog continue to race over the crest. We climb higher toward the summit of Mount San Jacinto. Socks on my hands, high energy food in my pouch, rain gear fastened down, I'm willing to make a go of it.

The wind howls. There is awesome beauty on this ridge! The manzanitas have half-inch-thick ice on their leaves and branches, which transforms them into clusters of flowers. The smooth, orange-red bark glistens. Bob is crouched by a bush, fumbling to make cold, stiff fingers operate his camera.

"This is crazy!"

"I know it!"

I go first, and Bob follows. We're searching for Apache Spring. Still ascending steadily, we enter a burned area and lose the trail. The gnarled manzanitas are burned off and charred. Limbs are stark naked and exposed, twisted like our stomachs. It is so grisly and rough up here, so inhospitable. When the trail reappears, we follow it for what seems like miles, losing elevation, life-forms changing, yuccas appearing.

"Bob, are you sure this is where we're supposed to be?"

"No. I'm following boot marks. They're all going this way."

We don't care if we're on the right trail. Now our number one goal is finding water. We approach every gully with wetted lips and hopeful hearts, but nothing. Finally, I spot a hole with slimy algae water.

"Tank up!" Bob says. "Double dose of iodine!"

"This stuff even smells like things are living in it!"

The tall pines disappear, giving way to chaparral. Our trail finally empties onto a road, where there is a sign stating, "Desert Divide Trail—PCT—5 miles." Holy hell! Five miles down the wrong trail! But we turn simultaneously and head into town. Tomorrow we'll find the trail.

A few minutes later we're racing toward the town of Idylwild, in the back of a pickup driven by some crazy rock climbers who evidently feel we need a good time. They kindly offer to be our chauffeurs while in town.

We plan on only staying one night in this small, Swiss look-alike town, which offers the best eateries since we began. But the storm doesn't abate. For three and a half days we hang out at the base of San Jacinto. As the rain falls on us, we can see the mountain shrouded in snow and ice, growing whiter every hour.

Every day the mountain spits out more hikers, either lost like us or forced down by the storm. Soon there are seven—me, Bob, Dan and Dale, Sue and Dave, a fair-haired couple from California, and their friend Melissa, a dark-haired, tan, Mexican beauty.

The rock climbers out here have a great game they play to stay limber between climbs. It's called Hackey Sack and is played with a small, leather ball that you hit to one another using only your feet. Counting the climbers that picked us up, there are ten of us, and for three straight days we play in parking lots, campgrounds, and along the highways, as we walk back and forth to our pig-out meals. A better time in town was never had.

One restaurant serves massive portions that even hikers have difficulty finishing. Its "Sunshine" omelet boasts three eggs, Monterey jack cheese, sour cream and chili peppers inside, with guacamole on top. Fresh fruit is on the side and all the homemade breads and muffins you can eat come with it.

We scramble into the restaurant, salivating like Pavlov's dog.

"Table for ten, please."

"Look, that couple is leaving! They left bread in their basket! Let's get it!" Scavengers!

Playing Hacky Sack

After this orgy, as we're dividing the bill, I realize that we didn't touch our napkins! They're still very neatly folded and tucked under the plates. Instead, bandannas and shirt sleeves took their place. I don't believe it! Two weeks in the wilderness and we're already animals!

The next morning, sun and blue skies grace us with their presence, but it doesn't make us eager to move. All seven of us are storm-shocked and apprehensive. The mountain is whiter than it was before the storm, and we're reluctant to leave the safety of this low, dry environment.

It takes hours, but this large group of hikers finally gets its gear packed up. We cram ourselves into the pickup, unload at the trailhead, and say good-bye to our rock-climbing, beer-drinking, Hackey-sacking friends. It's been a great four days!

The seven of us have decided to hike together for a while. Using a different route than Bob and I tried earlier, we are going to make another attempt to reach the high shoulders of San Jacinto. With our greater numbers we hope to find the trail more easily.

On this first day back, I am feeling the strain of carrying the added weight of my new supply of food. In addition, my muscles are soggy after four days of inactivity. I push to stay up with the group and keep the hiker in front of me within sight. They're going much too fast for my pace.

There are two other women, Sue and Melissa, in the group, a rare treat, for male hikers dominate the long trails. They come from behind, singing Joni Mitchell songs, hitting high notes, even on an uphill, taking their time, while the men go on ahead. Why is this?

Bob told me earlier, in his teasing way, "Everyone knows women hikers slow men hikers down." I think we choose to go slow. The three of us women have a marvelous time meandering up those switchbacks, stopping to notice birds, light patterns, pines swaying in the wind. I take my time. I can choose to run these hills like a gazelle or mope along like a steady turtle. Both are okay.

At nine thousand feet, we have rounded San Jacinto's summit and are approaching Fuller Ridge, a two-mile-long, snow-choked traverse. The guys go ahead to scout the trail's location. There are no markings or signs, no footprints or visible tread. Only snow. Because there are so many of us, minimal amounts of energy are wasted and we make good progress.

Jerry Benson, my old hiking friend and a PCT veteran, has been mailing letters to every post office drop, giving me information on relocations, hazards, hot spots. They have been an enormous help to the group. Jerry has written of an incomplete section just ahead. In fact, the trail just disappears a short distance beyond an intersection, where construction and dangerous blasting is going on. Most hikers who follow it become lost and pull out their map and compass to determine which way to go. It's against the code of the through-hiker to turn back when lost—one merely continues and finds a new way. Here, we can actually see our destination down the mountain, in the desert below: Cabazon, California. If we follow our compass, we will fall into box canyon after box canyon, where the only escape is to climb back out. We decide to continue cross-country rather than turn back because we had heard stories of some packers who drove a team of horses down this particular section of trail. It took them nearly a week to do the four and a half miles, and six of the horses died en route. Even if the story is only half true, it gives us reason to be concerned. At three P.M. we come to a new wooden sign marking the intersection. It states, "Pacific Crest Trail: Hurley Flats—4 miles, Cabazon—5 miles."

I've been warning everyone in our group that the trail ends ahead, but it never registers with Dale. He is off floating on some mountain in the sky. His descending footprints show he did take the new trail section, oblivious to what lies ahead. We sit at the intersection for some time, hoping he realizes his error and turns back, but he never does. We continue along the way that Jerry said to go, hoping Dale will be okay.

The town of Cabazon lies in the San Gorgonio Pass, a wide trough between Mount San Jacinto at 10,805 feet, and our next challenge, Mount San Gorgonio, in the San Bernardino Mountains, at 11,485 feet. Cabazon is nine thousand feet lower than either mountain but is separated from them by only a few air miles. Through this channel, moist air rushes from the ocean toward the rising fires of the desert. It's the first real break in the mountain wall.

"Cabazon! A furnace of hot, blowing air at sixteen hundred feet. Why would anyone want to go there?" Well, if you're on the

PCT, it's a nearby place to get food, relax, and wait for Dale. He doesn't show up. While we wait, we pool our money for chicken and salad and eat in the park by the volunteer fire house.

"Sleep behind the garage," the caretaker suggests. "There's a sprinkler system that comes on in the evening and you won't get wet there." After we lay out our bags behind the garage, we pick a picnic site and get the charcoal stoked up. All of a sudden, a geyser shoots up, soaking everything. We dive for cucumbers, tomatoes start to roll, lettuce flies. We run to another site, only to be drenched and chased off again fifteen minutes later. Finally, we resort to the gravel parking lot. One problem remains though— the charcoal. Dan volunteers to put his rain suit on and tend the chicken. There he is, flashlight in hand, singing, turning the chicken in the pouring "rain." When the stomach is empty, the will is strong!

Day #1

All the next day we sit around under pavilions in the shade, answering mail, drinking beer, writing in journals, darning socks, cleaning out packs, studying maps—typical layover activities.

Only now there are frequent interruptions. We lift up our heads repeatedly, glancing down the road, staring at that mountain in front of us. As though, if we concentrate hard enough, we could see Dale coming off its rocky face.

But will he show up? And how long do we wait, before we go for help?

Day #2

Night falls. No Dale. Morning breaks. No Dale. The desert sun explodes on the horizon. Lying there in the shade, we continue to stare at the mountain.

"We'll wait until tomorrow," the guys say. "Give him a chance to walk out on his own."

When evening comes, I feel we've waited long enough. I call the sheriff, report Dale's absence, and wait for the police to arrive.

At eleven-thirty, the sheriff pulls up. "Search-and-rescue team goes out tomorrow, if the kid doesn't show."

Day #3

Slept little last night. I continually pictured Dale sitting down, looking at and holding his foot. I feel certain he's hurt. Dan is concerned that he's dead.

Close to noon the search-and-rescue vans arrive. A base radio is set up, maps are studied, helicopters are brought in ($200 per hour), packs are stuffed with emergency survival and first aid gear.

We are asked countless questions about Dale's clothing, hair color, the pattern of his boot soles, and more. On the ground and in the air, search parties are sent out.

We're all pretty gloomy the entire day. We take walks back and forth to the radio, hoping to learn something. No one can do anything constructive. No one can think of anything but finding Dale.

One of the helicopters is returning! Everyone runs out. Hearts are hopeful. Eyes are searching. Refuel! They found

Rescue at Cabazon

tracks, but the prints seem to be going in circles. And they think they found his first night's camp in a box canyon, with fresher tracks leading back up the mountain. Oh God! The sheriff takes me for a ride in his car and gets as close to the mountain as a road can go.

"Look at that mountain. Doesn't look too terrible, does it? Look through those binoculars now. Do you see deep gashes on what first appeared to be a flat surface? They are box canyons, and there is no way out but straight back up. Now start at one point and follow a line down. How many canyons would you have to cross?"

"Four."

"That's right. And you have no way of knowing what you're getting into, until you're down in them. And rattlesnakes! Like you've never seen!"

Oh God, I feel worse. Before last week, Dale meant nothing to me. He was just a callous kid who was all wrapped up in himself. Now, my every thought is of him.

The radio is announcing, "We've spotted a hiker! He has shoulder-length, curly hair and a red pack." That's him! We run out to the field, just as the helicopter lands. Out comes Dale, smiling ear to ear, body scratched up, ankle sprained. He had fallen!

I hug him when I see him, throw my arms around his bony body. Pulling away, I realize how very badly I just wanted to see his face again, see his eyes shining, and have him be alive!

He gets lectured by the sheriff and then his hiking partner, Dan. "You've got to be more attentive, Dale. You must wait at intersections!"

Another saga over. We're reminded to take nothing for granted. Not one blessed, cool mountain day or one hellish, desert day or one sweaty, stinky, hiking companion. It is all a gift.

Dan and Dale will road walk to Big Bear City, our next town stop, sixty miles away, in hope of healing Dale's foot. We'll meet them in a week. And since Dave and Sue have decided to go off on their own for a while, that leaves Melissa, Bob and me as a team for the next stretch.

From the town of Cabazon, our course follows the convenient San Gorgonio Pass for twelve miles to the hamlet of Whitewater. Interstate 10 also takes advantage of the natural break. The pass is bound by faults, which made this huge chunk of earth drop way below the land around it. A graben, geologist Bob calls it.

A dozen long, sweltering miles await us. We start at five A.M. to escape the heat, by nine the sun is unbearable. Melissa and I walk together. Visors are pulled low, heads down, singing albums. Individual songs won't get you through a desert—this is long-distance singing country!

Whitewater's post office is a trailer, like so many others on this trail. Next door is an alcoholics' dry-out home. We sit on their wooden benches, in their shade, in their front yard. Our tired bodies rest. The patients, with their tan beer bellies, pass by all day. All are congenial. One insists we take some grapefruit. Eight of them? He has no concept of weight. Although it's ridiculous, we can't turn down food. We'll eat them all tonight. By six o'clock, it is cool enough to walk again.

I remember that my friend Jerry, when hiking the PCT, cursed Mission Creek and Whitewater Canyon in his letters. The next two days we'll be hiking along this creek. The guidebook says the trail will be difficult, if not impossible, to follow, which could mean more wasted miles. We don't get very far in a day as it is. The heat overcomes us around three o'clock and we experience the first signs of dehydration.

We follow the creek bed all day. The trail continuously switches from one bank to the next. Twenty crossings in one day! Scouts! Send out the scouts!

Bob, Melissa, and I are joined by two hikers: white-haired Howard and his grandson Miles, who are hiking as far as they can. They aren't much help in finding trail.

Howard is overloaded. His pack weight far exceeds what his body can handle because he's got most of his and Miles' collected gear. He wants Miles—his big, black, seventeen-year-old grandson who is on probation—to make this trip. Howard hikes bent

Miles (left) and Howard

over and walks straight into someone's back about four times a
day. He's not able to pick his head up. He staggers along. Howard
is hard of hearing, so we spend the day screaming at him each
time we locate the trail. He also has lots of close calls with rattlesnakes, which thrive along this river. "Big mothers," he calls
them. He couldn't hear their rattle if they did decide to warn. According to the trail guidebook, "An unsuccessful program in 1960
aimed at exterminating the rattlesnake resulted in killing most of
the noisy ones and left the silent ones to multiply. Now, there are
many that strike without a warning."

His trusty partner Miles isn't around to help him find the
way. Howard walks too slow for Miles, who is up ahead all the
time, sometimes taking the wrong turn, for he has no map or
compass and couldn't read them if he did.

We make our way up the canyon, seeing more snakes than miles of trail. Now I understand Jerry's loathing of Mission Creek!

One of the most amazing things to me, as an Easterner, is the varying life zones that we travel through as we hike up and down these mountains. Going from one thousand feet to ten thousand feet, we pass through nearly every major zone that you'd travel through if you went from Mexico to the Arctic! And we do it in two days! Imagine the variety of plant and animal life that we see. From lizards and snakes to deer, bear, and wildcat. From squat sagebrush to towering pines. From thirty-mile waterless stretches to cold snow fields. From 115 °F to 30 °F, all in a two-day hike. One day we're swabbing on the sunscreen and donning baseball hats and visors. The next day we're in long underwear and wool balaclavas.

This crazy Pacific Crest Trail doesn't let you get comfortable with any one life zone because it doesn't stay at one elevation for long. Certainly not like the long ridge walks in Pennsylvania.

On the Appalachian Trail you walk through West Virginia in a few short hours. It's going to take me close to a half year to walk through the state of California. Opposite trails, on opposite ends of the country.

The San Gorgonio Wilderness awaits us. Although Mount San Gorgonio is seven hundred feet higher than San Jacinto, we are not afraid of the snow. Our lower trail makes a wide arc through the San Bernardino Mountains, around the summit king, whose flanks are already riddled with hiking trails. We'll never get intimate with this mountain as we did with San Jacinto.

Continuing our ascent up Mission Creek, we find the desert in full bloom. Fields of grape-smelling lupine up to our waists. Tiny, miniature flowers, all colors, grow out of the sand.

Brilliant, pink, flowering prickly pear. We're ever higher, up into the forests where the Jeffrey pine grows abundantly. The pines look like sculptured columns rising to the heavens, for the first branches are far above the ground. I put my arms around one pine's trunk and breathe in the butterscotch-vanilla scent. How long I've waited to be up here!

A good part of the day Melissa and I sing John Denver songs about being in love with nature. "Oh, I love the life around me. A part of everything is here in me."

What could be more appropriate on this glorious mountain day, where the wind blows and the sun is finally a friend. I have to fight back tears all day. My God, I am happy!

Bob isn't with us this afternoon. He and Miles are up ahead, scouting the way for us slow women. Poor Howard is in the rear, killing himself to keep up, still walking into our backs. Bob is leaving crude arrows made of sticks at trail intersections to show us which way to go. Melissa and I don't take too kindly to this. We don't like being forced to follow him.

We arrive at Coon Creek Jump-Off. The trail forms a Y. Melissa and I get out the maps and realize that Bob went the wrong way. All together now: "BOB!" No answer. Over and over, we test our lungs. No answer. God knows how far down this trail they have gone. Some of us are sharing gear, so we have no choice but to go the wrong way also.

"We'll have to go all the way up this again!" we say, as we drop lower into the valley.

"Boy, it sure is nice not to have to use our heads! Just follow blasted arrows! We just spent two and a half days in Cabazon, waiting for Dale, who wouldn't wait at intersections. I guess Bob didn't learn anything from it!"

We finally meet up with the men. Sweet Melissa stops in her tracks, twenty-five yards from Bob, and screams: "Where the hell do you think the trail is, Bob? It's back up there!" I am still mad, but am now laughing inside. Bob is feeling awful.

"How about waiting for our two cents' worth," Melissa adds. "Just maybe we can see something that you can't."

We choose to continue going down this wrong trail. We need to find water and make camp. It's getting late. An hour later, we sit by a road intersection, trying to figure which way will take us back to the trail. Then Miles looks down at his feet.

"There's something written in the dirt with pebbles. 'PCT this way!' " All right, Miles! Others did the same thing and left behind a message after they figured it out!

We go up to Coon Creek Cabin, but find the area dry as a bone. Wonderful. No water for supper tonight. Freeze-dried food doesn't make the grade with zero liquid. Bob trots off with two water bags in his hands.

"Redeem yourself," I mutter under my breath. He does, too, coming back with five gallons. Found a pump half a mile up the road at a horse camp. I go over to his side and put my arms around him.

"I'm sorry I didn't wait," he said.

"I'm sorry I got angry with you."

"I love you."

"I love you, too."

On to Big Bear City and the break-up of our first trail family. We have been together off and on for close to a month.

Miles and Howard leave first. They don't wait for town but take off for the road the first time it gets spitting close and head on home. Miles has had his fill. I'm surprised Howard made it this far. I have a funny feeling he thinks you have to suffer out here. Dale and Dan, whom we meet again in town, are going to the Grand Canyon to wait for the Sierra snow to melt. Melissa's time is running out and she's making plans to leave also. The couple from California are choosing to stay on their own. So it's me and Bob again, just like before. I enjoy it like that sometimes. He's a lot more secure when it's just the two of us. He knows I need him, and I believe he gets a lot from my company. It's good to know we both make life better for each other.

I have been looking forward to Big Bear's town stop. Then again, I get excited about every chance to go into town. I have come to appreciate both wilderness and town and what each has to offer.

Of course, my heart will always be in the mountains, but I'm not fool enough to pass up a Mexican dinner or a shower or twenty-five letters from friends every two weeks. I'll do more than not pass it up—I'm going to wallow in it!

Big Bear City reeks with money. You don't see a car, it seems, that's not a Mercedes or a Peugeot or a BMW. The people are all L.A. transplants or weekend visitors.

Bob, Melissa, and I walk down the highway to "La Paws," a hole-in-the-wall Mexican restaurant that supposedly has more authentic food than Mexico itself. No one speaks English here. The food is excellent.

We walk back along the shoulder of the road to our illegal campsite in the town's park, falling into sewer grates as we're blinded by oncoming cars. With shrunken wool pants and flip-flops, we look like we're waiting for the flood. A group of long-haired kids yell to us.

"Hey! You guys hiking the trail?" How did they know? You can't see the muscles in our legs; we have long pants on. Our hair is clean and down. We're not wearing boots, and there's not a pack in sight.

We're walking! No one walks in this town. The only ones who enter town without a car come in on foot, which means hikers. Very good. Can't get away from it.

They ask if we know about the snows ahead in the High Sierra. We know. It's become the main topic of conversation these days. Rangers say the mountains are impassable. Worst snowfall in one hundred years. Spring snows. Won't leave before next winter. The trail registers are full of previous hikers' thoughts on the matter. Everyone is concerned and absolutely no one knows what to do.

4

Cindy's Circus

May 25

Bob and I are back on the trail. Alone. Soon, we pass a guy heading south who informs us, "There's a couple up ahead, Nancy and Skip. She just joined him and is slowing him down pretty bad."

Echoes. I hear echoes.

Later that day, we find them at Deep Creek's bridge. Both are

Skip and Nancy

very tall and look like they make a fine couple, with their matching athletic bodies and expensive packs. Nancy has very shapely
legs, which, she later tells me, won her a prize in high school. Although it's her first backpack trip, she's always been active and
teaches blind people to ski in the winter. She has short brown hair
and a smallish mouth that is always moving. She is so thrilled to
meet me, another woman hiker, that her voice is nervous with excitement. Skip is even taller than Nancy, with close-cropped curly
hair, glasses, and a slow, deliberate style of speaking. I am so flat-
tered by Nancy's delight in meeting another woman that we
quickly become friends. This is Skip's second attempt at the trail;
she's never had weight on her back and it's evident that she's not
doing too well. Bob and I decide to stay with them for moral support and company.

In private Nancy tells me that they were attracted to each
other at his going-away party, just before he left for the trail. And
once he was there he called her at every stop, till he finally convinced her to join him. He supplied half her equipment and all of
her food. But Nancy tells me she didn't realize the price of his
generosity, that he would play on her dependence to make her
into some sort of emotional hostage. Skip doesn't want them to
hike with others; he coerces her to cater to his every need.

To our right, a sheer cliff drops one thousand feet to Deep
Creek. To our left, a rattlesnake lies coiled one foot from the trail,
ready to strike. Skip does not want to hurt it, so he urges us just to
walk past it. Going first, he walks by unharmed.

"See, he didn't strike," Skip calls back. "Come across single
file."

"Forget it!" I yell. "He'll wait until the third or fourth person,
get angry, then strike!"

Nancy looks at me, then quickly adds, "I'm not going either!"
This is the first time she defies him.

"Just go to the right of the trail then."

"And fall off the cliff when he strikes? What makes more
sense, a dead snake or a dead woman?" I holler, as I pick up a
rock.

Deep Creek Gorge

"Don't!" yells Skip. "Take off your packs and pass them around the side of the cliff. You should be able to traverse it without a pack."

I don't agree but try it anyway.

Thank goodness no one falls. The snake's life is spared only for a few hours because three fishermen who came along after told us that they had smashed it.

The rest of the day I walk directly behind Nancy, talking the entire time to keep her mind off her painful feet. Skip is grateful.

"She never hiked this far in a day before," he says. "You're good for her. This is the happiest I've seen her yet."

In camp we eat communally. Nancy hates Skip's bland food (noodles with soup mix over them) and won't eat half the time. She gets deathly sick after supper tonight, suffering from vomiting and diarrhea. Drawing on his experience as an emergency medical technician, Skip concludes that she ate something she's allergic to. My dried rabbit stew, he says, the only thing strange at dinner.

We decide to move Nancy out to civilization the next morning. Since we're more than twenty miles from a road, it doesn't seem wise to stay put: she could get worse. We split up the contents of her pack between Bob, Skip, and me and begin the long, sweltering exodus. I give her my visor and shoulder to lean on. The plan is to walk to a road, get a ride to Silverwood Lake Campground, spend the night there, and find someone to drive her from there into the mountain village of Wrightwood for medical attention and relaxation.

Ours is the only campsite at Silverwood Lake with no Winnebago parked out in front. The older couple next door brings wood to us for a campfire, but twilight has already descended and after our twenty-mile ordeal to get here, we are all exhausted. Bed sounds good.

All night, monster tin cans on wheels roll into our campsite, high beams glaring because, seeing no cars, the drivers assume the site is vacant. Then they spot our tents.

"There's someone already here, Charlie," a woman cries out in surprise. They move along.

In the morning our neighbors try again to strike up an acquaintance.

"The wife bets you'll eat eggs if she cooks them," says the man, whose name is Clifford.

She was right. Although we had just finished breakfast, we were ready for round two. Eggs, bacon, toast, coffee, homemade preserves. Over breakfast Clifford pulls out photographs—pictures tattered from frequent looking and longing.

"The grandchildren," says Sybil, his wife. "We only had one

son. Few years back he was in an auto accident—paralyzed from the waist down."

"From then on," Clifford adds, "his wife kept moving. Keeps the phone unlisted, us separated. Haven't seen the children in years. Neither has their father." With tears streaming, he comes to each of us for an embrace.

"You don't know what it means to have you young folks here."

> *Strange is our situation here on earth. Each comes a short*
> *visit, not knowing why, but seeming to divine a purpose. One*
> *thing we do know: man is here for the sake of other men, and*
> *for those on whose love our own happiness depends, and for*
> *those countless souls we are connected with by a bond of*
> *sympathy.*
>
> —Albert Einstein

From Silverwood Lake, Nancy and I hitch a ride into Wrightwood, a village in the San Gabriel Mountains that is about twenty miles away by road. Since I have friends there, it makes the most sense for me to go along. The men will continue on the trail and will rejoin us in a couple of days. Last night, as I lay thinking about this plan, a wave of guilt flooded over me. Skipping trail! I am essentially a purist when it comes to walking the entire trail. I don't stick my thumb out as soon as my feet hit blacktop. Nancy needs my help now more than this section needs to be hiked. It will be a good excuse to come back someday.

Nancy recuperates quickly and by the time Bob and Skip arrive she is her old self, and I have made a forever friend. In Wrightwood we also hook up with two more of the Easterners, Bruce and Allison, who answered my ad for hiking partners. Bruce is in his forties. He seems quiet and modest, with tender eyes and gentle ways. Yet I sense a steady assurance about him that only comes with wisdom and years. I look to him for support, advice, unprejudiced compassion in the miles ahead.

Allison, however, is young and silly. Her round, rosy face is always blushing, smiling, giggling. Her body looks baby soft, even pudgy, though it is surprisingly sturdy. She lifts weights and works as a clown. Although she lacks hiking experience, I hope her passion for the hike will pull her through.

Unfortunately, her first test is a tough one. Not far west of Wrightwood the PCT heads up Mount Baden-Powell, our first nine-thousand footer since the San Bernardino Mountains. Named after the man who founded the Boy Scouts of America, this mountain is something of a Mecca for young Webelos and Explorers who climb its hundreds of switchbacks to the sky. At each switchback a sign announces the elevation and mileage for

Allison; Bruce

those exhausted scouts. Actually, the leaders are usually the ones dying in the rear.

So is Allison. At first she complains about the "narrow trail." It's plenty wide for a broad pack and is totally free of snow. Yet she still takes tiny, cautious steps, hugging the side of the mountain so closely that the trees hit her pack, knocking her frantically off balance.

Soon the trail disappears into snow. We cut straight up. I teach her how to walk, shoving the toe of her boot forcefully with each step for a firm grip. On the summit, we stare down thousands of feet to the sweltering Mojave desert. Roads cut squares of land in measured precision. Up here, there's only cold and snow, a frightening place for our newcomer.

During the day I check on Allison for signs of hunger, altitude sickness, blisters—her general well-being. When the snow finally gives way to clean "cruise trail," I take off. Little Jimmy Campground, thirteen miles from breakfast, is our only water source. Everyone votes to camp there. Skip brings up the rear. An hour of solitude in the pink glow of sunset is all I want. Los Angeles smog and dust do wonderful things for a sunset's color. Except for the wide, brown line above, you'd think the hues were of divine origin.

Night begins falling. We stumble into camp and quickly fetch water. I expect Allison to be tired, but she comes to me clutching, sobbing. She had a terrible time the last hour and lapsed into the beginning stages of hypothermia. Skip forced candy bars down her throat, threw a wool shirt on her, and made her rest.

Nancy gives her a vest and a hat. Bob sets up her tent. I cook her supper, calm her down and hug her, give up my warmer bag for the night.

Whimpers come from the tent. Now it's Bob's turn to comfort Allison. Lying half in the tent, half out, his comforting words rise in the night like wood smoke. When I retire, she begins crying uncontrollably.

"I feel so vulnerable. So weak," she sobs.

I prop up her feet so that the blood drains. All parts of her body are sore and aching. A very grateful girl, feeling wretched and weak, finally sleeps. I lie awake, distressed, feeling responsible and wondering what I'm getting myself into.

Like a mother, I worry over my fellow hikers as if they were my children. It's my nature. My own mother is a strong care giver and she set an example for me. This large, extended family is taking its toll on Skip. He's been complaining of a hurt knee lately and is really hanging back. He gives Nancy strict instructions not to go past certain points on the trail without waiting for him. She knows he's just trying to lose the group. If he goes slow enough, he'll fall behind and the two will be alone again. This is the last thing Nancy wants, she says, so I encourage her to continue, and he's forced to follow.

The San Gabriel Mountains are wide open, sparse, barren. Tall pines clump only at the highest elevations. Oppressive sun drains you of all pep. Heat sucks your energy like a hungry mosquito.

The miles feel twice as long. I watch rust-colored grasses blow, swaying with what little breeze there is. White skeleton pines tower, dead from a burn. Fires run rampant in the San Gabriels.

Everything is so dry that the steep, chaparral-covered slopes often burn like torches. When there is shade, it is mostly from live oaks. Their dry, fallen leaves litter the trail, so that it sounds like we're crunching potato chips when we walk. The light beneath the oaks is diffuse and comes through in blotches. Still, the trees provide some shade.

Bob and I leave the crowd behind. My brother-in-law John is flying into the town of San Bernardino on business and renting a car to take us from the San Gabriel Mountains to his Holiday Inn for dinner. The whole circus can't come, so I choose my old buddy Bob.

We set up shop by the Angeles Crest Highway. Sitting on a foam pad on the gravel shoulder, staring into every passing car, we discuss menus for tonight.

Three and a half hours crawl by, no John. The sun sinks lower.

The temperature finally drops. "Maybe he had to work late." As darkness falls, we wearily look for a flat spot to camp, collect brown culvert water, eat a very unappealing meal.

"If you don't mind, I'll cuddle up with you tonight," Bob says. Maybe the evening won't be a total loss! This is the first time we've been alone in weeks. Being in a group makes me view him from a different perspective. Sometimes he drives me nuts with his chauvinistic insecurities. Other times, he is so endearing that I am fearful of caring too much. But all we do is touch knees! Through five inches of down! This is the extent of his affection and he encourages no more.

Days later, we discovered what had happened to John. The highway we had directed him to had a landslide a few years back. The highway department decided not to fix it, for it blocked only a short segment of road and there were other side roads that intersected the highway. A warning sign greeted John down below, but he cruised by, hoping to weave through. Less than one mile away from us, however, defeated, he turned around.

The next day, Bob and I are back with the group in time for our evening meal. Allison dumps herself on a picnic table. "What's for dinner? I'm starved!" Complaints spout forth. "Everything aches! I don't think I can make thirteen-mile days."

I told Allison to prepare for this trip. I told her that she'd be joining a group already strengthened by miles. She never exercised, never broke in her boots, gained unnecessary weight, and now can't keep up. Bruce offers to hitch with her into Acton, our next town stop, where they'll rest and wait for the rest of the group. Good old Bruce. He's quick to help someone in need. His assistance relieves me of some of the responsibility and pressure of Allison.

At Mill Creek Campground, we all do our separate things. Skip is on his foam pad, bathed in evening light, practicing yoga. Nancy is by the faucet, washing things out. Bob is at a solitary picnic table, engrossed in an adventure novel. I look back at them as I walk down the road. We four, it's so easy. The men hike fast, play cards when they wait. Nance and I chat, sing. She and Skip still fight, but they're managing.

The full moon rises over the desert. Today flew by. It felt so comfortable, so much like home. Finally, I am getting strong. We are nearly through southern California. So much of it I tried to hurry through. So much felt uncomfortable. I stare down at the Mojave. Soon we will be in its hold. I'm determined to enjoy myself. I'll mail everything I can ahead. No stove, no cook set; all cold, dried food to lighten the pack. We'll walk early in the mornings, late in the evenings. Experience desert stars, sunrises, evening winds.

Suddenly, I feel the passage of time. I hang in this moment like the moon in the desert sky. This trip seems so short now. Some days felt like eternity, but now it's really going by in a flash. Savor this moment! Soon I'll be back in that other life!

Full of emotion, I return to the group. I hug Nancy and thank her for being with me. I hug Skip too, for the first time. He was never eager to hike in a group. He tolerates it because Nancy needs my company.

"Nancy should thank you," he says. "She probably wouldn't be here if it weren't for you." I keep my distance from Bob. He doesn't seem receptive lately.

Six A.M.

Early start into Acton, where some friends of mine live. The guys estimate three to four miles, two hours maximum. I'll do some moving, push for once. The trail winds in and out of gullies, as though in a maze, getting nowhere fast. Foxtails—the dry seed heads of various wild grasses—puncture my socks. A pin cushion—that's what I am! In southern California, the only thing that keeps me walking is town.

Milkshakes! Friends! One goal at a time. Otherwise, the immensity of this journey would overwhelm me.

I don't try to keep clean out here. I don't enjoy smelling bad, but I don't mind dirt. No other time in my life is it okay to be filthy, so I take advantage of it. (Maybe that's my problem with Bob!)

Before town, I try to wipe off. Move the dirt around, spread it thinner. Three black rings remain around my neck.

At my friend's house, the crew bugs me to shower first. Skip is the loudest. He thinks I'm messy just to torment him. For example, Nancy says that he's laid awake, distraught over my cooking habits. It's true that I randomly throw in spices, let the soup spill down the sides of the pot, or let the spoon lie in the dirt. These things aren't important to me. Getting along is. Much of my day is spent as a peace maker. If it's not Allison, it's Nancy. But although we must help each other, no one can pull another along. Every day there are trail problems, but their conflicts overload my spirit. In caring for their needs, I forget my own.

5

The Mojave

June 9

On a hill, outside the sleepy village of Lake Hughes, I catch my breath. Last hill for a while. Panting like a dog, head exploding with heat, I look down on what the trail is dishing out next: the Mojave desert. I see my comrades stretched out in a line below me: Bob, Bruce, Allison, Nancy, and Skip. Heat waves rise from the desert's bowels like a hot tar pavement. Three to five inches of rain drop here annually. Gone are its short-lived results: flowering cacti, blankets of sun-colored poppies, cool days.

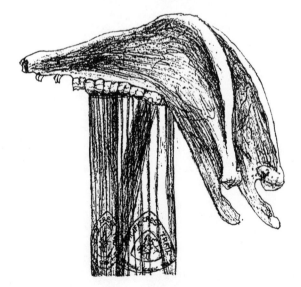

Jawbone on PCT sign

All through the mountains since the Bernardinos, we traveled an east-west track, with the Mojave to our north. The Pacific Crest Trail is not a straight shot from Mexico to Canada. It weaves and winds, zigs and zags, but staying in the mountains and as close to the crest as possible. Now we jog north, cutting straight across Antelope Valley, the westernmost arm of the Mojave desert.

Much of our route here will follow the Los Angeles Aqueduct, which carries water to Los Angeles. A string of sun-hardened folks live along the waterway, some of whom allow hikers to crawl under their trees and sip iced tea during the lethal hours of the day. Since their homes are spaced about a day's walk apart, we plan our miles accordingly.

> *In the desert, one is sensible of the passage of time. In that parching heat, a man feels that the day is a voyage towards the goal of evening, towards the promise of a cool breeze that will bathe the limbs and wash away the sweat. Under the heat of the day, beasts and men plod towards the sweet well of night, as confidently as towards death.*
> —Antoine de Saint Exupery

The desert day follows a pattern. The sun dictates how we walk and when we walk. Our eating and sleeping habits are arranged in relation to the heat. The days follow the same pattern.

Four-thirty A.M.

We awaken before dawn. Wind blows the tent like a sail. We help each other fold. Only a hint of light glows on the horizon, a smear of color. It's as if an artist took a thin sable brush, loaded with pinks, and streaked it across the blackened canvas. Walking toward a new day.

It got cold last night. Hat weather. The desert cools rapidly at night. There are no clouds to keep heat in. The chilly air rushes down the mountains to fill the vacuum below. This morning I hike with a long-sleeved shirt on. I button my collar and sleeves and walk off at a brisk, hurried clip. Our pace will increase through this section. We're racing with the sun.

Before long, a flaming, orange disk peeks over the horizon. As it moves quickly up the sky, we too lose no time. By eleven o'clock, the sun will be intolerably high. The chaparral is backlit and looks like Moses' burning bush. No trail is visible this morning.

We head cross-country between two buttes. They're ruddy complexioned from the iron content and from years spent baking in the sun. They've taken on the sun's color permanently, absorbed it. As we watch our progress by these isolated hills, they strike us as being much closer than they really are. What appears to be five miles away is actually twenty. The atmosphere distorts the space between your eye and the object. Dust particles and sand load the air and affect your perception. What seems real becomes uncertainty.

Ten A.M.

We hit road. Amid miles of irrigated crops, we march our straight-line course. Never failing, never deviating. Perpendicular rows of telephone lines cross our path every few miles. Beside them are numbered streets. But no cars! No buildings! I wondered about these roads as I looked down on them from atop Mount Baden-Powell. "What goes on down there?" Now I know. Growth! Huge, mobile irrigators, poles on wheels, stretch for hundreds of yards, greening the arid soil.

We run into the sprinklers and soak ourselves. A spray under the armpit! A shot down the shorts! We hesitate to drink because diluted fertilizer may be in the water. A small taste. Gulp! Gulp! Gulp! At the time, heat stroke and dehydration seem more serious than poisoning.

Nancy and I sing oldies as we push down the road and even dance and skip a little. Allison tries to join in, but is too young to know any oldies. She's keeping up for a change. Seems to walk faster when she wants to. Don't we all! Something must drive you onward. Today it's the approaching heat.

Eleven A.M.

Air and time stand still. The singing has ceased. We drape bandannas around our necks, foreign-legion style, and others over our faces. I walk with my head down. No sense greeting the sun. My nose acts as a trough, channeling sweat from my scalp and brow. A rivulet runs off my chin. Torrents stream down my neck, collect in my cleavage, like a dam. Up ahead Skip lies under a moisture-starved bush. Blackjack cards, chips in hand, he plays poker with himself to pass time. Always waiting for us. We throw off our packs and collapse in the fragmented shade.

We should have been to the next house by now. We promised ourselves not to be out here past eleven. With no idea how far the next house is, I tighten my pack straps and stretch my neck to the horizon. Looking for a dark clump of trees. Under it will be a house. No springs along the way. Live trees mean someone opened the earth to pump water out and built a life around that tiny hole.

I stop to lower my head to fight off the faintness and dizziness. Glacier goggles slide down the nose. It's so bright out here! The intense light is not just from direct sunlight, but is reflected off the bright sand. There's no dark place to cool your eyes. Same with the heat. It radiates unobstructed from above. There are no trees to shield you. Then the land absorbs the heat, and it rises from beneath you. Double dose!

Two-thirty P.M.

We stagger in. Trailers and mobile homes clutter Mrs. Davidson's yard. The men hug the aluminum sides, hide in the three feet of roof overhang. This is not a natural oasis. She steals water from the aqueduct after five, when the patrol goes home. All the folks who live along the way do that. The patrol knows it. It's been going on for years. Mrs. Davidson is just a small mosquito sucking the blood of a giant monster, which is Los Angeles. She is a desert survivor, behaving the way any other creature of the desert would.

Nancy Davidson greets us with arthritic hands, fudge, iced

Nancy Davidson's trailers

tea. The girls take over the screened-in porch, hiding from no-see-ums. Nancy and Allison stretch out on lounge chairs. I lie down on the indoor-outdoor carpet. I feel like I've been at the beach all day—wiped out from the sun. Country music floats through the thick air, and I try to sleep, waiting for the sun to sink.

Six-thirty P.M.

The breeze starts. As the sun gets lower, the land begins to cool. Air is moving in from higher, cooler places. The distant Tehachapi Mountains pass by at our side. They remind me of the

Shenandoah ridge because in this low light I can't distinguish barren land from lush woods. Someday, the trail will traverse them. Landowners and the lack of water force us lower. Down here, we get water from the aqueduct's maintenance holes. Every so often the metal lids are left unlocked. We lie on our bellies, gritty concrete scraping our skin, to lower a cord tied to a plastic water bottle. When it hits the surface, the swift current tries to snatch it away. The water smells like a swimming pool! Heavily chlorinated water is better than none at all.

Bruce and I walk together. He asks to join me since we haven't gotten a chance to talk since he joined us in Wrightwood. Moving this complicated group up the trail seems to consume the entire day. There is talk of the life we left. He tells me of the research he's been doing on osteoporosis back home at the University of West Virginia. He designs metal pins to implant in bones. The conversation rolls out as the miles roll by until he's all talked out. You don't need to converse with Bruce to communicate, to feel connected to him. Here, there is time to be quiet. Time not to talk. At

Aqueduct water hole

home, with friends, we cram in as much conversation and news as possible. Out here, silence becomes communion.

I feel extremely comfortable with Bruce. He has a girlfriend back home whom he's deeply in love with, so I can hug him or lean against his knee without having him get the wrong idea. I don't pass the miles with him as I do with Nancy and the others, but I am so happy to have him with us. He adds a peaceful note to this otherwise chaotic circus.

The sky turns brilliant orange behind the hiking family. The hotter the day, the thicker the air becomes, for there is more dust and sand in the air as it rises and cools. This produces haze and incredible sunsets. The dark bodies of my companions silhouette the glowing horizon. Some are tall and thin; others are short and wide. They have different leg shapes and different ways of walking. Such individuals! They all influence me — their problems and pains, their ways of looking at life and this trip, their needs and desires, their expectations and moods. Somewhere, in the midst of all that influence and close living, is my own voice. A whisper: "Oh please, take time to enjoy!"

Nine-thirty P.M.

Distant lights switch on. Huge mines, factories glitter in the distance. We stare at them, mesmerized. They didn't exist in the daylight. We still wonder if they're real, for it seems that they never come closer. With darkness falling, we walk with a keener awareness of snakes and begin looking for a place to camp.

We carry fresh food through this stretch. Water weight is the same in an apple or a bottle of liquid. Salad is on the menu tonight. Since we're not cooking, we have no pots or lids or bowls. Instead, plastic bags and empty cookie boxes take their place. We're making do.

One A.M.

I awake from my sound sleep. Down feathers nestle around each curve of my body. But Nancy Davidson's iced tea demands an exit. I crawl out of my tent into the night. The wind is silent, still. Billions of stars fill the heavens. The Milky Way is wide and incredibly bright. In the distance, the lights still flicker like jewels. Coyotes wail in the night.

The town of Mojave lies in the distance. Tin roofs shine brilliantly, reflecting the sun. They hypnotize me, lure me. Bob is setting the pace. My legs pump like the pistons of a machine, moving twice as often as his long strides. I eye Joshua trees along the road. Oh, to crawl under there for five minutes!

"Look at that, guys!" I get Bob and Bruce to pause for just a second. Leg muscles shake, go into spasms. "Would you get my water bottle, Bob?" Anything to get them to stop.

I hold their pace all morning. Finally, I relax, fall behind. Good God! Twelve miles before nine o'clock. No wonder I'm beat! I catch up at a McDonald's golden arches. Dry, salty sweat tightens my face as I smile a smile of relief. As soon as I stop, my legs cramp up.

Fifteen-mile days at a two-mile-per-hour pace are now easy for me. At day's end, I am not exhausted. I'm barely even fatigued. If I do not push myself, I will merely maintain this strength, all

Joshua tree

that is necessary for a long hike. That is when hiking is pure en-
joyment—when no pain is involved.

However, I've been fearful of what lies ahead in the Sierra. To
get stronger, to reach higher levels of fitness, I must push through
this pain. Before, in southern California, this could not even be
considered. Pain chose me in those soft days. I had a hard time
just seeing through it. Now, I am choosing pain. For I know that
in the miles ahead, in the mountains of snow, there will be a need
for enormous stamina.

At McDonald's, customers turn and stare. I walk confidently.
Stomach in. Chest high. Our packs force good posture upon us.
We walk tall even when they're off. Heavy boots make us place
our strong legs very deliberately. My suntanned skin glistens,
wisps of bleached, golden hair frame my face.

Outside, I raise my arm, tilt the milkshake back, and suck the
last drops. I see a beautiful, sensuous line reflected in the window. It follows the top of my arm and curves down onto my
breast—my pectoral muscle. Most women have never seen their
pectoral muscles. Lift a sixty-pound pack many times a day and
they will be resurrected.

I feel good about the way I look. I enjoy being noticed. We are
living as we should, close to the earth, breathing clean air and
pumping blood through our muscles. We look strong and
healthy.

Out here, there is no choice. Get strong or go home. The trail
sees to it.

Mojave's post office is a haven of cool air. Each hiker picks up
his supply box, packed ahead of time, and mailed out by a support person back home. We stretch out on the lobby's cool linoleum, each in his or her own spot, reading mail, separating
meals, breaking open care packages. Hikers tend to take over a
place. We're used to lots of space.

Nancy takes off her boots and elevates her feet to reduce
swelling. She's been suffering for weeks and may have tiny stress
fractures throughout her toes. I lean my bare back against the
chilly tiles and read the trail register kept at post offices. Through

these notebooks, we can communicate with one another and keep tabs on who's ahead. My AT friend Todd says hello and wishes all those behind happy traveling.

Suddenly, Allison bursts in. Furious and talking a mile a minute, she storms up to me. She's wearing an aqua blue sun hat and silly-looking flip-up shades. I can't tell if her face is red from the anger, the heat, the reflection from her shocking pink bandanna around her neck, or all three. Soon a wave of body odor, coconut oil, bug dope, and garlic catches up.

"What's the matter?" I ask.

"I never saw the note! I walked out of my way and had to come back!"

Allison and Nancy walk the trail blindly, never inquiring where it goes. Today I drew arrows in the sandy road every fifty yards. Certainly, the route was obvious—follow the road. There was nowhere else to go. When we finally did turn, I left three arrows pointing right and a large note under a rock. She must have stepped right on it!

Skip arrives next. "You guys ought to go outside. Air the place out for a while."

I look around. People file past, ignoring us, as though we aren't obvious. Others glance our way, with frowns on their faces. We don't notice any smell. We're accustomed to it. Not until you go outdoors and come back in does the wave of odor hit you.

Moving along on a hot desert day, we can sweat up to one liter an hour. Our bodies cannot replace all those fluids immediately. Even if we could drink all we need, we would be so diluted, so drastically lacking salts, that there would be little improvement. Cramps would develop. So, after drinking about half of what we need, our bodies stop thirsting, even though we're still dehydrated.

And our systems wait for food, containing the necessary salts. Then, we resume drinking. Every day we become dehydrated. Every night we rehydrate.

The "family" is really coming around. The wide open spaces of the desert make everyone relax. It's hot, but the course is set.

Percy on desert road walk

Follow a road. People hike at their own pace. More independence and freedom equal less pressure. We begin loving one another. If we express anger, then we must also express love. Not long ago, I realized it isn't sexual attention I need, but blessed human contact: touching, hugs from my friends. Bob and Skip had a hard time accepting that. They weren't brought up that way. My Polish-Italian heritage taught me otherwise. The guys come to collect hugs now! The second hardest way to hike along a trail is in a group. The most difficult is alone.

Percy, the new hiker who's been hanging around, realizes that. He came to me today and asked if he could join our group. He's fearful of going through the Sierra alone, although he doesn't come right out and say it. It's fine with me if Percy tags along, but the guys aren't real excited about it. Percy is sort of strange. He hikes in long pants and a sweatshirt and carries an umbrella.

In camp, he wears a floor-length gauze caftan from India. He shaves daily, actually sets up a mirror and meticulously grooms his face. He massages Vitamin E cream into his face and neck. He's at that "dangerous age," the mid-thirties, when wrinkles first appear. He takes quite a liking to me. Calls me "dar-link" and "love," in a put-on French accent. It amuses and flatters me and for some unknown reason, I find him strangely attractive. Everyone else merely tolerates him. I tell him there are responsibilities that go along with this group. Sure we have fun, but we help each other when there's a need. He assures me that he will do everything to help the group.

Jawbone Canyon, where the Allens live, is the obvious exit out of the low Mojave desert. From here, we will begin ascending through a contoured desert into a land of canyons and a maze of washes.

The trail guide reads: ". . .we continue hiking north on KC Road 5599 up Alphie Canyon, watching the east-facing slopes to find the mouth of Butterbredt Canyon. It presently appears, though its devious course and bland color make it almost indistinguishable from the slopes that surround it."

Skip, Allison, and Nancy leave the Allens' first. They want a head start. Bob, Bruce, Percy, and I follow their sole prints all morning. This is Bureau of Land Management property—public land. The wide, open spaces are abused. Hundreds of dirt bike trails scar the hills. Signs are riddled with shotgun holes. We walk single file in a tire rut. The sand is a few inches deep, and we get no traction.

Sometime during the morning, the footprints disappear, which means that someone is lost, either our group or the one ahead. We continue walking up washes, which look as if flash floods ran through them an hour, rather than months, ago. A four-wheel drive slides by in the sand.

"What canyon is this?"

"Butterbredt."

At least we aren't the ones who are lost!

Staring at the desert hills that surround us, I imagine Skip and the girls topping the horizon like Indians in a Western, coming from another canyon.

We stop at a mud hole for lunch. Cattle hang out in the waist-high, slimy water. Bob climbs the windmill and manually turns the blades. Fresh water for pudding! As I shake the pistachio mixture, the cattle move to arm's length.

"You like pudding?" I ask the beasts.

By the windmill, we leave a note for the lost trio: "If you find this, you are no longer lost."

At the head of the canyon, I see for the first time a massive mountain wall of rock. My mouth drops open. The Sierra! Is that light color granite or snow? Lord God, I hope it's not snow.

It's everywhere!

The Weeds are our hosts tonight for our last stop before Weldon. Their charming little house has a patio and garden. Old Man Weed hobbles out to welcome us.

"WATER'S INSIDE!" he screams, sure that we too are hard of hearing.

"THANK YOU!" we automatically respond.

Toward dusk, the lost hikers stagger in. What a carrying on! Allison, in her high-pitched voice, talks a mile a minute, her face scarlet. Nancy, equally hysterical, yells at the same time.

Skip looks exhausted.

Nancy says, "I held my tongue all morning. I knew we were lost, although Skip insisted that your group was. I hijacked a dirt biker to look for you. He drove sixty miles an hour! My legs were flying in the air! I asked Skip about the windmill and the pond. There's supposed to be one in Butterbredt Canyon,' I said. 'Probably dried up,' he answered. Then we met some people, and I asked them where we were. They said that the canyon was not called Butterbredt. Do you know what Skip said? He said, 'They're always changing these canyons' names!' That was it. I lost it!"

I ask the Weeds if I can come inside to write. The light is on, and a table is a luxury.

"We left the low desert today. Climbed two thousand feet. It was a good feeling to turn around and gaze down, back toward the desert. It feels good to know we are moving north, making progress. I found the Mojave to be a good experience. I went in with a positive attitude, was touched by the host families' generosity, and learned to adapt to desert conditions by changing my hiking style."

Old Man and Old Lady Weed sit on their rockers by the wood stove. Four feet apart, they holler at the tops of their lungs.

"WHAT'S THE WEATHER FOR TOMORROW?"

"I DON'T KNOW!"

"WHAT?"

"TURN THE RADIO UP!"

Time for bed.

The Sierra Nevada

6

The Foothills

June 15

Two million years ago the unborn Sierra Nevada lay beneath a sea. Then, like the yawning of a great crocodile, the land slowly lifted up, gently sloping in the west, but baring its teeth in the east: steep, jagged, abrupt. About the same time, the Owens Valley sank, giving this range greater local relief than any other mountains in the lower forty-eight.

The Sierra is a massive range about sixty miles wide and four hundred unbroken miles long. For two hundred of those miles the Pacific Crest Trail stays near the crest, traversing a wilderness so deep that not a single road crosses it. Wilderness rangers have their provisions dropped by helicopter.

The Sierra Nevada is a weather barrier, catching nearly all the moisture that supports the largest trees in the world, the giant sequoias, which reach heights over two hundred feet and diameters up to thirty-six feet.

The Sierra Nevada was also a barrier to early explorers, settlers, and gold miners heading west to California. Indians knew enough to cross the range during the summer. Only the white man was foolish enough to attempt the Sierra during the winter. The Donner Party got trapped in the winter of 1845. Thirty-five died, and the living resorted to cannibalism to survive. More than a hundred years later, we must confront this same barrier.

With these thoughts, I stumble into the post office in Weldon, a tiny town at the southern end of the range, near Walker Pass. The guys are engrossed in the register. Their sweaty, dust-covered bodies huddle around the book.

"What's it say?"

"Nearly everyone skipped the Sierra. Took a bus north, to a much lower elevation!"

My friend Todd and his group had skipped also. They arrived here three weeks ago. Conditions in the mountains were pretty bad. Only one group went through, very early in the season. The Steiner party was equipped with mountain skis, snowshoes, and long ropes for river fords. We're next.

In 1981 the range got twenty-three feet of snow. This year it's buried under fifty-two! Much of that is still there! Are we crazy? Should we even try? What makes us think we can get through when so many other parties jumped ahead six hundred trail miles just to avoid the snow.

When you give, you get back in kind—maybe not from the same person or in the same way, but the goodness completes the circle. When I completed the Appalachian Trail, I set up housekeeping near it, so I could bring hikers into my home, like so many did for me.

Once I had seven hikers crowded into my home. Two women were from California. As soon as they heard I'd be on the Pacific Crest Trail, they began making elaborate plans to meet me along my way. Not a one-shot deal, like their visit, but continuous service throughout the state. One was Cathy, the girl who drove me from Los Angeles to Mexico and who brought Bob to meet me in Anza.

Farther north now, her partner Marianna is taking over. She set us up with friends in Acton and visited with us in Mojave. Now in Weldon, the seven of us—Nancy, Skip, Bob, Allison, Bruce, Percy, and myself—are all going to her home in Ridgecrest, fifty miles away. She makes two round trips in order to bring all of us and our gear. For this single visit, she drives eight hours, four hundred miles in total. Yet she barely knows us. To these two exceptionally generous women, I am forever indebted. They brought much joy and comfort to my trip.

People who bring hikers into their home should be ready to provide constant service. Our needs are extraordinary. Everyone bathes. Everyone does laundry. Some need a patch to repair ripped pants, or boxes, paper, and tape for mailing equipment home. Someone else wants their hair cut or scissors to trim a beard. There are stamps and postcards to be bought, drugstore visits for lip balm and boot liners, camera store visits to clean out the mechanism, buy film and a polarizing lens for the snow. And countless phone calls home. . . Where is my whatzit? Why wasn't it put in the box?

Then there's the grocery store scene. Everyone gets a cart, immediately going off in their own little world. What a heavenly world that is! Food everywhere! Mouths agape, like country bumpkins in New York City, we look at everything. "Imagine making that into a meal!" we think. Periodically, we pass other bedraggled hikers, but our eyes are still fixed on shelves. "How many suppers do we need for the next stretch?" "Getting any bread?" All the while chomping on cookies. We ring up the empty cellophane at the check-out register.

If we aren't visiting someone's home, we have a community meal. Nancy and I are in charge. We ask for menus, gather the food, collect the $1.75, and of course no one has change for a traveler's twenty.

More often than not, salad is on the menu. Your body craves the things it needs most. Entering town, we immediately inhale ice cream, cottage cheese, yogurt. Calcium is the main deficiency in a long-distance hiker's diet. Fresh fruit and veggies are a close second.

Marianna and her husband Campy are extremely patient and understanding. They run a mountaineering shop in their home. Everyone piles in with questions. Tonight, Campy is demonstrating ice-ax self-arrest—in case we fall on a steep traverse. A mountaineer and a Sierra Club hike leader, he knows his field. An ice-ax looks good to Nancy, but Skip insists that she take two ski poles instead.

Couldn't save her life if she did fall.

For dinner tonight, Marianna cooks a huge feast. She and Campy have a beautiful custom when they have guests over for dinner. All join hands in a circle around the table and say grace.

Everyone is present except Percy, who is out in the yard, repacking his gear. Marianna calls him twice, but he doesn't listen. I leave the circle and go out to fetch him. With disgust in his eyes, he yells at me for hassling him and says he doesn't care about the prayer. The dining room table is next to the sliding glass doors that empty out onto the patio, and I know our hosts are watching.

When Percy enters the dining room, he turns on a sickeningly sweet smile and is very apologetic. For the first time, I question his sincerity. Bob and Skip sure don't like him, and I'm starting to think the men are right.

After dinner, Campy goes over maps of the John Muir Trail. For more than one hundred seventy-five miles, we'll never be near a road, never go below seven thousand feet. We discuss possible bail-out routes for help or supplies.

It's easy to share my fears with this couple. They know the

danger is real. They know the importance of being prepared, making wise decisions. More important than being successful, they say, is having the courage to alter plans, instead of staying in a situation that is dangerous or with which you're grossly unhappy. It's not failure to say you've had enough. We're not sure of our limits, so we'll try our best to succeed.

Skip

Weldon marks the symbolic end of the desert. Good-bye chaparral. Good-bye heat. The southern five hundred miles is complete. Now we begin a new leg of our journey, the High Sierra, where we will climb into the high country and remain there.

From the town of Weldon to Trail Crest, where the John Muir Trail crosses the Sierra crest just south of Mount Whitney, it is a climb of nearly eleven thousand feet. Along the way we'll walk through five life zones, each with its own characteristic climate, soil, vegetation, and wildlife. Ecologically, the journey will be like traveling from Mexico to the Arctic. Each thousand feet we climb will be the equivalent of walking northward for three hundred miles.

We'll first climb up onto the Kern Plateau, then into the High Sierra. The land around Weldon is hilly. Some places are covered with dry, buff-colored grasses. The rains stopped in March. The flowers died in early June, three weeks before our arrival. All our familiar friends are here: live oaks, chaparral, sagebrush, and heat.

Up ahead, Skip sprawls on the trail, leaning against the hillside, still saddled to his pack.

"Can't take it off," he slowly says. "Weighs ninety pounds."

"I know how you feel, Skip. Mine's close to seventy." I collapse in the dirt beside him, throw off my pack like it's the enemy. "My favorite conditions, up hill in the heat with a heavy pack. Can't beat it."

"Yeah I can," he says. "How about a swig of warm, iodized water? My favorite drink under these conditions."

I quickly swallow the brown-orange liquid. Such a repulsive beverage. Tastes like metallic medicine.

There are cattle-grazing allotments on the Kern Plateau and in the Sierra foothills. Their organic debris riddles our campsites and pollutes the streams. In John Muir's day, thousands of sheep trampled the Sierra. But cattle are the modern day "hoofed locusts." Because of this, and other nasty things like amoebic cysts, giardia, and hepatitis, we carry glass bottles of caustic iodine crystals. Dilute the crystals in water. Shake. Add the saturated solution to your drinking water. Wait, then drink, carefree. Ugh!

Even when cattle are not present, waste from humans and wildlife may contaminate the highest snowfields and run-off streams. The sensible thing to do would be to purify all drinking water. But since there is nothing more delicious than high mountain water, many hikers take their chances and only purify their water when pollution is clearly evident or there is an excess of people or animals.

We sensed a change before we got into the transition zone or lower forest. We felt the transition, the moisture in the air, the lower temperatures . Atop the Kern Plateau the trail levels out for a while, leaving us energy to enjoy this cool, new forested wonderland.

The forest is a hospitable place, easy and gentle for living. Summers are pleasantly warm and there is plenty of moisture. Deer graze. Meadows fill with wildflowers. John Muir's descriptions of the Sierra forest come to life before my eyes. It's truly a paradise worth the five-hundred-mile walk to get here.

Jeffrey pines

Trees have appeared. Ponderosa pines dot the forest. They are big trees, with yellow-pink, deeply grooved bark. These dark brown crevasses, up to several inches wide and five feet long, look like incisions. The forest floor is clean, void of undergrowth. Beneath the trees are carpets of apricot-colored needles.

We've noticed a definite change in the daily weather pattern since we climbed the plateau. Brilliant blue skies greet us in the morning. As the day progresses, cottony cumulus clouds build. By midafternoon thunder rumbles, and we're driven under cover. Rain and frozen ice balls beat the earth, bounce off our reddened skin. Every day this happens, just as John Muir said.

As the day progresses, we realize that we haven't seen Allison. Numerous cow paths have cut across the trail, but arrows are left at all intersections. Bob's been ahead since Weldon. I mentioned to him—wishful thinking—that I'd love for us to go off by ourselves together for a few days. Conditions in the group are getting tense. Nancy and Skip are more miserable than usual. Enough time has gone by for Allison to be physically equal, but she still can't hold her own. I spot Bob up ahead. He flings his arms around me when I reach him, surprising me.

"I haven't seen you in so-o-o long!"

"Hey!" Skip yells. "I didn't get my hug for the day either!"

Such changes! It wasn't long ago that Skip despised the group and resented me for coming in between him and Nancy. Her affection was directed toward me rather than him. Skip's asking for a hug makes me believe he genuinely cares about me, and that makes me feel wonderful.

Bob and I walk down the trail arm in arm. A storm stirs the heavens. The sky begins to darken.

"Allison is lost, Bob," I say. "I have the tent. She has the cook stove, but she doesn't know how to work it."

Bob goes back to search for her.

The next morning they arrive in a car on a near-by road. Allison bursts from the car, giggling, relaying her adventure. Bob walked six miles last night. Skip walked an additional six miles this morning, on a different trail, to find her. She never said "Thank you," never muttered an "I'm sorry."

I walk at an angry pace, while Nancy tags behind, describing her most recent fight with Skip. Though I'm usually understanding, I turn and say, "I can't do anything. I'm sorry, but I don't want to hear it." I need to escape. This group is closing in on me.

For the rest of the morning I hike alone. I follow Trout Creek, but I swim in fields of lupines. A deer trots from the waterside. I never see such things when I'm with the group. Someone is always talking. Soon Nancy catches up to me with the latest drama. Allison lost her glasses while crawling over a log on a stream crossing. The men are in the water, combing the creek bed, feeling in between rocks for the lost spectacles. Allison's blind without them. Maybe she'll go home!

The Kern River lies ahead, one of the widest, deepest fords on the trail. Cautiously, I find my footing amid the boulders. The surface is deceptively slow. Underneath, the current pulls at my legs. As I progress, the water rises to my hips. Allison has a hard time crossing with a guy on each arm to hold her up. Making Skip carry her pack, Nancy crosses in her underwear. Bob, Percy, and I watch them from above. "Either the girls go or we're splitting," they inform me.

Skip is again talking of leaving the trail at Kennedy Meadows, the next bail-out point. We've heard this at every town stop for the last few weeks. Nancy wants to remain on the trail.

All day long we continually lose the trail. The guys opt to cut across a meadow. "We can see the Kennedy Meadows store from here," they insist. I march through the open meadow like a trooper.

It's raining and I haven't eaten. The group is amazed at my pace. The meadow is full of gullies and knolls and takes twice as long as it looks, but I'm out-running everyone. My stomach feels empty, but I'm not weak. It's churning like the rest of me. Something else powers me through the rain, over the hills—adrenalin, anger, utter frustration with this group.

Crowds of weekend campers stare when at dusk we arrive at Kennedy Meadows campground in our soaked coated nylon. We rage through the tiny store, dumping armloads of food at the check-out counter. Outside, we make sandwiches on the dripping wet picnic table, share beers. Tonight, *Mr. Smith Goes to Washington* is playing in their outdoor theater. We lounge on our pads on the soggy ground, leaning against railroad ties in the dank night air. We pass cookies back and forth. Nerves are calming. The beer is working.

Some people view long-distance hiking as a vacation, a romantic adventure. However, expectations can be crippling, disappointing, ofttimes false. It is best to have no expectations, to be open, receptive, ready to change.

Allison has decided to go home. She expected a fun vacation. She expected me and the group to care for her, guide her, mother her. She thinks of me as a tower of strength. This trip is demanding. Every night as we sleep, our bodies build themselves back up. Our minds relax, become free of cares and the day's troubles. Come morning, we can go out to battle again. But some days, it's all I can do to make myself continue. Pulling another human being along is simply too much. She doesn't want this hike badly enough or she would find the strength. It's a question of passion.

My spirit feels only slightly lighter upon hearing her decision. While I separate food, divide provisions in half for her long bus ride home, I realize that she may be the fortunate one. She is leaving; we still have to face the high country. The snow makes me nervous. Everyone notices my quiet mood. Skip comes to the rescue with a joke.

"How much room is in that bus, Allison?" he asks. I manage a chuckle. "Let's go canoeing in the Boundary Waters," he adds. Everyone suggests their own favorite peace-filled vacations. They must be as nervous as I am.

It's been hours since the sun rose. We should have hiked a few miles by now. Everyone is airing out their clothes, sleeping bags, tents; writing letters; chatting; putting off the departure as long as possible. Their actions speak louder than the words, "I'm scared."

Eventually, after saying good-bye to Allison, we set off. Life around us quickly changes as we climb the steep trail off the Kern Plateau. Lodgepole pines appear, none measuring more than ten inches around. Their bark is gray and scaly. Gone are the towering trees that offered protection from the forces of nature. Life is getting scant. Rock outcrops are more extensive; soils are thinner. Temperatures are lower, even during the day. Nights are downright chilly.

While skirting Olancha Peak, our first close view of the High Sierra bursts before us, a solid wall of snow. It's so much higher than we are, although we've been climbing for days. I just sit there, staring. Bob joins me and we both gaze, silent, entranced. An excited fire lives in his eyes, a growing concern in mine.

As we continue our gentle ascent to more than 11,000 feet elevation at Cottonwood Pass, the snowpack becomes deeper and covers more area. Ahead of me the guys leave footprints four inches deep in the snow. By the time I arrive, the snow is weak and rotten and cannot support me. A leg punctures through. The other one joins it in the next instant. Under the dense red firs, snow does not melt uniformly. Large mounds remain in the places where the sun never reaches. Climbing up and over these miniature mountains wears down our diminishing stamina.

In order to follow the now totally obscured trail, we make mental notes, try to watch where it goes, where it first appears, and then try to guess where it goes next. If it curves, we spend even more time and energy locating it. It makes one very weary.

At Chicken Spring Lake, the sky splits open. Hail pellets pummel the ground. The temperature drops quickly, to the mid-thirties by eight o'clock in the evening. Evening brings cleaned, scrubbed air and patchy sunshine.

Siberian Outpost is named for its desolate appearance. Giant, twisted foxtail pines share our campsite. Nothing else grows on the ground: no shrubs, flowers, grasses, not even young trees.

Most of the pines, whether outstretched or still towering, seem completely stripped of bark, their naked limbs twisted by the wind. Even the exposed roots are spiraled, strengthening the entire tree. The color of the bare wood is warm and glowing, a cross between yellow ocher and burnt sienna.

The next day Bob informs me that he is going off alone again. I find it more difficult to part from him. I worry over his safety and miss him terribly. We also need him to help us find our way on these difficult stretches. I feel resentment, but try to overcome it.

The atmosphere is relaxed at our Guyot Creek campfire. Nancy brushes and French-braids my hair by firelight. Percy gives me a foot massage, and I cook dinner. When Allison left, I sent my tent home. Percy invites me into his. Together we share our meals and chores.

Nancy thinks Bob is putting space between us because of Percy. But why should he care? He's never shown me abundant affection. I think he just likes to be in the mountains alone.

The group discusses plans for the following days: when to climb Mt. Whitney, where to camp, what kind of mileage to make. The peak lies about seven miles off the Pacific Crest Trail, on what will soon become the John Muir Trail. We decide to bypass the summit. Instead, we'll cross over the Sierra Crest to the east side of the range and descend eight miles to Whitney Portal, where Marianna will meet us with supplies. My friends from New England will also join us there.

Our self-confidence grows. We have crossed rivers and survived. We've been higher than eleven thousand feet, the elevation of much of the John Muir Trail, and even at that height the snow was mostly patchy, though the patches were sometimes vast. Perhaps we can do it. Perhaps the High Sierra will be a wonderful, exhilarating experience.

Every opening in the trees makes me strain for a glimpse of Mount Whitney. When I finally break through the forest on a ridge top, a steep snowfield stretches before me. Forgetting all else, I look the situation over.

"It's okay! It's soft!" Nancy yells from below. "Look, Cindy!" She points. "Mount Whitney!"

My eyes widen. The west face! Jagged, gray rock, but no snow! Not a bit of snow! I leap down the snowfield. Hurrah! Fourteen thousand, five hundred feet and clear!

Crabtree Meadow is a lush, green paradise and home to deer and marmot. Flowing through the meadow is a crystal-clear stream whose icy water was snow just hours before. The backdrop of this heavenly scene is Mount Whitney, the crowning glory of the Range of Light.

The High Sierra! New life! A cleansing celebration! It seems the most natural thing to do. We strip down and clean our bodies. Wash the dirt and all our cares away. We take turns pouring water over reach other's heads until our brains freeze and we can no

Sunning at Crabtree Meadows

longer stand it. We wash all our clothes, string a rope to hang them out to dry, stretch out in the sun, naked. Soaking up the warmth!

The meadow is empty of all intruders. Just the animals and our little family are here. We feel like we are the first ones in this pristine wilderness. I comb my long, wet hair over my face and see Mount Whitney through the sunlit strands. I lean back on my elbows. This is a wonderland. Every half-turn of my head presents another idyllic picture-postcard scene.

Climbing out of Crabtree Meadows, we see life diminishing with each step. Lodgepoles reach only eight to ten feet high, growing to the level of packed snow. Avalanches will roar over and behead anything taller. As we climb higher still, we find stunted whitebark pines scattered in patches, misshapen by the cold, harsh winds. They grow in clumps around mountain tarns. You can tell which way the wind blows, all the trees lean that direction. They are gnarled and stooped, like old men and women. We have reached timberline, the upper edge of the forest, the highest point at which a tree can live.

Down lower, whitebark pines grow to greater heights. There is no competition here from larger trees, but life is hard anyway. At timberline their branches are low, sprawled over rocks, looking like desperate hands and arms trying to hold on, grasping for security. Snow cover is more frequent. The hearty alpine flowers haven't arrived yet. Clear patches of trail have nearly disappeared. The ground that is uncovered looks brown and dead.

Tonight we are sleeping in a glacial cirque, an amphitheater-like bowl scooped out by ice. All that remains is Guitar Lake and the ice's mark on the smooth, polished rock piled on the lake's rim.

June 28th is still winter in the alpine zone. Nothing is growing. We are in another world. Frozen, snow-covered ground is everywhere. Even the lake has huge ice chunks floating in it.

There is a four-foot strip of matted, frozen grass along the lake. We set up camp on its shore, the only clear spot. When the

Guitar Lake

temperature drops sharply, we huddle around our stoves for warmth.

There's no fuel for a fire up here. Long underwear, gloves, and wool balaclava ward off the cold, and we sip rapidly cooling tea that took an ungodly amount of time to boil. Orange peaks surround us, brilliant, fiery granite reflecting the setting sun. Soon the color turns to shocking pink, then melts to a soft pale hue. The glory of alpenglow! We sit in silence, mesmerized by the show, until someone yells, "Yo, Bob!" at a tiny black speck on the mountain. Somewhere up there, he's viewing this spectacular show alone, the way he likes it.

Six A.M.

I force my eyes open. They're plastered with sleep. Icy condensation coats the tent wall. I blow out air and see my breath. From my down cocoon, I emerge into the frosty Sierra world. The lake froze solid during the night. So did my water bottle. The sun is coming up through a gap in the rock cirque. Brilliant white light breaks forth, so pure and clean, void of all dust and dirt. Guitar Lake shines a pale, opal blue.

The mention of breakfast sounds disgusting. Eating hasn't interested me since we've been at this higher elevation. A fourteen-mile day lies ahead. Already I feel sick from the altitude. We cross an expansive snowfield and head toward Whitney's west face. The field is filled with sun cups, six-inch depressions in the snow, caused by the melting action of the sun. They are hard and rigid, still so frozen in this early hour that we can walk on their rims.

Every step makes me sicker, yet I'm barely climbing. I lean my head on my ice ax; I'm so dizzy and nauseous. The altitude is really getting to me. Bruce and Percy are way ahead. I've been pushing to keep up. When Nancy and Skip come from behind, I relax. Nancy sounds like she's hyperventilating. She's always trying to catch up. Skip explains the importance of taking our time. The air is thinner up here—not as much oxygen—so we're not getting enough into our bloodstream, he says. The more we exert, the harder our hearts have to work, the sicker we feel. Our heavy packs don't make the job any easier.

Somewhere on the wall lies the trail. Skip's been here before. Granted, the trail was clear back then, but some recollection remains. We stop in our tracks and search the bouldered slope.

There! Way up high! A thin sliver of a trail snakes back and forth.

The trail is dynamited out of the rock and switchbacks up the steep wall. In the places where the trail is buried under snow, we must traverse the ice-covered slopes. Back and forth we go, first on the left, then on the right. Thank God someone was here yesterday and made these footprints when the snow was soft! Yesterday's sun smoothed them into little depressions. We gently place our feet in the cast concrete. Still, we are shook up. Especially Nancy, with her two ski poles.

Every snowfield crossing is an ordeal. We tense up when we see one ahead. We lean on our ice ax and poles, gathering strength, the little that remains. Every traverse takes more out of us.

Finally, at Trail Crest, we meet the rest of the gang and Bob. It's the first time I've seen him in days. I mumble a faint "Hello."

"You should eat something," Bruce says to me. "It's lunch time."

"Not really interested, Bruce."

"At least take some sips of water."

Even that sounds grossly unappealing.

On the other side of Trail Crest I gasp in horror. A two-thousand foot drop! Straight down! Covered with snow! The men are going to glissade, slide down. The trail is under there, they say.

Sliding is the fastest way to go. We'll even cut off a few miles. Bob shoots down the slope first. In a matter of seconds, he's beyond our field of vision. Percy goes next. Nancy and I gain no courage while we stand watching. Only terror builds inside.

"What do you want to do?" asks Bruce.

"Do I have a choice?"

Glissade on Mount Whitney

He and I will go down side by side. Nancy and Skip will follow.

Going out to the chute, my legs shake revoltingly. Oh Lordy! We stand out there for what seems like forever, staring down. "Let's go, Bruce!"

We slide twenty yards, then dig in with our ice axes, which act as rudders. Stop! We're not letting ourselves go far each time. We're trying to maintain control.

As it gets steeper, I go faster and for much longer stretches than I care for. The packed snow under our butts holds us up.

"I'm really getting tired, Bruce."

"Me, too."

The next time I take off, I go totally out of control. I wildly fly down the slope, far away from Bruce. Screams rise from my gut. My legs are airborne. All my concentration is centered on keeping them in front of me. "Just keep them straight!" I tell myself. "Dig that ice ax in!" I bounce over sun cups, my glacier goggles plastered with snow. I see nothing. My rain gear makes me slide like a greased pig. My speed builds. Whimpers come, and I call to God for help. Over and over I mumble, "I'm so tired, so tired." My arms are exhausted from digging that ice ax in.

Finally, I stop. Everyone is a long way behind. Dazed, I lie back in a sea of blinding snow, content to have it be over. Within seconds, Skip is at my side. When he saw me take off and heard me scream, he pushed off and glissaded quickly to my aid.

"Are you okay?"

"I lost control, Skip," I sniffle.

"I was calling and calling you," he says. "You wouldn't answer. I was afraid you'd fainted or were hurt." I am touched by his concern. He really is a good guy, even though his inconsistencies are hard to handle sometimes.

For two hours we just sit here, baking in the high afternoon sun. The reflection is incredible from the snow all around us and our location closer to the sun. There's a rock outcrop paralleling the chute. Although it's more treacherous, Nancy chooses that route, instead of the snow.

"A coward is the first to die!" Skip yells back to Nancy.

"Don't say that to her, Skip. She can't help it if she's scared."

Our bodies are covered by rain gear, wool gloves, goggles. The temperature rises inside, like an oven. It feels like the sun is two yards from our faces.

"I've got to get out of here, Skip." With the slope now more gradual, I am able to race safely down the mountain. Four o'clock and I haven't eaten or drunk yet! The same pit is in my stomach that was there that day in Kennedy Meadows. By a waterfall, Percy sits cooking soup and biscuits. He heard me scream earlier and waited to see if I was all right.

Down below my friends are waiting. Together we fly down the final switchbacks. "You sure can hike fast if you want to!" Percy exclaims.

"I don't feel well up this high. I want to get down as quickly as I can," I say. When the parking lot comes into view, I break into a gallop, pack and all. My friend from New England, Beth, runs to meet me. I lift her up, swing her around. Donaldo gives me a tremendous bear hug, pulls away to look at me, then embraces me again.

"You look so good! So tan and healthy!"

Within minutes, my head is reeling. I run to the bathroom. Not a drop comes out! Over and over this happens.

Nurse Marianna is highly concerned. "You're dehydrated, girl! Your body is absorbing the liquid in your urine!"

The dizziness forces me to lie down, and I drink and eat small amounts as my body allows. I relate all that happened to my friends. "What a day! What a day!" is all I can say.

Climbing Mount Whitney

7

Mount Whitney

Inyo—"the dwelling place of a Great Spirit." The Paiute who lived in the foothills of Mount Whitney and the valleys below, gave the name Inyo to the High Sierra. Namunana, the People Father, the guardian of their travels, lives up there. Mount Whitney at fourteen thousand, four hundred ninety-five feet lies within the national forest of the same name. We're going up to visit.

June 27, four and one-half miles
"There's a good rock!" With my pack frame still on, I lift my-

self onto the flat rock and ease down. The pack's weight shifts from my shoulders to the cool granite. It's so heavy, I can't take it off unless I have help to put it back on, and our entire group of eight, including Beth and Don, is strung out over the trail. My hands push down on my knees, my arms are braced to hold the weight behind. A sticky plastic bag dangles in my face when I lean forward: smashed grapes, apples, peaches from Marianna. They didn't fit in the overloaded pack but certainly couldn't be left behind. Every fifteen-minute break I consume a few more pieces and reduce the amount of weight I must carry. At this rate, diarrhea should follow shortly. Day hikers in sneakers cruise by.

"Hi!"

"You're a PCT hiker, aren't you?"

"How did you know?" Peach juice and sweat runs down my chin.

"You look like one. You look like you're dying."

Once they're well out of sight, I hoist my injured ego and my stocky frame up by my legs, which grow more massive with every step. My body rebels at carrying seventy pounds, food for sixteen days. My feet shuffle over the trail, an inch above the ground, kicking up dirt. I feel like I'm being pushed into the earth.

There aren't any roads where we're going, the high country of the Sierra Nevada. No place to resupply. The food on my back must sustain me for one hundred and forty miles, until my next food drop in Mammoth Lakes, California. This pack is the heaviest I've ever forced my body to carry, especially while climbing the highest mountain on the entire trail. Fourteen miles of ascent to reach Mount Whitney's summit, which seems an eternity away.

Steps from behind. When I step aside, I see it's Percy, looking awfully silly with a strap around his head, connected to his pack.

"What's that for?" I ask.

"Sherpas in Tibet use their heads to help carry heavy loads."

Sounds like a good idea. My arms are going numb from these thin shoulder straps. I'm getting pack palsy. The weight is cutting off my circulation and damaging the nerves in my arms.

At Outpost Camp, we set up the tents. We're four and a half miles from Whitney Portal. Not many miles, but a lot of pain. Beth and Don have slight headaches from the altitude. Those two amaze me. I stumble in, looking and feeling as though I've gone through the wringer. Beth looks like she's going out on a date. Cotton polo shirt and belted khaki shorts, with matching ribbon in her brushed-back hair. She always looks good, even through the sloppiest trail conditions, on the most rigorous climbs.

Donaldo is equally well groomed. With his poker-straight brown hair, sleek jaw bones, and large brown eyes, he reminds me of a Middle Eastern priest, for he is half Indian. He does tai chi and meditates frequently. He's quiet and feels very deeply about things in life. Occasionally though, he comes out with a remark that sets us rolling.

We've covered many happy miles together, Beth, Don, and I. We're totally different people, but a common thread unites us — shared memories in the mountains. We'll take it slow these first days, so the Sierra newcomers can acclimate and we can enjoy each other's company.

June 28, two miles

The next day we hit snow. We take small baby steps, sliding our feet into the footprints. We lean forward as we climb, moving our faces closer to the snow. Ultraviolet rays reflect back. The inside of my nose and the roof of my mouth are beginning to burn. We walk with our mouths open, breathing heavily from the weight and lack of oxygen.

Don stays close, as he did on so many of our climbs back East. Our breath is too short to talk, too shallow to get out a full sentence.

"Look there," I say to Don, pointing to mare's-tails moving over the peak. The long, wispy clouds that curl up at the end are usually the forerunners of a storm front. Bad weather should arrive within twenty-four hours. At least it does back home.

"Doesn't look good," Don sighs.

By the time we reach Trail Camp, the final place to camp before the climb to the summit, clouds are pouring over the peak. The wind picks up almost instantly. The temperature drops quickly, and we hurriedly put on coats, hats, and wind gear. Previous climbers have built shallow rock walls around level, sandy spots. In one of these the group huddles, waiting for everyone to arrive so that we can decide to stay or go back down. We lie on foam pads in the gravel, bodies close, trying to keep in the heat. We can't stand up. The wind is gusting too strongly. It knocks us over. They make room for me, and we all stuff food down our throats. It's too windy to start a stove.

When everyone is present, we decide to stay put. Frantically, we run around, trying to find a sizable tent site out of the wind.

I help Percy tie his tent down with guy lines, reinforcing his

The group (clockwise from top right): Cindy, Bob, Skip, Beth, Don, Nancy

aluminum support poles. They continually collapse under the wind's force. Snow and hail begin falling as we struggle with freezing hands. Wind blows right through our gloves. Snow plasters our faces. When the tent finally goes up, I fetch my pack. Hunched over in the driving wind, shivering uncontrollably, I feel weak and helpless. There it is! I sit down to rest and immediately want to sleep. Oh no! Hypothermia! I force myself to walk, so that my body temperature doesn't drop too low.

Storm clouds race over our heads and drop into the valley below. We watch them as they build, turn the sky navy blue, and pour down rain. Down below, to the east, the storm clouds are dissipating over the desert. The land down there is bathed in sunlight, with a pale blue sky. It's astonishing! Here we lie in fog and blowing snow, observing the weather move along its course thousands of feet below. Patches of blue occasionally break through. We watch the storm blow by the summit. What, O mighty Namunana, have you in store for us?

June 29, zero miles

The storm really moved in last night. All night long the wind howled ferociously, slapping sleet and hail against our tent walls. I am still sleeping in Percy's tent. Bob is sleeping alone in his one-man bivvy sack. I longed for ear plugs to escape the deafening roar, but crumpled toilet paper had to suffice. Percy's tent is not meant for winter mountaineering. Its body consists only of mosquito netting. with a coated nylon rain fly. The snow blew under the fly, spraying into our faces, and accumulating almost as much inside as out. The few cat naps I managed to take were interrupted by the tent dropping flat on my face when the poles collapsed. But Percy and I merely had to reach out, push the poles up, and our roof would spring back.

Today, we're spending time reading, writing letters, recording in our journals, and visiting the other tents. Our group's tents dot the barren landscape with color: Skip and Nancy in their royal blue dome, Beth and Don in their lemon yellow tent, Bruce in his forest green two-man, Bob in his kelly green bivvy sack,

and Percy in a light tan net tent. I fall into Don and Beth's tent, full gear on, letting my snow-covered boots dangle outside.

"What are you guys up to?"

"Not much," says Don." We both read the entire guidebook for something to do. Beth's got a terrible headache. I feel like I have a hangover." Not one of us remembered to replenish our supply of aspirin.

Questions fill our heads. How many days do you think this will go on? Should we stay put? For how long? Should we go back down to resupply and lose two more days? Beth and Don only have so much time. No one knows what to do. My dear friends. They flew all the way across the country to be with me. From the desert to the snows of Mount Whitney in a matter of days. They wanted an adventure. It seems that they're getting their wish.

"Card game in my tent!" Bruce yells. Five of us pile into the two-man tent. Heads, backs, knees protrude into the tent wall, stretching the nylon. Our knees serve as the card table. Every time someone gets a cramp and needs to stretch, all five must re-arrange. Sure is toasty, though!

In the last few days, Percy and I have been eating my lunch food. His meals require a lot of prep work and long cooking, which is difficult under these conditions. Already I'm running low and we've only progressed six miles. I will be dependent on him for the rest of this stretch, a situation I don't like. Right now, I'm starving for something hot, so I go outside and brave the weather to make my emergency freeze-dried supper. I sure hope the stove works in this weather.

"When will it be ready?" Percy asks, awakening from a nap in his tent.

"Must be nice having a servant," Don whispers to me teasingly.

I'm starting to resent Percy. He won't even get out to clean dishes, even though I cooked! Just calls me "luv" and asks me sweetly to do it. I swish the pan in the granular snow, scour it with the frozen pellets. I hope this storm clears up by morning. Life in the tent with Percy is getting old fast! I wish I hadn't left

my tent behind. Right now, four pounds of tent seem worth the price of independence.

But I look around and it seems hopeless. The mountain is socked in with snow and fog. The clouds are so thick you can't tell the difference between the white, snow-covered ground and the sky above. A white-out is not safe for travel. I feel as though we're on a major climbing expedition, biding our time until the storm clears, so we can make the summit.

June 30, Summit Cabin, seven miles

Snow has fallen softly all night, burying what little trail remained. But the sky looks promising, so we dig out camp. Clouds are blowing by at high speeds. In between are large patches of blue. Every now and then, the valley breaks into view. In a matter of seconds, though, the clouds roll in, and we're alone in our world again.

"Let's get going!" Bob yells. Seven miles remain to the summit. It may take all day to get there. If we wait any longer, we'll lose another day's food and not gain a single mile. Besides, the weather does look like it's breaking up.

Bob goes first. Bruce, Don, Percy, Beth and I follow. The trail zigzags up a spiny backbone of granite, which parallels the two-thousand-foot slope we glissaded down a few days ago. The trail is open! We could have gone this way!

We spot four backpackers roped and pinned to the slope. Don't they know the trail is open? They look like they're having trouble. No one is moving.

Four inches of snow lie on the trail, but, for the time being, we can find our way. We stare down at Trail Camp, trying to spot Skip and Nancy. Their tent is still up. They'll probably wait until morning. Beth and I take turns singing lines of a Cat Stevens song: "Miles from nowhere, not a soul in sight. Oh yeah, but it's all right. Look up at the mountain, I have to climb. Oh yeah, to reach there."

Before long, bad weather moves in again and the trail disappears in snow. Adrenalin surges through my body the moment I round a corner and see one stretch of steep, icy traverses ahead of

Traversing to Trail Crest

me. I chop narrow ledges into the ice with the side of my boot for footholds, making sure they are secure, but not wanting to dawdle. The longer you take, the more chance your foot has to slip. But the more you hurry, the less cautious you become. A catch-22. The narrow ledges exhaust us terribly, mentally and physically.

We cannot believe, after walking only four feet, that we are gasping for breath! We're not even going fast. Every few yards we must stop, lean on our ice axes, and try to down more air. At high altitudes, our blood actually thickens and slows in our veins, no matter how hard or fast our hearts pump. We'd develop more and richer blood if we stayed longer, but we don't have that kind of time or that much food.

Women naturally have fewer red blood cells than men. These cells are responsible for absorbing oxygen into the bloodstream. As a result, Beth and I are suffering far more from altitude sickness than the men are.

Two new guys have joined us, teenagers just starting their trip on the John Muir Trail. Percy hangs back, teaching them to traverse. They are scared and appear very weak. Most of the time,

Bob leads, little sparkplug that he is. Occasionally the fog breaks, revealing our way and a startling new world. The rocks are not solid gray, but every gorge, crack, and depression is filled with new snow. All the crevices and cracks in the rock are etched in white. Raised crags and pinnacles stand out dark and ominous, dusted with new snow. It looks so dramatic and forbidding!

The fog rolls in again, and we are completely disoriented. Which way is Trail Crest? How far is it? Should we take the ridge? Will it be too jagged and dangerous? Bob drops his pack, takes two ice axes to chop footholds and scales the snow wall, looking for the top. The longer we watch from below and the smaller he gets, the more we realize that we don't like the way this looks. Bob backs down, and we pray for a break in the clouds to give us just one glimpse of where to go!

We continue. Our route is suddenly obstructed by an ice waterfall, which we are compelled to climb. The guys pull our packs up separately. "Please, God, keep us strong. Give us courage," I mutter to myself.

When we finally make the top, we collapse in the snow. The ice below us breaks way, just minutes after we crossed it. Never have I prayed so much as I did today. Unceasing prayer, the only way to keep down my fright.

We let out a roar when we see the sign at Trail Crest and topple into the snow. We can't rest for too long. Precious body heat is being sucked right out of us by the cold snow. Below us is the two-thousand-foot slope. The roped-in backpackers are still there. It must be tremendously difficult to ascend.

The long trudge to the summit cabin remains. Another two miles, another thousand feet to climb. Climbers generally try to ascend only a thousand feet a day, in order to acclimate. We are far exceeding that. At sea level, your blood is saturated with oxygen. The higher you climb, the less oxygen there is, the lower your blood's oxygen level drops. When it goes below sixty-five percent, exhaustion results. Below fifty-five percent, you're risking unconsciousness.

Beth and I have been sticking close together all day. After what seems like hours of suffering, she collapses.

"Sure would be nice to lie down and die."

I wholeheartedly agree. How strange! How can death look so good? This must be how a dying person feels on his last days: weak, just seeking rest and peace, release from the enclosing pain. Just wanting it to be over.

A scream startles us. "Send help!" Bruce yells from behind. "We're in trouble!"

We yell up to Bob and Percy. "Somebody, quick! Bruce needs help!"

Bob and Percy charge past us down the trail. Soon, the two young teenagers appear, without their packs, being pulled by our men. The two kids are out of it. They were trying to sleep in the snow. Bruce is shook up, too, but for a different reason. He was alone back there and didn't know how far ahead we were.

Beth and I let out a whoop when we see the roof of the cabin. It's over! We put the two hypothermics into sleeping bags, light the stove, and shove soup, tea, and food down their throats. The results are immediately noticeable, and the boys quickly recover.

This mountain was named after Professor Josiah Whitney, California's first state geologist and the man who supervised the first geological survey of the Sierra Nevada. The stone shelter was erected in 1909 by the Smithsonian Institution to study water vapor in the atmosphere of Mars! In 1913, it was used to study solar radiation. Since then, the shelter has seen a lot of use, a lot of storms, and a lot of frozen, exhausted hikers.

There are three little rooms in the shelter. Ice coats the floors like a skating rink. The doors are off the hinges, but we lean them up against the openings. We spread out all the ground cloths and space blankets that we have. The foam pads go down next, and then we climb into the sack to make supper.

Bob is acting spacey, stumbling and stuttering, probably from overexertion.

"Bob, sit down," I say.

He comes over and puts his arms around me and we cuddle. I tell him I love him and sincerely mean it.

Later, I begin shivering and feel sick. I notice Percy is flitting around like normal, so I ask if he'll cook dinner.

"How about if you do it, and I'll help?" he replies.

"How about if you do it all by yourself," I answer. And he does.

The storm clears completely while we eat supper. Suddenly, someone realizes that the sky is ablaze with color! We clamber about in our insulated down booties, skating on the slippery floor, taking pictures through the sole remaining glass window. Bob digs celebration beers out of the snow. I mix up an instant cheesecake and go around feeding huge spoonfuls to everyone with my wooden spoon. We all drink hot chocolate by cozy candlelight. Melting the snow to make the chocolate puts a big dent in our fuel supply, but we're dehydrated and need the liquid.

The orange glow begins to fade as we brush our teeth with snow. Save that water! I feel privileged to be here with these people. They've made all the difference in the world. Climbing into my bag, I mutter a prayer of thanks for getting here alive and in such good company.

Beth and I slept intertwined last night. The ice floor underneath was so cold. We laid rain gear beneath us in the middle of the night, in the hope of better insulating the floor. Still, we felt the cold. The shutters banged continuously from the wind. With the cold and the banging, we slept little. We peeked out to see if the world was growing any brighter, waiting for morning.

At four o'clock I had to make a trip outside. As soon as I sat up, I felt instantly dizzy and nauseous. Relieving myself outdoors was a feat. I came back feeling as though a train had hit me.

This morning I can't get breakfast down. Vomit rises as soon as I raise the spoon to my lips. Packing up, we discover that everything is soaked! We slept in puddles! Our body heat melted the ice.

Outside, the view is gorgeous.

Jagged mountains extend as far as you can see. The sky is a shade of deep, dark blue that you will never see at lower elevations. There's nothing green anywhere. Just steel gray granite and snow so brilliant that you cannot venture forth without wear-

Summit of Mount Whitney

ing glacier goggles, complete with leather side pieces. We stroll around the summit, taking rolls of pictures.

It seems to us that there is no higher place in all the world. This is it! The top of the earth. The next flight up is heaven. We feel favored. The mountain has showed us who is boss these last days, but it did allow us to gain the summit and see this extraordinary sight. I do not want to linger, however. I don't want to spend hours in repose, soaking up the view. I see the beauty, but sickness and cold speak louder. Our time here must be short.

As I race down Mount Whitney, my headache lessens. I begin to feel strong again. But, as soon as we have to climb over a windswept cornice or even go uphill, the sickness floods back.

The trail on this side of the crest has about six inches of new snow, which crunches loudly beneath my feet as snow crystals break in the cold. The sound gradually decreases as the day warms up and the crystals soften and become flexible.

Our trail mostly traverses Whitney's gently sloping west side, just below the crest, but narrows to three feet as it passes through gaps, or windows, in the pinnacles. One foot to our left the east face of the peak drops two thousand feet to the rocks below.

Eroded cliffs and couloirs flank this face, where the technical climbers ascend.

Beth hates the windows. She thinks of what could happen if she were to slip in the snow or if a swift wind were to knock her off balance. Gingerly, I step across and peer down thousands of feet to the desert. This place didn't even faze me yesterday in the fog, when we couldn't see the exposure. We weren't conscious of the height and steepness and potential danger.

Finally reaching Trail Crest, we turn west on the John Muir Trail and switchback steeply down to Guitar Lake, where we had camped six nights before.

Here, we take a long break. The elevation—about 11,500 feet—is low enough to make us feel better. We bask in the sun, drying our soaked gear. Air Force jets scream overhead and fly so close to the crest that it looks like they'll crash. They make steep bank turns and swooping dives. Engines roar, the sound of war. It brings us back to reality. There is another world besides the mountain.

When you're up there, though, there is nothing else. Just the mountain and survival.

North slope of Forrester Pass

8

Siberia

July 2

With high gaiters to her knees, only Nancy's shapely, bronzed thighs are displayed. Her long legs step high over sun-cups, prancing into lunch like a show horse.

"Nancy! Where've you been all these days?" we ask. Bob, Percy, Beth, Don, and I stop spreading peanut butter, stop reading guidebooks, and cutting fingernails. Her tale unwinds.

"We were ready to pack up at Trail Camp, when the weather moved in again. Skip stared up at you guys climbing on the rocks, as the fog rolled in. 'Come on,' I said. 'Let's get going.' All of a sudden he started screaming and pointing. 'They're going to die up there! They're all going to die! I'm going back to the Portal and get a bus home!'

"I was so upset," she continues. "I didn't want to quit. I knew I'd never see you again. I didn't have your address. I knew I couldn't follow you alone. I really started crying. Well, he got so angry with me, he picked up boulders and crashed them into the ground. Even killed a marmot. Screaming the whole time. I just didn't know what to do. I was really afraid to be alone with him.

"Just before that outburst he ate an entire can of cake frosting. Nine hundred calories of sugar. I've been noticing that this is when he gets these incredible mood swings. Usually he's nice, but then sometimes he goes on these sugar binges and then behaves so strangely.

"Anyway, we went back down to Outpost Camp that night, and the storm finally cleared. Skip promised me that he'd bring me to you guys and then get out the first chance he has. I never hiked faster than I hiked today. I was so afraid I wouldn't catch you! So here I am. Skip is just behind."

It's three o'clock and she hasn't eaten all day. Nor has she stopped walking. It's amazing how strong people can be when they want something greater than their fear.

I manage to get breakfast down this morning, but as soon as I begin climbing, the sickness floods back. We walk in the direction of the wall, Forrester Pass, thirteen thousand two hundred feet.

Up through the frozen, desolate country. The landscape opens up. No animals are in sight. Most live in more hospitable environments. No trail is in sight either, but none is necessary. We walk enchanted, staring at the barrier, as if some superhuman, magnetic power is drawing us against our will. I search its serrated crestline for what could be the pass, the low point.

"Are you okay?" asks Nancy.

I shrug. Tears stream down my face and I'm glad she's behind and can't see me crying. I'm so tired of all this snow.

The gradually switchbacking trail, which was so painstak-
ingly dynamited out of the granite, is totally buried by snow.
What remains is an ice wall. We pick our way slowly, trying to
climb at an angle, but sometimes heading straight up. We rest often. Skip is now close behind—right where you'd want an emergency medical technician.

Near the top, our trail crosses a couloir, a narrow ice chute
that drops thousands of feet. It cannot be avoided. I cross without
thinking, never glancing down. Nancy is next.

"How is it?" she asks.

"Not fun. Just go for it. It held me." We both know her two ski
poles won't help if she falls. After a half dozen adjustments of her
glacier goggles and licking her lips, she steps to safety.

Boulders lie exposed at the top of the pass, poking out of the

Nancy traversing

snow. The hot, noonday sun strikes them directly, melting the snow quickly. The air is dead still, strange for this elevation.

The group is scattered on the rocks, and surprisingly enough, there is a ranger here also. He was just dropped in by helicopter and is on his way to his station. I look past the group out to the expanding new world. A new set of ranges, canyons, and pale, frozen lakes. Always snow.

"What's the report up ahead?" I ask the ranger. "The passes get lower to the north. Is there less snow?"

"Afraid not," he replies. "Just got a report from a pilot who flew over yesterday. The range is buried. Elevation doesn't matter. Spring snows hit north of here."

In a daze I drop my pack. Oh, dear God. There is a long, uncomfortable silence.

"Where're all the people we've heard are on the John Muir Trail?" Percy jokes lightly. "Guidebook says there ought to be traffic signals, there're so many."

"It's like Siberia up here," adds Skip. "We're the only fools here."

"You're the only fools I've seen," says the ranger, smiling.

I sit off to the side, blinking back tears and watching marmots that now come out of their holes to investigate us. A half dozen pop out to lie in the sun. They look like large groundhogs but sport long, bushy tails. Fat and clumsy, with yellow-brown fur, they're the only color in this stark environment. A warning whistle from a nearby marmot startles me and reminds us to push on.

Stepping down the steep slope, I sink in to my thighs. Abrasive ice crystals cut into my red skin. My running nose forces me to sniff back the tears.

"I'm worried about Cindy," I overhear Skip say to someone behind. "She's crying all the time."

I'm worried about me too. I'm getting burned out. I'm tired of being scared, of deep snow, of traversing. I'm tired of feeling sick every morning and not being able to breathe when I climb. I need a break. Beth and Don are getting out at the Kearsarge Pass trail tomorrow, ten miles from here. They've had enough. They've been trying to talk me and Nancy into going with them, but we know that we'd never come back up here alone. Skip says that the Bishop Pass Trail, fifty miles from here, is a good place for us to get out to resupply. It leads to the big town of Bishop. There's even a bus station for him to catch a bus home. If I don't get away and forget my fears for a while, I'll have to quit. Bishop looks like a good target.

It isn't long before we meet Bruce, whose tent is already set up—although the sun is hours from setting. He pitched it on the first dry spot he came to. A little bit of heaven in the middle of hell. He figured I wouldn't want to go far, the way I was feeling.

Tonight, Nancy and I stay up late by the burning embers of the campfire. "Don't think about it so much," she advises. "Don't try to outguess yourself. That's when you'll get hurt."

"You sound like Skip. 'Get scared and you die.' He's right though," I admit. "I'm obsessed with this fear."

I remember reading an account of Jim Podlesney, another PCT hiker, who said: "Nothing can prepare a hiker for the despair, the alienation, the anxiety, and especially the pain, both physical and mental, that slices to the very heart of the hiker's volition, which are the real things that must be planned for. The ability of the hiker lies in his personal adaptations. The desire to do the long distance hike is the only thing that can get a person through."

There has to be a passion, even before one starts, an insatiable desire for that goal. It must be strong enough to carry a person through all the hard times. It must be strong enough to keep one's vision clear. Right now, my desire to do the hike and my desire to go home are running neck and neck.

The next morning, everyone discusses plans for the coming week, where each of us is getting out to resupply. Everyone wants to do something different. Bob wants to go on ahead, and Bruce would like to join him. No one wants to get out at Bishop, except Skip, who is going home, and Nancy, who gets more scared than I do. Skip thinks we're crazy to attempt to get any farther on what little food is left. Supplies were depleted by the storm on Whitney and, in my case, by Percy. I must get out at Bishop for food and for my mental health. Won't anyone else come with Nancy, Skip, and me?

The log beneath my bottom is cold and wet, yet I scarcely notice. Already packed up, I sit and wait for the others. Everyone mills around, folding tents, stuffing sleeping bags, not noticing me. Suddenly, I feel very alone in the world. I have put so much energy into this group. I have tried so hard to keep it together. I don't want to quit. I just need a break. Nancy says she'll never leave me, but Nancy and I can't make it alone. I need to know that someone who is stronger than I am will be there should I need help. I cannot stop the tears. I hold my head between my legs and sob.

Bob comes over to talk. He's going off on his own—for good. He doesn't want to be held up by the group any longer.

"I thought this was supposed to be a loosely knit group," he says with a smirk on his face, his chiseled jaw protruding even further.

"Fine," is all I can answer, and I feel a knife go through my heart. Bruce comes over next.

"I'm going to stay," he says. "I'd just as soon get out at Bishop anyway."

My face lights up! "Oh, thank you, Bruce!"

"Come on," he says. "I'll walk with you today."

There are four men camped at the Kearsarge Pass Trail when we arrive. Each one has a muscular body that makes him look like Charles Atlas when compared to our skinny, undernourished guys. Our poor men look as though they're feeding on muscle. They don't eat enough. Vast amounts of calories are needed out here, and lately we've been starving. I say my teary good-byes to Beth and Don and go over to chat with the newcomers.

It's a warm and balmy night. I sit on a high rock and let the landscape soak in. A misty fog rolls in, making the foxtail pines look as though a white organdy veil has been dropped over them.

The farther you look in the distance, the milkier the landscape becomes. One of the new guys comes over to my side. Sandy-haired Derreck and his buddies are out for a week. We exchange information, talk of our homes, the kind of work we do. Because he is a stranger and is so taken aback by what we are doing, it's easy to talk to him. He does not find me a coward, nor weak. He's impressed and honored, he says, to meet a woman like me. He helps me understand what I'm going through out here, for he sees the entire drama from an unprejudiced point of view.

The moon rises, full and luminous, while we talk. With the light reflecting off the fog, the night is even brighter. We stand to say good-night in the damp evening air. We quickly embrace, and I run off to my tent.

"What were you guys talking about?" Nancy inquires, as I pass by her tent.

"Fear."

Skip wants to know why I allow myself to have these fears when they can be so destructive.

"Men are raised differently than women," I explain. "From an early age you are taught not to show your fear. Courage is synonymous with manhood. When women put themselves in vulnerable situations, when we're suddenly confronted with new fears, we often react emotionally. Every pass I go over, every snowfield I traverse will make me more confident. One day, the high passes will become a pleasure, not something to dread."

The next morning I join the new men for breakfast. On my way back to our site, I pass Percy. "Got a fan club?" he asks, as he packs his gear.

At the top of the pass, the guys catch up with our group. Derreck comes over, and we share his lunch and my foam pad. He asks me for my address and mail drops. Percy sits removed from the group, sneering at me. He's been cold to me for weeks, shares no thoughts or fears, just his tent. When I ask him what's wrong, he says he doesn't know. I resent the way he treats me just so that he can join the security of the group.

"You guys want some salami?" Derreck's buddy asks. "Here, take the rest. I've got some extra cheese you can have too. We'll be

The "new guys" at Glen Pass

heading out soon. Probably been a while since you've had fresh food."

Our guys say their thanks and pack up. They won't even talk with the newcomers.

The guys all come for parting hugs and kisses. I hug Derreck, then he turns away, then turns back. "Come see me in L.A.!" he says.

"You've got a date!"

How light my heart feels now! Bounding down the slope, weaving through the partially frozen Rae Lakes, I stagger like a drunk, from the deep snow and the high, happy feeling in my heart. I realize that Glen Pass didn't even faze me! Those guys were so good for my self-confidence!

A new problem has entered our little lives: hunger. A hiker can burn more than six thousand calories a day, trudging up and over these snowy passes. We're trying to function with a daily intake of fifteen hundred calories. We're falling way short of needed calories.

It's still slow going, trudging through snow, but we're trying to push now. Seven- and eight-mile days are full and exhausting. Fourteen-milers are on the present agenda to get us to Bishop sooner. Another day on the trail means three more meals and a multitude of snacks. If we can't make fifteen miles, we'll have to hike without food, a feat next to impossible in my opinion.

Between passes, the trail drops into high valleys and basins, where we find warm, comforting environments, shimmering aspens, spring flowers, and wild onions that we pick by the potful in an attempt to stretch our meals. No matter if we're preparing macaroni and cheese or freeze-dried lasagna, it's seventy-five percent onion and predominantly green.

Lately, I've been sharing Bruce's tent. Percy told me he had bad gas problems and that it might be in *my* best interest to sleep elsewhere. His subtle hint is the get-away I need.

Today, Bruce and I awake before the others. I need an early start for a big day, since I'm the slowest of the group. Bruce says

The great basin below Mather Pass

he'll keep me company. The rest of the group will catch us later in the day. But Bruce and I lose the trail and fall behind, stupidly following footprints that we assumed were heading toward our destination—twelve-thousand-foot Mather Pass. By the time we discover our mistake and get to the base of the path, it's already four o'clock. Only now does Bruce notice that he left his ice ax at our last rest spot, a mile back. So while he goes back to get it, I huddle alone on the last bit of dry earth before the next pass—Mather Pass. I tuck myself into a ball, knees tight together to keep in heat, like an alpine flower nestled under a rock. I bury my hands in my pile jacket, pull my wool hat lower over my forehead, and stare into the upper basin, watching for Bruce. Clouds are moving in, dark gray and threatening. The world around me is frozen. I can't believe this is July!

Is that my name I hear faintly when the wind blows? All day long I have imagined voices, thinking the gang was close by. We were never sure if they had gone ahead or were following our footprints, getting lost themselves. But my name was always on the wind. Sometimes we thought we saw tiny figures, waving their arms to us in the Upper Basin. But they were always firs, waving in the wind. This time I hear it distinctly. "Cindy!"

Up on the pass! A tiny speck of a man, waving his arms! "Take the snow! Don't take the rocks!"

Confusion races through my mind. What snow should we take? Which rocks shouldn't we take? Both cover the entire wall. I search for a clue, then spot two more specks hanging on the side. One is higher and is moving down to the lower one. Moving down? Is that Nancy? Is she in trouble? I watch for an hour. They barely move. My God, it must be difficult!

By the time Bruce returns, the two have disappeared over the pass. The sky has grown darker, and the air is frigid. Bruce is so exhausted, he has to give me instructions on how to set up his tent. He can barely move, and just lies there in the gravel on his foam pad. Supper is a somber affair. We sit with our feet wrapped in coated nylon stuff sacks to keep in warmth. We wolf down our evening rations and sit staring at the wall, wondering where to go and how to do it. This is our first time without the security of the group. If we get in trouble, no one will even know.

In the tent I pound my clothes bag pillow to make a depression for my head, draw my hood tightly, so that only my nose is sticking out. Last night it was so cold that my body burned up the calories from supper before I even fell asleep. Images of my possessions flash in my head. Whom should they go to if I die up there? My silver and turquoise jewelry to my Mom. My backpacking gear to my AT partner. Divide up my artwork. I turn in my mummy bag to whisper these ridiculous things in Bruce's ear, but he's sound asleep, snoring softly.

I sigh and wonder how long it will be before the snow begins to melt. Can I hold out that long? I'm not ready to quit yet. I've come so far and gone through so much to get here. It's three long days to Bishop. I'll just try to get through them.

From the moment Bruce made a commitment to hike with me, he has always been there when I needed him. When I am scared, he never leaves my side. If I need to talk, he listens. And on ascents when I am too scared to speak, he jabbers on, telling stories, which is quite unnatural for him. He speaks so softly that I can hardly catch enough to comment on—it's all to keep my mind occupied.

When we hike together, he considers my fatigue and asks if I need to rest. The quietest member of the family is becoming my greatest strength through this most difficult part of the journey. Today is no exception.

Climbing rocks is reasonably safe, as much as Nancy despises it. You take small steps, cautious and slow. Big leaps only force you to exert much more energy and swing your pack over your head, which throws you dangerously off balance. We take our time climbing Mather Pass. So far, it's not too bad.

When we reach the snow, another vertical stepladder awaits us. The prints of those who walked this before us are deep, frozen solid, and quite capable of holding our weight. The snow must have been very soft for them to sink in up to their hips. Pulling

The pass

yourself out of a hole is very dangerous on a slope this steep.

The snow stops at a rock outcrop. There is a two-inch ledge we must traverse. It's too narrow to walk straight across — our packs would hit and throw us out into the air. We cross facing the wall, on our boot tips, arms outstretched, gripping the rock. Bruce takes my ax so that I can use both hands and I nervously manage to cross to safety.

There is an overwhelming sense of excitement and anticipation as you near the top of a pass. When you take those last crawling steps, stand upright on level ground, and peek over the edge, it's as though you are the first to discover the world beyond. Nothing on this trip can surpass this feeling.

The Palisades Lakes stretch down the snow-covered valley and by one there appears to be a grassy stretch where we could camp. Is the group down there?

Nancy yells when she sees our little pack bodies dropping out of the sky. "Get up, you guys! They made it!" They placed bets on the time when we'd be in. Two o'clock was the general consensus, but we were four hours early.

We zigzag down the dynamited Golden Staircase, built on the cliffs of the Palisades Gorge, the last part of the John Muir Trail to be constructed. The trail is submerged by rushing, flowing snowmelt that runs like a creek, taking the bends on the trail just as we do.

"Percy didn't want to wait," Nancy reports, as she sloshes through the water. "He and Skip had a fight over it. Skip yelled, 'You're not going anywhere! We're a group and we're staying together! They may need our help.' He was prepared to wait until two and then go back to find you."

My heart warms.

Skip is really going home this time, Nancy says. He's worried about his mental health. One afternoon as Nancy was cutting cheese, Skip seemed to go berserk at the sight of her holding the knife. What did he think she planned to do with it? He's had such drastic mood swings—violent anger, then deep depression. It could be a reaction to his diet. He consumes huge amounts of sugar. We speculate that he could be hypoglycemic. Skip can be difficult, but he's really a nice guy. I hope he can get some help.

Our trek through King's Canyon retraces the route followed by the Spanish explorer Ensign Morago, who camped along these banks in 1806. He arrived on January 6, the same day as the feast of the Magi, who visited the infant Jesus. He named the river Rio de los Santos Reyes, River of the Holy Kings. And it is a canyon well suited for royalty.

Walking along the river's bouncing, spraying water, a feeling of immensity overshadows you. When you look up, the canyon walls tower more than eight thousand feet above you and you're two thousand feet deeper than you would be in the Grand Canyon! You feel as though you are in a colossal funnel. Avalanches have roared down the polished walls, leaving large bald scars. The violence of winter!

Peace is a state of mind. It has to come from inside your soul, they say. Adversity shouldn't affect it, not if its source is deep and steady. Or so I thought. Not until I descended from the snow and cold of the high country, into the gentle warmth of Le Conte Canyon, and breathed the perfume of the wildflowers, not until I watched deer graze in Grouse Meadow, backlit by yellow sunshine, and felt the aspens shimmer while running my hand along their pale, green bark, not until I heard the surging waterfalls of the King's River and drank its aquamarine water did I realize how much environment could affect my peace. It was as if my spirit lay dormant and starved under that twenty feet of snow. I feel as if my senses thawed out and came to life. I break into song. A smile covers my face. The harsh, frozen world I left behind has no strings attached to my heart. This, to me, is paradise.

Getting out of the mountains from here is not easy. You must hike an eighteen-mile side trail up and over another pass just to arrive at a primitive dirt road miles from the nearest highway. And from there it is many more miles to even the first small store. The town of Bishop is more distant yet. Even so, this route over Bishop Pass is our choice. Our depleted food sacks contain only spices and one spare gravy mix. They say the town of Bishop has everything!

When you stand at the top of a pass in this open country, it's not difficult to find your way. It takes no skilled map reader to see that the trail wraps around the left side of the lake, cuts through the outlet, and goes around to the right of the next lake, just as it does on the map. Beneath Bishop Pass the trail winds through a string of sapphire glacial lakes whose basins were sculpted in the Ice Age. The first one is frozen solid and has a snow survey marker nearby. The California Department of Water Resources sends snow survey crews into the mountains monthly to gauge the depth and water content of the snowpack. They can predict the amount of water likely to run off in the spring and determine how much the reservoirs downslope will accumulate. If it's a heavy, wet year, the reservoirs can remain open longer to prevent spring flooding.

The farther we descend from Bishop Pass, the more defrosted lakes we find and the more people we see. At the South Lake trailhead there are pack horses and manure everywhere, staining the brilliant snow brown and polluting the lake's immaculate waters. How did they get here? We find it hard to believe that pack animals can traverse. When we walk through narrow aisles of snow, with walls up to seven feet high on our sides, we realize that the trail has been shoveled right down to the ground!

I ask each person that we encounter on the trail about the good places to eat in town. Bakeries, pizza parlors, salad bars, ice cream shops. I want to know them all: places to stay, places to dance, movie theaters, department stores. I want to do it all!

I'm used to stashing my pack somewhere safe and going off with a stuff sack for a purse. If there is no designated place for a wandering mountaineer to stay, we usually can find some secluded picnic area or a dimly lit baseball field to camp in. Bruce is uneasy about this though.

"Bishop is a big town," he says, "probably with an active police force that has never heard of the PCT." Bruce prefers a motel, which cuts into our partying money, so he offers to pay the major part of the bill.

It's a little frightening to enter a backpacker's motel room. Parachute cord is strung from door to curtain rod, tents and sleeping bags are unstuffed and left to air on the line. The sink contains drying cooking gear, and soaking water bottles line its rim. The sink's bowl has a black water ring from the greasy carbon on the pot's bottom, and ten-day-old socks soak in the water. Wash hangs on our towel racks, while Nancy's boots soak in the tub in the hope of stretching them out. Dirt from the groundcloth that Bruce shook out clings to the ceramic sides of the tub. White face towels are used to clean boots and other sundry items. After bagging our supply box, instant oatmeal and potato flakes litter the shag rug and look like confetti. We lounge on the unmade bed, watching cartoons and old movies. Maps and guidebooks take up the remaining space. Since the air conditioner is on in this desert motel, our very stale, used-up air has no place to go. Takes some getting used to when you first enter.

Bruce and I, Skip and Nancy are sharing this palace. Percy is off on his own. He made friends with the outdoor store's manager the moment we arrived in town. We have all had our fill of his borrowing habits.

Getting a cash advance on my credit card enables me to gorge on chocolate eclairs and apple strudel at the bakery and a steak dinner at the Ponderosa. I even bought sterling silver earrings at the jeweler and thought twice about purchasing mascara. Night falls and I am ready for dancing. Bruce is busy writing a long letter to his girlfriend, while Skip lies on the bed, engrossed in a submarine war movie. Nancy is ready to meet some Bishop men but feels obligated to spend Skip's last night with him.

So, I cruise into the bowling alley nightclub wearing my "in town" khakis, a T-shirt, and sneakers. The men turn and look as I go by. No tables are empty. A small one with two chairs has only one guy sitting at it.

"I've got some sand in my sneaker," I say. "Do you mind if I sit down and remove it?" The guy turns out to be really nice. He "hates bars and hates to dance" but has no idea how else to meet girls. We get into some good talks, and before we realize it, the night is over. He's danced nearly every song and enjoyed it!

At two o'clock I slide into my motel bed. The late show is long over.

"Have a good time?" Nancy whispers from her bed.

"You bet!"

There are tears in Skip's eyes as we pack up and say good-bye. John Denver's "Back Home Again" is playing on the radio. It's best for him to return home, I suppose. Bob left first, now Skip.

Percy must sit and wait in town until his money arrives, living off the kind heart and wallet of the storekeeper. He may even decide to go home. Bruce will be our loyal companion for the next one hundred miles to Yosemite, where the High Sierra and the John Muir Trail end. We three quietly smile at each other as we take the sunny drive back up to the trail in the shuttle bus.

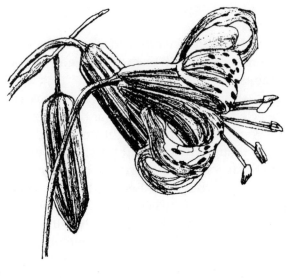

Tiger lily

9

Spring Arrives

July 14

Spring creeps very slowly up the Sierra. Evidence of its arrival does not even reach the alpine zone by the time things begin to die in the foothills. In Siberia, we were barely conscious of the changing season. Time stood still, preserved, in that frozen world. We saw some changes when we descended into the river basins, but we never remained long enough for the sun to warm our bone marrow. What occurred in the mountains, while we frolicked in Bishop, was nothing short of an explosion.

July is the hottest month in the Sierra. The greatest snow melt occurs then and all but the high peaks wake up and come alive.

The range has the mildest, sunniest weather of any major mountain range in the United States. Only five percent of the range's precipitation falls in the summer, leaving a clear, sunny atmosphere to radiate heat.

The six-foot-high, shoveled snow walls we descended through on our way to Bishop melted to waist level! Inches haven't disappeared, feet have! The snow is mud black from horses' hoofs and hikers' treads. This reduces the snow's reflectivity and holds in the heat, helping it to melt even more rapidly. The guidebook says mid-July is the safe time to go into the high country. That wasn't true four days ago.

An army of footprints goes over the passes, some prints high on precipitous slopes, others meandering haphazardly up the basins. Gone are Bob's prints. Atop snow-choked Muir Pass, a hummingbird dives into Bruce's back. His sunflower yellow sweatshirt, with its violet hood and magenta sleeves, is the closest thing to a flower up here. A hungry hummingbird can go comatose if the temperature drops below fifty degrees and his tummy's not full. He won't find much to eat on Bruce!

In some places enormous slopes are covered with sun-cups. The sun-cups can grow as deep as three feet, turning into miniature mountains and valleys that are quite treacherous to walk on. They begin as little irregularities on the snow's surface, formed by rain or debris. When warm summer air blows over these raised areas, they diminish by evaporating. The hollows, in turn, are protected from the wind, soak up more heat, and melt faster. Since greater energy is required to evaporate snow than melt it, the hollows sink deeper, getting far ahead of their rims.

We walk on the cup rims in the early hours of the day, when they're still frozen from the night's low temperature and rigid enough to support us. Later in the day, we must step into the holes, for the rims soften up and collapse. It's slow and deliberate walking.

In gullies where it looks like a stream could be buried underneath the snow, we look for streaks of pink on the surface. The color looks like someone trickled watermelon juice down the de-

Walking on sun-cups

pression. This algae is actually green, but coats itself with a pink gel for protection from intense solar radiation. We don't dare eat the pink snow, for it acts as a laxative.

The biggest clue in the high country that the season is advancing is water. It runs under the snowpack, carving the snow into gullies, canyons, and bridges. The same erosion is at work on the earth, only now its medium is much softer and more pliable than the granite beneath it.

As the passes get progressively lower, our trail descends deeper into the middle forest region. The guidebook continually speaks of "formidable" stream crossings ahead. Until now, fords weren't even on our list of concerns. If a ford is too imposing, however, Bruce always rests at the bank, waiting to assist.

Ice is breaking up in the high lakes. Sections of the trail pop out of the snow in the places where a patch has melted through. Surprise! It's like seeing an old friend, and it feels good to know you're right on course.

Meadows are the first areas to spring forth with new life. Even before the snow leaves, the soggy ground begins sprouting.

With only six to eight weeks to complete their cycle, the flowers bloom furiously. After only a few days, it seems, the ground is bursting with their color. No time is wasted, for Mother Nature made them predominantly perennials. Their root systems, shoots, and buds develop before the snow leaves. Snow melt, not rain, is their source of moisture and a high water table keeps them moist.

Once you descend away from the deep snows and runoff, you see few meadows. The Sierra summers are much too dry to produce such lush, water-loving vegetation without the help of snow.

Tonight the snowy high country is exactly where I want to be. A tiny creek meanders four feet from our tent. Water laps gently against the bank. Nearby, a gorgeous waterfall crashes to the canyon floor. Frogs harmonize in the lake before me and complete the wilderness spring song.

Evolution Lake in Evolution Basin is the kind of place I'll hold close all the days of my life. The beauty here is supreme. The lake is nestled in an amphitheater of peaks named for Darwin and all the thinkers and pioneers of evolution. Darts of low evening light spotlight the soggy meadow I sit on, intensifying the green and gold alpine grass that has just now begun to grow.

Now that I've witnessed spring's arrival, now that I've seen the snow melt and the lakes defrost and feel confident that I will be safe, I do not want to leave! Such fickleness! I've heard that people become mystically attached to the Sierra—a devotion that takes some time to develop. I can feel a little bit of that happening, now that some fear has left and spring has made room in my heart for love.

Other changes have taken place since we left Bishop. There are two less people now. Skip and Percy are gone. Only Bruce, Nancy, and I remain. With Skip gone, Nancy is much more relaxed and fun to be with. She doesn't complain at all and is discovering all sorts of new things, like taking charge of route finding and being able to choose the way to go. This new-found freedom is giving her the confidence she needs.

Bruce, Nancy, and I have made a pact to put every effort into enjoying ourselves. Walk slower. Look around. Lounge in the flower meadows. Eat more food. Make more drawings. Quit early in the day. We chuckled when someone in Bishop exclaimed, "Think of the fun you must be having!" Fun? That word hasn't been in our vocabulary as of late. So we've decided, after eight hundred miles, that we're due for that little bit of fun everyone assumes we've been having.

Bruce walks ahead, scouting the trail. He goes off on his own a lot. Nancy hikes second and, although she has slowed down quite a bit, her uncontrollable fear of being in the rear and losing us drives her to walk faster. It turns out that Skip was the source of this fear. In his efforts to get her to leave with him, he had repeatedly told her that we would leave her behind to die. I did not realize how seriously she took this warning until I came upon her one time as she was hastily and awkwardly urinating beside the trail, her clothing and pack still on, just so she wouldn't be left behind. To make her feel easier now, I often saunter along in the rear.

Life is mellow and easy. There seem to be thousands of alpine lakes, too numerous even to name. Wildflowers of every color crowd the meadows. Incense cedars, with their bases charred black from ancient fires, fill the air with a spicy aroma. Ground squirrels pop up in the grass. Deer seem tame. A refreshing breeze blows constantly and the trail is clear and open. In an environment like this, it's easy to relax and let the conversation flow. Nancy and I could talk our way to Canada if time allowed.

On the agenda today is the Bear Creek ford. We ask everyone going the opposite way about trail conditions. The horror stories are accumulating about Bear Creek. We're talking white water, waist-high white water. And someone supposedly died while crossing it last week! This worries Nancy. When we arrive at the surging, swollen stream, I attempt it first. I take off my boots, tie the laces in a knot, and hang the four-pound weight around my neck, leaving my hands free. A third of the way across, I realize that the current is too strong. I can no longer keep my balance. About face!

Bruce helping Nancy

Next, we three try together, holding hands and crossing in a line for strength and support. Bruce leads and, when he gets to the very point where I turned around, he does the same thing. "We've got to find another place. It's too dangerous here!" We walk down the river until we find a better crossing. Nancy puts her hand in mine and it feels lifeless. She is terrified.

When crossing a stream hand in hand, you should move very slowly, one person at a time. Instead, Nancy tries to hurry. While she pulls one way, I get separated from Bruce, Soon I'm straddling a rock and cannot move. "Hold it, you guys! You're pulling me apart!" Nancy continues to move farther away, anxious to get to land, until I feel her hand slipping through mine. "Hold on!" I scream. She starts to go down in the water! A look of terror and helplessness covers her face. She tries to let go so she doesn't drag us in too. I pull her shaking body up and manage to get safely to shore. She takes a while to compose herself and dry everything out in her pack. We stumble on, weak-kneed.

We're descending on a side trail along Bear Creek to Mono Hot Springs Resort. At seven thousand feet, the first mosquito hatch has just taken place. Clouds of insects fly in our faces, crawl in our scalps and our dinner, bite through layers of clothing and a half inch of pile! Fifty dive into our tent with us! "Enough!" we say. It's time for this day to be over!

Lately, Nancy and I have been feeling some distance between us and Bruce. We two women are inseparable when we hike, passing the miles with all kinds of chatter on topics that Bruce isn't particularly interested in. His girlfriend back in West Virginia sends him wonderful care packages, with homemade breads and cookies that he promptly and proudly shares with us. His face lights up like a sunbeam when he gets her mail and he reads her letters over and over at rest stops. I think Bruce is lovesick. Besides being inadequate substitutes, Nancy and I burden him with a lot of responsibility.

The guidebook warns of more high-water crossings, avalanche danger, and hard-to-find trail in the next section, which crosses the Silver Divide. Nancy and I have been doing our own route finding lately. We try to follow the line shown on the map, even though the trail is once again buried beneath snow. Bruce goes in the direction that looks quickest and easiest, but then sometimes uses more energy trying to relocate the trail and get back on course. Nancy and I are convinced that the trail was built at these particular spots for good reason.

The trail doesn't always cross a pass at the lowest point. Bruce wants to take a short-cut over Silver Pass, instead of climbing five hundred more feet of trail. We convince him to join us and discover that the actual pass now below us has a dangerous, overhanging cornice and an ice chute leading down to the lake that we're heading for. Nancy and I are proud of our disciplined belief in the guidebook and the trail. Still, I am concerned about what

Cornice on Silver Pass

lies ahead. After all, Nancy made no commitment to me to stay to the end. I may very well be on my own soon.

It probably sounds as though I'm scared all the time. First the snow, now the fords. But there is nothing in this life on the trail that can be taken for granted. Nothing that doesn't change.

Every day your path takes you to new territory. Every day the weather throws different patterns out to you. Every evening you lay your head on a different spot of ground. Back home, some people's lives remain essentially unchanged for years, with every day being nearly the same. Out here, every hour is an adventure. You get bombarded with so many adventures sometimes that you just try to cope. Anxiety and concern, unfortunately, cannot be avoided here, but still a definite sense of freedom flourishes.

Our next town stop is Mammoth, California's hot spot. After the shuttle bus takes you from Red's Meadow resort to the Mammoth ski area, you still need to cover the five miles that remain to get into town. You are forced to find your own way. It looks bleak. Who goes to a ski lodge in midsummer anyway? Nancy and I split off from Bruce to hitchhike. Three people with three large packs is more than most cars can handle. We agree to meet in the next town.

Within minutes, a guy in a Datsun pulls up. "One pick-up at your service," he says. He is applying for a job at the building site and is left with time on his hands. First stop, Mammoth's post office, then breakfast, a visit to the bookstore, and then to the laundromat. There are four more outdoorsy-type guys doing their laundry.

"Been out for a while?" one asks, smiling at our filthy clothes.

"Only two and a half months."

As we talk, I realize that they passed us back on the trail. They walked right past Nancy and I while we were taking a break and never stopped to talk or give trail information. They just yelled "Hello!" after they had passed. Now, they seem to have time.

We sit in front of the laundromat, sipping beer, telling stories, and getting to know each other. I like Neil, our chauffeur, so much that I say, "Come hike with us!" never dreaming he'll really come.

"Okay!" he replies. "Will you go to the outfitter and help me pick out some gear?"

This cigarette-smoking, twenty-nine-year-old hasn't back-packed since his Boy Scout days, yet he's willing to try. By the time we return, Mitch, the dark one, and his buddy decide to go back and walk the trail they just finished, to be with us! Hurrah! More company for the next stretch!

The northern section of the John Muir Trail is not in the heart of the highest mountains. Banner and Ritter peaks shine white and brilliant in the background, while Thousand Island Lake wraps itself around the scene. All the lakes are now free of ice, and the trail is clear. Because of this, the number of hikers grows larger as we get closer to Yosemite.

Weekenders come to us for directions and their mouths drop open when we tell them what the high country is like. They don't know how to react, especially toward Nancy and me. I suppose we intimidate them. When they see us with our glacier goggles on, they get self-conscious seeing themselves in the mirrors. My goggles are not prescription, so I wear them and my regular glasses, looking like some four-eyed alien. Usually a twist-tie holds the two together, but at this stage of the hike, none remains. Instead, I use a hair elastic with a blue bell the size of a nickel on the end. Marianna sent it as a joke. For use in bear country. It hangs from my glasses and sits on the tip of my nose, ringing everytime I move my head to talk. People just stare. No one dares ask "Why?"

We descend from Donahue Pass into Lyell Canyon, and bear country. Where there are people, there is food, and so there will

Cindy with bell on her glasses

be bears—bears that are not afraid of backpackers. Their aim is to eat, and you must be the next thing to an engineer to hang your food safely in a tree.

At our campsite tonight are the very same teenage boys we rescued on top of Mount Whitney, one hundred seventy miles ago. After taking two hours to hang our food, we listen to all they went through and how they changed. Neil sits back with a beer and a cigarette and is duly impressed. This man, who good-naturedly said back in Bishop, "I shouldn't have any problem out there," has since admitted that everything but his ears is sore. He's loving it though.

Meanwhile, Nancy has fallen for Mitch. His buddy got lost and turned around to go back to Mammoth the first day with us. Mitch will be leaving with Neil at the road at Tuolumne Meadows, the gateway to Yosemite Valley. Here, in the largest meadow of the Sierra Nevada, the PCT continues ahead, while the John Muir Trail descends for twenty-five more miles to its termination point in Yosemite Valley. Bruce's hike will end here, along with Bob's, who is waiting for us in Tuolumne Meadows. We haven't heard from him in weeks. In Muir hut, atop Muir Pass, a hundred miles back, there was a register—he could have said hello, but he didn't. We all look ahead to Tuolumne Meadows with mixed feelings.

From our drop into broad, glacier-carved Lyell Canyon, the mountains change again into smooth, white, granite domes. These were not sculptured by glaciers but, rather, by the exfoliation, or peeling away, of successive layers of rock. As one layer pops loose and falls away, the one beneath, no longer compressed by the rock above, pops loose in turn. In this way the domes are peeled like onions. Over thousands of years, each peeling has produced a smoother, rounder, and more erosion-resistant dome.

Along beautiful Lyell Fork, the trail is deeply rutted with many parallel treads. Since the water table is so high, the many hikers trample the sensitive ground until they are actually slogging through mud. Then they walk on the dry grass above it, which soon becomes another rut. The park is relocating the trail away from these fragile meadows in the hope of restoring them.

The closer we get to the road, the worse the trail becomes and the more numerous the people. One brightly dressed, middle-aged hiker with a pot belly pumps me for answers as he points to a map, a youth group of twenty-five trailing at his heels.

"Where'd you camp last night, Upper or Lower Basin?"

"I don't know, we just pulled over when we got tired."

"How many miles did you come today?"

"I don't know, two or three."

"What'd you get, a late start?"

"No, about nine."

"Did you start at Red's Meadows?"

"No."

"The last road crossing?"

"No! Mexico!"

"I didn't think women hiked that trail."

"Yes, we do!" I say and walk away.

At Tuolumne Meadows, Mitch and Neil exit. We both enjoyed their company, especially Nancy, who is as love starved as I am. Even so, I am a little afraid to see Bob again. Afraid of rejection, I suppose. But I'm more confident now. There's a note on the outdoor bulletin board that says he's in the backpacker's campground. I fear that the note is old and he's long gone. But, here he comes! So happy to see me and so affectionate. Same old Bob, a bit of a hotdog, telling of his adventures in the high country. His eyes are even bluer than I remember.

Nancy and I used to talk about him a lot when we hiked. Was there really a potential for us as a couple, or was I making it up? Would there be this attraction had we met in that other life or was it that opportunities for romance are so slim on the trail? No, we went through a lot together, and some kind of love grew. Seeing him again makes me realize that we're just not right for each other. I'll love him as a friend and look for a soulmate elsewhere. From the looks of all these climbers, Yosemite is a good place to begin!

Glaciers did more to carve the Sierra than any other natural force. They're largely responsible for the gouged canyons, the steep, jagged peaks, the alpine lakes, and the meadows. During the Ice Age, glaciers advanced at least six times. About 20,000 years ago, the last one filled Yosemite Valley to the rim. When it retreated, it left behind a huge lake that has since filled in with sediment, creating the broad, flat valley that exists today. John Muir recognized the valley's unique splendor and dedicated his life to getting it protected, along with many other wilderness treasures.

Yosemite Valley lies twenty-five miles off the Pacific Crest Trail, a two-day walk. Many Through-hikers pass it by because they're in a hurry. But I had read about it and dreamed about it for so many years that there was no way I could come this close and not see it. We plan to walk down Tenaya Canyon, then climb Half Dome to get our first view of the main valley.

There was a letter from Beth and Don waiting for me at the post office in Tuolumne Meadows, saying that Beth panicked

Toasting Bob's birthday (left to right): Bob, Nancy, Cindy and Bruce

while climbing Half Dome. She had to back down the cable ladder bolted to the rock. Donaldo crawled around the top on his hands and knees, fearful he would fall off.

I've come too far not to see it, and what better way to experience it than by climbing it and spending the night on top? Nancy is skeptical.

My big visit with Bob is about to come to an abrupt end. He wants to go off on his own again, after one day, and meet us in the valley below. I'm beyond caring. The clouds start moving in as we leave Tuolumne Meadows. The impending rain doesn't bother me. Thunder rolls. Drops wet my skin. The rain turns to hail. One by one, freezing cold, wet day-hikers come out of the high mountains.

I walk through the fir forest, needles on the ground, on a wet soggy trail that reminds me of Maine. Suddenly, I spot Bruce, Bob, and Nancy huddling under a tree. All wear sheepish grins. A bottle of champagne sticks in the snow and they have a carrot cake! It's Bob's birthday. He was going to spend it alone atop some peak, but had second thoughts. He just may enjoy our company after all. After a toast with our Sierra cups, we stagger drunkenly into the forest, looking for a campsite. It doesn't take much booze when you're not used to alcohol. "Is everybody happy?" Bob yells back, as I narrowly miss a fir. "You bet!" we yell.

Bears are the number one nuisance and hazard in this national park. Its many visitors provide a plentiful source of food for these large animals. Bears ravage the campsites in the valley and the backcountry alike, trying to satisfy their acquired sweet tooth. When a bear gets in trouble more than a few times, it is marked with a red tag and helicoptered into the high country, away from the myriad of people. If it continues to be a nuisance, it is shot.

There is a complicated way to hang your food bags so as to make them supposedly "bear proof." Two bags (or a bag and a rock) of equal weight are tied on opposite ends of a rope that has been flung over a tree branch. The branch must be strong enough to hold the weight but not so strong that a bear can go out on the limb and grab your food. The branch must also be sturdy enough that a bear cannot push it down so that the food sacks slide off. Mother bears have also been known to send their cubs out on thin branches to retrieve the food bags. As a result of the animals' ingenuity, it can take hours to find the right tree with the right branch. The men work on it for nearly two hours each night. One more thing for Nancy and me to worry about once Bruce goes home.

We find a beautiful spot near the Cathedral Range to camp for Bob's birthday. The storm is just clearing as we arrive. Cathedral Peak, with its lofty spires, looks like a massive church carved out of a single rock. The light moves quickly over the peaks, as it shoots through the breaking clouds. Snow-covered summits are lit up like beacons, with a backdrop of a navy blue sky. We plan a great pig-out dinner for the occasion. While the men climb a nearby knoll for a sunset, Nancy and I cook chicken a la king. As we sit there stirring, I spot a bear about fifty yards away. As calm as I can be, I remark, "Look, Nance, a bear." She's never seen one before and is quite startled to see it walking around on all fours. When he turns to the side I see a bright, red tag. Oh boy, this bear's been tagged as a menace.

"He's coming over here!" Nancy says.

"No, he's not." I reply, but in the next instance I realize that, sure enough, he is. He walks in a long arc, closing in as he moves, glancing at us from time to time. We're able to watch him until he gets to the ridge on which we're camped. Then out of nowhere, he's twenty yards away, coming straight toward us.

"Oh, my God!" Nancy says, "He's right there! What are we going to do?"

I begin yelling at him. "You better get going! You're going to get a rock in your face! Ever have a rock in your face?" The bear totally ignores me and continues moving in. I frantically scream to Nancy, "Get the pots and pans and start banging!" We grab lids and cups and start banging like crazy. Still he advances toward our supper, now only fifteen feet away!

"Bob! Bruce! There's a bear down here!"

"How many?" they yell.

"FIVE!" I want them to hurry.

We run back to our packs, where our week's food is stored.

"What should we do?" Nancy gasps. "He wants our food!"

"He can't have it all," I reply. "Maybe our supper will keep him busy while we round up the rest and put it in a tree."

As the men approach, the bear disappears. They're a bit perturbed, for they were almost to the top when they heard us yell. Now, there's no bear in sight. Just us standing there, holding their smashed pots and pans. Ours have food in them. We hang the food very carefully tonight, but I am still uncertain. This bear means business.

Evening finds me sitting outside the tent, writing in my journal. Everyone else has already retired. I turn and see the bear ten feet away! "Get going!" I yell, and dive into the tent. He's in our packs, putting tooth holes in our water bottles, in our soap containers, and lemon-scented shampoo.

Soon we hear a loud thud from the direction of our food tree. Was that the food? No, we can still hear him in the tree. Nancy is scared and wonders if we're next. My mind flashes to the greasy pemmican that melted on my sleeping bag in the heat of the desert. We hear cracking branches and then another thud. "He's got it!" we all say in unison. Soon we hear him ripping open stuff sacks.

"Oh, my Fig Newtons!" Bruce sighs, "and my butter pecan pudding!"

"My boysenberry jam!" Bob adds, laughing. "I hope he gets the hot salsa!"

I snicker. Nancy finds nothing amusing and, despite all the activity, is still hopeful.

"I don't think he's got the food," she remarks confidently. "I think he fell out of the tree and he's dead."

When morning comes, we all parade to the battleground to see the remains. The tree's bark is scarred with claw marks. Three broken limbs lie on the ground, along with our shredded stuff sacks and unappealing food. He didn't eat everything. He was downright choosy — and skilled. He opened the cracker box at the lid, like a person would, and one sleeve of crackers was taken out and consumed. He had one taste of Bruce's French bread, all the jam, cookies, pudding, a little plastic from the peanut butter container, along with its contents. Even freeze-dried dinners were pulled open at the top, as we would have done. This bear has had lots of practice. He earned that red tag on his ear!

The first time I lay eyes on Half Dome a sudden rush of warmth and love goes through my body. Another dream of mine is about to come true! Cold reality hits me, however, when the rock monster comes into close range. I'm going to climb that? It's incredibly steep and doesn't look to have enough room on top for us all to stand. Nancy is going wild. If Beth couldn't do it, Nancy

Ladder up Half Dome

concludes, she certainly can't. For Beth climbed Whitney in a blizzard on her first days out, along with a dozen other frightening things.

Heavy construction is going on at the lower part of the rock, where trail crew members are lining the trail with granite blocks and jackhammering steps right into the side of the mountain. Time to make the trail out of something lasting.

On Quarter Dome we hang our food on the bear cables provided by the park and ready ourselves for the next part of the climb. Bob and I plan to sleep on top. Bruce and Nancy will only come up for the sunset. We put our stuffed sleeping bags in our zippered jackets and tie the arms around our waists. We'll need our hands to pull us up the half mile of cable ladder bolted into the smooth rock.

From a plateau at the base of Half Dome, you can see little bodies the size of ants, crawling skyward. It looks like the trail goes straight up! Two twelve-year-olds walk by on their way down.

If they could do it, so can we!

I tell Nancy that she is going in front of me. If she thinks she's turning around once we're halfway there, she's mistaken. On the ladder, there's room for one body width at a time, and I'm not moving aside.

At first the ladder is not too steep, and you quickly learn the easiest way to climb. The cables are waist high and go through poles that stand upright and are bolted to the rock. You slide your hands forward on the cable, then pull yourself up, walking flat-footed, up the rock to join your hands. Every twenty feet there's a wooden slat laid across the rock for you to rest on.

The problem places are where one cable ends and another begins. Your hands have to go down to the rock itself, as you walk in a low, crouched position, holding yourself on the mountain before changing to a new cable. Shoes that have good gripping soles are a necessity.

Soon Yosemite Valley bursts into view. The sides are so steep, so exposed that I cannot bear to look. We are in the bright sun, but the valley is so dark blue, so deep in shadow that you know it's a long way down. The far end of the canyon looms at your side. More mountains, more domes, with their faces lopped off by the glaciers. They feel so close, yet there is this huge chasm between them and you. Keep going, girl. Don't think about the five thousand empty feet below you—just climb. Still, I can feel those empty feet as I climb higher into the sky. I wonder if we really belong up here on this stairway to heaven.

The dome rounds off and we push onto the top, which actually is quite spacious. I run around, drinking in the view and gasping, "My God, I don't believe this!" It's even more fabulous than I'd imagined. To stand here and know that glaciers came through to the point where I stand and just sliced off the faces of these rock mountains! North Dome sits across the valley, with a totally vertical rock face and a curving, forested head. Down the canyon rises the sheer wall of El Capitan, the most sought-after big-wall climb in the country. The rock that I stand on was smoothed and polished by glaciers. I run my hand over the sheen and think of the ice that pushed by. Water flings itself over the cliffs and floats down to the valley, thousands of feet below, in clouds of mist.

I am overwhelmed, humbled. I look at this spectacular canyon and see God's mark. Nothing man-made can compare to Yosemite's beauty.

We crawl on our bellies out to the edge of the dome and peer into the valley a mile below. The buildings look the size of Monopoly houses. The Merced River is reduced to a tiny, shimmering snake. Directly below, on Half Dome's face, hang some technical climbers, bivouacked on the vertical face of the rock, where they are forced to cook, eat, sleep, and even urinate from their hanging sacks. Unable to make the climb in a single day, they must hang there through the night.

"Come on down for a cold beer!" they yell to Nancy and me.

As the sun sets, the high peaks to the south turn rosy, and long shadows cast by El Cap and the other rock giants fill the canyon. It's time for Bruce and Nancy to reluctantly head down. Far-off storm clouds concern us slightly. At the first sign of

Yosemite Valley

approaching bad weather, you're supposed to descend. There are no trees here to shelter you, only rock walls built in half-circles by climbers to keep the worst of the wind off. There's no earth to secure any tent stakes. Bob and I decide to stay.

The earth colors evaporate while the color in the sky grows more intense. Close to the horizon, a strip of yellow appears, then orange, then red. Above that, the pale blue melts into the deeper blues the farther you tilt your head back. Stars pierce the sky one by one. A warm breeze soothes us to sleep. It feels very right to be out here. During the last few weeks I have felt more and more comfortable in these mountains. It has taken a long time, but the Sierra is now in my blood. These mountains have made their mark on my soul, and I will never be the same again.

We awake to a soft, pink sky. The sun is not yet up and the breeze is turning into a wind. The work crew starts at eight A.M. Anyone not down before then must remain on top until work ceases.

With no food or water, it doesn't sound like a good idea.

Descending is even more interesting than climbing up. We lean forward to grab the cables and lower ourselves. Early-morning shadows hit the surrounding peaks and domes as the sun pops up. North Dome's face is bright with light, while its dark green, forested head is deep in shadow.

Once off Half Dome, we join Bruce and Nancy and head for the valley, following the Mist Trail by beautiful Vernal Falls and Nevada Falls. The closer we get to the water, the more soaked we become from the airborne spray. Kids scamper by. I lower myself and my huge, top-heavy pack cautiously down the drenching wet, stone steps, fearful of slipping head over heels. The heat is intensifying. Where is Yosemite Village? The air gets thicker, heavier, hotter, and more humid. The dirt trail turns to blacktop.

The lower we descend, the more people we see. They obviously come from many different countries, for we hear different languages, see different clothing. We smell different perfumes, hairspray, after-shave, shampoo. Our senses are bombarded! We probably smell just plain nasty to them!

Yosemite Village is like a small city composed of several individual towns. It has three post offices, six gas stations, two golf courses, a hospital, four swimming pools, five gift shops, two hotels, a motel complex, and thousands of campsites. As many as fifty-five thousand people shuttle through it on a big holiday weekend.

It is difficult for us to handle these extremes, going from Half Dome's loftiness to Yosemite Village's problems. We have been in the mountains for so long now. We were just up in the air that angels breathe, and now we're choking on carbon monoxide. The park was developed so that it could "be seen and enjoyed by all." To open the park, an environment had to be created so that huge numbers of people could watch the natural wonders without missing out on comfort. With all the development and side attractions, it is difficult for even the clear-eyed traveler to grasp the exquisite beauty of Yosemite. For me, a long-distance hiker, this is a matter of the heart. It brings me pain to see a place like Yosemite so exploited.

Out on the trail, we long-distance hikers, for better or worse, set ourselves apart from other more casual, occasional, or inexperienced hikers. Unlike them, we have given up all that we've known and associated with before—our jobs, our homes, our friends and family. Yet we still feel the need for a sense of belonging and community. Therefore, we pride ourselves on being Through-hikers rather than Weekenders, Greenhorns or—God forbid—Yahoos.

Weekenders are hikers who, as the name says, come into the mountains on weekends. We feel friendly toward them, yet we are also bothered when they pour into the mountains each Friday night, like water spilling from a dam that just broke. We sometimes get a little stingy when it comes to sharing "our world," for we are spoiled by its normal solitude and peacefulness. Most of us started out as Weekenders, and when our trip is over will become Weekenders once more. Even so, our memories of what it's like to hike long distance, to stay out here for extended periods—they will always separate us from all other hikers.

Greenhorns are beginners, inexperienced hikers. Everyone starts out like this, no matter who they are.

And then there are the Yahoos. They are Greenhorns who are so out of touch, so aggressively stupid or insensitive, that their ineptness seems more like an attitude problem than a simple matter of inexperience. They are the hikers who leave dirty diapers and empty cans scattered about their campsites or who flick cigarettes into dry woods and meadows. That's what we Through-hikers find so objectionable—their lack of caring, not their lack of experience.

On the shuttle, and in the entire valley, the four of us stick out like sore thumbs. We feel like foreigners!

Nance and I find it very difficult getting anything accomplished in the three days we are in the valley. Around twelve o'clock it starts getting very hot. I feel lethargic. Nancy gets bitchy.

We ride shuttle buses all day, doing our chores and seeing some sights, too burned out to walk.

The campground we are staying in is like a town—the low-rent district. Hundreds of tents crowd together so you can see everything everyone does. Two motorcycle guys with tremendous beer bellies and tattoos of eagles and naked women up their arms come over to talk. They inquire about the trails in the high country. As politely as possible I talk them out of going.

The time has come to say good-bye to Bruce and Bob. We embrace, a much too casual response to the extraordinary role they played in our trail lives. But there is too much going on in the valley. There is no time for deep-felt reminiscing; Nancy and I are already looking ahead.

I saw a beautiful, moving film of John Muir's High Sierra in the park last night. Johann Pachelbel's heavenly "Canon in D Major" was used as background music. The film showed many shots from the summits of mountains—clouds moving in, frozen alpine lakes—an eagle's view or a PCT hiker's. I feel so privileged to have been there, to have seen and felt those mountains first hand. Why do I feel such a kinship with them? Why do my eyes water when I think of crossing brilliant snowfields or of the drama of topping a pass? Will I ever repeat those hundreds of miles of High Sierra snow?

Back then I didn't want to. Nor am I ready to go back now. Yet I am amazed at how my attitude has changed since I left the East. I realize now how very much the Sierra has changed my life. Nothing can compare to the amount of personal growth that I have experienced while traveling through these mountains. At first I thought the snow was a curse; now I look back on it as a blessing, a gift, for I am not the same person. This trail and the Sierra Nevada are making me a better person. Perhaps this is the best reason of all for being here.

There is a drawing of John Muir in the show. His soft, deep eyes captivate me. It is as though I could look into them and see the beauty that he saw in nature reflected back to me. His eyes really seemed to be mirrors of his soul, which was packed with goodness and the love of nature. If I met a man with eyes like that, I would follow him to the ends of the earth, if he wanted me. For now, I only follow Nancy.

10

On Our Own

August 2

"Get that spot! You didn't get that spot!"

"I'm trying, but it's getting all over my socks!"

Nancy and I are peeing in a circle, directly below our hanging food bags. Someone told us that the smell of urine keeps bears away. We're trying everything. It's easy for a man to direct his flow, not so for a woman. I waddle a few more steps in a squatting position.

Nancy's muscle

We choose our campsite when we find a good food storage tree. Never mind the location or availability of water. Priorities! Nancy ties a heavy rock to the end of the rope. We have to take turns throwing and need to rest often. A dozen throws apiece, then we're successful. We heap pots and pans on the ground beneath the sacks and gather a rock artillery. They're placed outside the tent by our heads, just in case a bear visits us in the night. The tent is positioned so I can lie in my bag and merely open my eyes to check on the suspended bags, which I do a dozen times a night.

No bear comes. In the morning we untie the food sacks and the rope gets snagged on the branch. It wraps around the limb and no matter how hard we pull, it won't come free. We need the rope to hang food and maybe get across some formidable fords. Nancy climbs on my swaying shoulders, but she's still too short to reach. I hoist her up the tree but there aren't any lower limbs to grab.

What can we do? That's Skip's two-hundred-dollar climbing rope up there! We just can't leave it. We look for a stick lengthy enough to pull it loose. None is any longer than three feet, so we decide to connect four pieces together with surgical tape from the first-aid box. Looks good on the ground, but as soon as we raise it, the sticks bend at the joints, never reaching the branch. Soon two men come by. They find a stick that is more like a small tree and retrieve the rope.

"Steep, spectacular, glaciated canyons" ahead, the guidebook says. You feel as though you're walking straight up. The canyons run west to east, and since we're heading due north, the ups and downs cannot be avoided. On each canyon floor we face a stream crossing that "could be dangerous if you're unroped."

You get to a point in a long hike when you expect to feel comfortable doing long days. You expect to be in good shape and not have a climb devastate you. After making it through the High Sierra, we expect to have reached that point. Not so. We're trying to do too much in a day. Brian, a friend of mine from San Francisco, is bringing us a food drop at Sonora Pass, seventy-five miles north of Yosemite. We plan thirteen- to fourteen-mile days and don't think this goal is unrealistic. The descent is so steep, however, you can't merely walk downhill, but must step one foot at a time, like a toddler. Ascending is like climbing stairs. The trail has become excessively rocky and eroded. Dropping down and crawling out of a single canyon is about all we can manage in a day.

Today, we met our first south-bounders. Skipping around the Sierra, they had walked north to Canada through the Cascades. Then they took a bus back to Belden, California, to walk south through the Sierra. All this was done to bypass the High Sierra's deep snows and dangerous fords. But they escaped the High Sierra's snow only to find another sort of hell. The northern Sierra and Cascade range is much lower, but the country is steep and thickly wooded. Snow hangs under the shady forest until late in the season and never softens up, making progress difficult. What's more, you can't take compass readings in that forest, unlike the open basins we traveled in.

Todd Gladfelter, my AT friend who's been hiking ahead of us all this time, did the same skipping around. Before I left the East, he said he'd look for me, and I'm so looking forward to a familiar face!

But these south-bounders say Todd broke his foot and had to go home! He and his partners reached their thirteen-hundred mile mark and celebrated that night by their campfire, saying, "Halfway! Nothing's going to stop us now!" The very next day, Todd was traversing a steep ice slope and fell. His crampon bit into a tree as he fell into the melt hole around the trunk. His leg twisted, but his foot remained rigid, planted in the bark. He had his leg put in a cast and returned home to Pennsylvania, a very sad man.

For the first time in a long time we don't have to wear long underwear to bed. It's beginning to feel like summer. The passes are much lower and forested. We travel by shallow little lakes with grassy margins. Fallen trees can be seen beneath the surface, and swarms of mosquitos hover on top of the water. Wildflowers are abundant, especially the mule's ears, with their showy yellow, daisylike flowers and their big velvety leaves in the shape of their namesake. The creek crossings are quite manageable. We are a little late for peak runoff, and previous hikers have laid logs across the streams that were a bit deep and treacherous. Nancy nearly panics at all of them, even the step-across fords. I must go first every time to show her where to step and see if any rocks are wobbly. Then I stand on the far bank and wait.

"I can't do it!"

"Yes, you can. Calm yourself. It isn't dangerous."

"I'm going to go in! I'll drown!"

"No you won't. Just come on," I say and begin to walk away.

I don't want to stand there and watch, to make her self-conscious and unsteady, so I go ahead a bit and wait. She always makes it. Nancy's theatrics really don't bother me, because I know she's merely acting. The fact that she is out here with me and responsible for herself says a lot.

August 6

We awake to find dripping rain. An aura of dread hangs over us in weather like this. We must move quickly. The day is not relaxed. Breaks are short and hurried. Gloom fills our spirits, as it fills the sky.

We are eighteen miles from Sonora Pass. There's no water or place to camp on the entire ridge top. We were supposed to meet Brian at the pass last night. We hope he understands and waits until tonight. This section has been far more difficult than we anticipated.

We leave behind the glaciated canyons and begin to see some signs of volcanic activity. The rocks are gray. Flowers grow abundantly in this soil, but there are no weeds or grasses. It looks like someone's cultivated garden. Raindrops cling to the orange and red straw flowers and fuzzy, pink pussypaws. The air is misty and cool, for the first time since I left Mexico. Our food is down to the minimum again. We were figuring too closely. We didn't con-sider the arduous climbs that increased our hunger. Crackers soaked with gasoline from a leaky fuel bottle are all we have for lunch today.

The wind is blowing sleet against us as we climb. We're at the deciding point. Should we put on rain gear and sweat or just walk fast enough to have our body heat dry us and keep us warm?

There aren't enough calories in our stomachs, however, to produce much heat. We stand on the ridge, shaking, red skin raw from the driving sleet. Time to put on plastic.

Six miles of exposed ridge lie before us. We attack them vigor-ously, as if to make the distance go by more quickly. We want the day to be over, to see Brian, to be warm, to eat. The side of the crest where we walk is gentle and sloping. I peer through a cloud break and spy Levitt Lake far below. Up here the mountain is jagged and devouring, as though the earth has cracked open and I am looking past its teeth down into its throat.

The snowfields begin to increase at ten thousand feet. I don't feel like leading and kicking steps, so Nancy says she'll go first. Her willingness and lack of hesitation prove that she's not the same fearful woman who carried two ski poles on Forrester Pass. Our arms tire quickly, unaccustomed to using ice axes. The mus-cles have gone soggy in the last snow-free weeks. The weather is getting colder and we're increasingly fatigued. What little warmth was present during the day has dissipated. By six P.M., we round some corners, fly down a few switchbacks, and spot the road below. Is that Brian's truck? Is he watching for us? Then the trail curves around into a tremendously snowy bowl, stopping us dead in our tracks. The guidebook mentions short-cut trails and advises us not to take them. The PCT cuts across the snowbound bowl, through hundreds of yards of steep snow, looking like it adds miles of unnecessary walking. A set of prints from a rock outcrop come our way, although they seem to just stop. Someone else was here.

Above us, the slope looks more gradual. We'll start high and walk down to meet the rock outcrop and follow the prints, just as we have so many times, over so many passes. The snow has always been soft enough for us to take plunging steps down the slope. Even today, with overcast skies, we've been able to kick good steps. No reason why we shouldn't now.

Nancy leads, angling up with every step. She can't seem to go down! Ascending slightly seems much easier. I follow right behind, placing the sides of my boots in her footholds. About twenty feet out, she starts losing control. Her whole body starts to shake.

"You're doing fine," I assure her. "We're getting there. Just take your time and stay calm."

I really feel quite confident. The end is in sight. I can see Brian's truck down below on the road. It's so close. Besides, I'm in the rear, the easy part. Once again, I think she's overreacting.

"I don't think I can go anymore," she concludes.

"Okay. Try to move up and I'll go by and lead."

"I'm really scared," she whispers, as I pass. "This is the hardest thing I've ever done."

I hurry a little, but not enough to be careless. I slam the side of my foot two or three times into the slope before taking a step. I can't seem to get a good foothold. There's only about a half inch to stand on. Suddenly, my foot slips! My heart sinks and I catch myself.

"Be careful!" Nancy screams from behind.

Boy, I didn't like that one bit! It shocks me into realizing the seriousness of this traverse. We're moving closer to the center of the bowl—the steepest, iciest section. There are chutes of ice that are too slick to stand on, so we must step over them, forcing our feet too far apart for good stability.

Across one of these chutes, my rear foot goes out from under me again! But this time it pulls the other one along! In a fraction of a second, my feet are racing down the slope, with the rest of my body trying to catch up. I look up at the hand that holds my ice ax, watch it pull loose from the slope. My mouth opens in a scream and I go down.

On my back I race downward at blinding speed, desperately trying to shove my ice ax and heels in the slope. It's no good! The ice is thick and offers no grip. I skid down the slope like a hockey puck, hurtling toward a rock outcrop. I make one more mad attempt to stop myself, but my feet succeed only in spraying snow on my glasses. Suddenly, time stops, and I remember nothing else.

Nancy: *I can't believe what I'm seeing. 'Dig in! Dig in!' I yell, but it's not working. Cindy seems to give up and starts barreling down the slope. As each second passes, she gains tremendous speed! She is flying down the mountain right towards the rocks! I shriek at the top of my lungs, over and over, 'Oh, my God!' The moment seems to last forever. Memories from the last months race quickly through my mind. And now it's all coming to an end. Cindy is going to die. This must be a bad dream. Please God, wake me up! But it isn't a dream. Cindy has crashed into some rocks.*

She's so far away, I can't see what part of her body took the impact, but it looked like her backpack hit first and that she flew in the air and landed on some more rocks. Nothing. Not a sound. I'm standing in the dusk, looking down, and I can barely see her body. Is she dead or unconscious? What in the hell am I going to do? I am alone, desperate. I have just watched the most important person in my life crash to her death.

When I finally come to a stop, I just lie there in a dark void. There is a pain shooting up my limbs. There is a pain in my hand. I take off my snow-caked glasses and move my legs, back and forth, bending them at the joints. Everything seems to be working. Suddenly, I hear this frantic scream above me. Wiping my glasses clean, I turn around to see a steep wall of snow and ice above me. Nancy is so far away, she looks like a tiny speck on the mountainside. I fell all that way? As my eyes move up to her, they stop on an outcrop of boulders, where skid marks scar the snow. My God, did I go over that?

Nancy: *She's moving! She's standing up! This is a miracle! How can she possibly stand up after the fall she just took? This can't be possible. But it is, she's alive! 'Cindy!' I yell, 'Are you all right?' What a stupid question, but I'm in such a state of shock. 'I'm all right!' she finally answers. I don't believe her, but at least she's up and moving, and we're close to the road to get medical help. Then I realize: How am I going to get down? My*

*body starts to shake uncontrollably. I have been through an incredible
trauma and have little strength left. No way can I traverse all that distance and with each step relive the horrifying image of Cindy falling to
her death. I know that I'll fall too, but I'll never get up again, as she has.
It's all over. I guess I'll just sit down, dig my ice ax in, and hope for the
best. 'Can I glissade down?' I yell to her. 'No!' she yells back. So I try to
keep strong and start taking steps. My entire body shivers like a leaf.*

I sit here watching Nancy, listening to the lonely sounds of
her boots thrusting into the ice and her ax jamming into the bank.
I'm glad I'm here and not up there trying to tackle that horren-
dous ice field. Then I hear a voice from below. "Are you all right?"
"Yes!"
"How is Nancy?"
"Not so good!"
Brian tells me not to move, he's coming up. I look up and see

Brian's rescue on Sonora Pass

Nancy continuing, angling up the entire time, overshooting the rock outcrop and getting into a broader expanse of snow. He screams up to Nancy to stay put, but she has her hat pulled tight over her ears and hears nothing. I act as the mediator, yelling up messages, which throw her dangerously off balance every time. She's heading toward the worst part of the bowl! Oh, God! How is she going to get down? I sit down, crying, looking out at the clearing sky and spots of sunshine.

"Why? Why do we do this to ourselves?" I ask out loud.

Brian is wheezing as he runs up the snow. He has sneakers on, but is flying over the surface. I'm content to stay put and let him come to me. He hugs me, demands to know if I'm all right.

Then, trading his tire iron, which he grabbed as a makeshift ice ax, for the real thing, he goes up to get Nancy. Once there, he chops a platform in the slope for her to stand on and takes her pack.

He spends quite some time talking to her, calming her down. Then they descend backward, Brian leading, chopping steps as he goes.

It seems to take forever to bring her down. At least an hour to cover the space it took me two seconds to fly over. She keeps yelling down and asking me how I am. I'm walking around fine. I'm safe. I just want her to be safe, too.

They make it over to me, and Nancy, who is usually not so affectionate, throws her arms around me and bursts out, "I'm so glad you're alive!" Brian gives Nancy's pack back to her and insists on taking mine. Besides being a little shook up, I feel fine. I don't get the chance to walk without a pack often, so I consent. "You've taken quite a fall," he says. "You deserve to walk without a pack for a while."

Taken quite a fall? I'm not aware of it. Then they tell me what really occurred. They said I flew in the air, flipping over two times! I hit the first set of rocks with my feet, my knees buckled, and the force hurled me into space. I somersaulted over the rocks, landed on my stomach, and flipped again before stopping on the second set of rocks.

"It was the most horrifying thing I ever experienced," Nancy said. "Here was someone I'd lived with for three months, flying to her death. It was petrifying to watch."

Brian also thought it was all over for me. "I had just pulled up in my truck when I saw two people venture out onto the snow-field," he said. "I yelled up, 'Don't go out there!' but you didn't hear. I'd been up there earlier, trying to go south to meet you and had to back down. I wasn't sure it was you, but whoever it was, I knew they'd need help. So I shot up the mountain. At one point, I was in a gully, and just as I rose out of it, I heard Nancy scream and saw you fall. Then I realized who you were. I felt sure I'd have to carry you out on a stretcher."

Both say that if I could have seen what my fall looked like, I'd realize how fortunate I was to be walking around now. Except for a tremendous knot in my stomach, I feel incredibly good. If my glasses hadn't caked with snow and my body hadn't gone as limp as a rag doll, I would probably have struggled and fought and hurt myself. Having Brian arrive at that precise time to help Nancy to safety seemed too much of a coincidence. It was as if I was picked up and guided by divine hands. That night I write a passage from Psalm 36 in my journal: "With the Lord shall the steps of a man be directed, and he shall light well his way. When he shall fall, he shall not be bruised, for the Lord putteth His hand under him."

Living in San Francisco, Brian is close enough to keep in contact with life out here. He loves the mountains, the trail, and hikers. If hikers need supplies, equipment, information, or care he is there for them. He answered my ad in the *Appalachian Trailway News Magazine*, just like Bob and Bruce did. He is tall and wiry and built like a runner. His pale skin, earned by too many days spent in a closed-up legal office, gives no clue to his talent as a mountaineer.

Brian stays through the entire next day's hike. The trail goes above ten thousand feet one last time, and he wants to help us over any rough spots. Paranoia has struck Nancy and me. It is more than the fear we experienced in the High Sierra. Now snow absolutely terrifies us.

Brian guides us around drifts, chops steps before we arrive. But even dirt trail that is badly eroded and slips beneath our feet makes our hearts race. One snow slope is nearly horizontal, with no chance of falling. We don't like even that. We do not want to deal with the snow at all. We don't want to do anything even vaguely difficult. We want the trail to be easy from here on in. We have simply had enough.

Atop the ten-thousand-foot saddle, Brian turns around. I look down at the ground, draw in the dirt with a stick. Nancy hugs her knees, pulls her jacket around her and stares back at the snowy mountains.

"Look out there, you two!" Brian points ahead. "The mountains are considerably drier. Only very tiny snow patches can be seen."

"All it takes," I say defensively, "is one north slope where the snow lingers all summer long."

"Sonora Pass is a freak," he replies. "They built that section in the forestry department's office, with only a map in front of them. They never went out there in the spring to see how the snow lingers in that bowl. It's poor engineering. It should have been built down one of those spur ridges, where the short cuts were. The guidebook even reads, 'If you fall here, it could be lethal!' "

I look up. "You're kidding! We never read that! Still they keep the trail there?"

After Brian leaves, we hit a patch of snow. Nancy travels on her rear, I crawl on all fours. Now, no matter how gradual or short a snowfield, we'll go to extremes to go around it. Sonora Pass has destroyed our faith in the trail.

Nancy relives the nightmare of my fall every evening in the tent. In great detail she describes the horror on my face and the fright in my eyes as I went down. She's kept up nights, haunted by it. After hearing it repeatedly, my sleep too is affected.

We talk much of our traveling plans once we get off the trail. Getting off and being safe sounds more and more attractive. We decide to quit a week early from my halfway goal and end in Belden, California. I've been getting letters from Derreck, the blond fellow I met near Glen Pass in the High Sierra, and Nancy has been swamped with letters from Mitch. Both live in Los Angeles, as do Cathy and Marianna, my two buddies who helped me so much. We decide to have ourselves a great time in L.A. Look out, men, we're going to celebrate getting through this trail alive!

These last days have been glorious ones. We've been traversing the western wall of mountains around Lake Tahoe. The trail stays high, right near or on the ridge, affording excellent views of the pale blue lake. It seems like a mirage down there, so large and airy looking. Strange volcanic-rock formations, called dikes, poke out of the mountain ridge. They look like fins sticking out of the mountain's back. A closer look reveals small, smooth rocks fused into the solid mass, which was once liquid lava. The lower slopes are covered with mule's ears, their flowers dying, leaves drying. When the wind blows, they crackle like the corn fields back home in the fall. The season is changing. The days are rolling by.

We see the end today. We top a ridge and there, jutting into the sky, are the Sierra Buttes. Rising behind them looms Mount Lassen, the first Cascade volcano in a long string to Canada. Our trip will terminate between the two landmarks. We've been through so much together. We've really learned to get along, to compromise, even down to little things like breaks. Nancy loves the sun and sits eating lunch with her face jutting up toward the sky. I hate to be hot and gravitate toward the shade. So we have lunch in the shade-sun line, moving ourselves and all our lunch food every ten minutes so we can be together and talk. She rolls her sleeves up for an even tan; I sit bundled in my pile jacket four feet away. We've learned the secret of living together.

We met a bedraggled hiker coming up the hill this afternoon. He's skinny enough and dressed strangely enough to be a long-distance hiker. It's Steve Pack, one of Todd's partners. He's been traveling alone for quite some time and his excited, nonstop talk makes it obvious that he needs some company. The fall snows in the High Sierra are scaring him. He's afraid of getting pushed out so close to his goal, so he chooses to move on and pass up camping with us. Before separating, I ask to take his picture. He takes off his Bing Crosby hat with the feathers, slicks down his greasy hair, smooths down his once-white T-shirt, now black where his shoulder straps have rubbed for four months, straightens his sweatshirt around his skinny hips, and crosses his bean-pole legs. What a sight! It's late in the hike. You can tell.

Sierra City is a gold town, lying right along the Mother Lode. "Ninety percent of it is still up there!" the miners tell us. Gold mining is the standard occupation in this little town, nestled deep in the northern Sierra by the Yuba River. Here, in 1869, in the Monumental Mine, the largest gold nugget in the country was found, a nugget that weighed one hundred forty-one pounds! It's a town brimming with charm and history.

We sit on a grocery store bench, eating ice cream and getting to know the town. Miners in old cowboy hats and beat-up boots, looking like pictures of forty-niners, come and go from the store.

Shortly, a man nicely dressed in khaki approaches us. He asks if we met a guy named Steve traveling south. "He spent a night at my house," the man says. "You're welcome to say at my place for the night, too." The man's name is Bob. He works for the Forest Service as a "fire-prevention technician," putting out forest fires, educating campers on campfire safety, fining violators, checking on people cutting firewood, and performing related duties.

He tells us about the three skull fractures he received from motorcycle accidents, injuries that left one side of his head numb. He has trouble remembering things, he says, and at first he does seem a little slow. But after we know him better, we discovered that he is actually very bright. After talking to him for a while, we decide to take him up on his offer.

Bob rolls out the red carpet. We're treated to an impressive

Sinbad and Bob Frost

dinner of spaghetti with clam sauce, homemade bread, homemade lentil soup, corn on the cob, salad, and beer. Bob allows his
dog and best buddy, Sinbad, to stand on top of the wobbly table
while we eat and share his meal with him. We try to act noncha-
lant. As we talk, Bob whips a corn cob across the room. It flies
through the air and hits the carpet, while Sinbad leaps off the
shaking table and dives for it. Nancy and I grab toppling water
glasses but Bob never stops the flow of conversation, never even
looks in the direction of the dog. Must be normal practice.

In the morning, Bob makes a huge cast-iron skilletful of pota-
toes and eggs, pours us glasses of milk, cuts oranges into seg-

ments, and is off "to keep the forest safe from democracy!" We truck downtown to do laundry and write postcards.

The town dog, a beagle named Low Rider, lies in the gutter across from the laundry, one long ear draped over the curb. After putting our laundry in to wash, we sit down on the post office steps to write our postcards. A few young guys who turn out to be miners come over to chat. The longer we talk, the easier it becomes to convince ourselves to take tomorrow morning off. The plan is that the miners will put me in a wet suit and take me under water to see how they dredge the streams for gold. Nancy will stay on shore. Afterwards, the guys will drive us to the top of the Sierra Buttes so that we don't get behind schedule. Eight days from now, we are supposed to meet Brian in Belden, a town more than one hundred miles north, where we'll end our trip. He will take us to his home in San Francisco.

Tonight the miners insist on showing us their claim and camp. The river roars five yards away and looks like rushing quicksilver in the moonlight. The men sit on lawn chairs around the campfire. Orange flames are reflected on their faces. Their eyes look wild and fiery beneath their cowboy hats. Beers in hand, playing cards, smoking joints, they talk about their shared obsession — gold dredging. I make my way through the round white river boulders, and find a chair. A dark, mysterious man stares and smiles at me from across the fire. I hold his gaze. Sparks shoot from the embers into the dark night. They pass around little glass vials of water, containing floating gold nuggets. They carry them always, in leather cases or on chains round their necks, never daring to spend them. They love their gold. They spend every weekend and sometimes an entire summer on their claims, dredging for the beautiful nuggets.

Our hosts, Mike and Ed, want to show us Donnieville, a quaint, old gold-mining town ten miles away, where a walloping street party is in progress. We race down the highway in their souped-up pickup, dancing in our seats to the Marshall Tucker Band's gold-mining song: "Six long months on a dust-covered trail; they say heaven's at the end, but so far it's been hell."

All the bars have bands. Some play country, others rock, but we choose one with a jazz band whose sax player looks and sings like Louis Armstrong. A wild guy only five feet tall, wearing a red football helmet with steer horns jutting out the sides, keeps asking me to dance. Big flashy smile, little dark moustache. But he doesn't need a partner, or even music, to dance. He does his own thing, even when the band is on a break.

Next morning the guys are supposed to pick us up at eight o'clock. After waiting most of the morning, we decide to hitch-hike to their camp. We are mad. It turns out they had tremendous hangovers and had no intention of coming. But Mike apologizes and reluctantly agrees to take us to the trailhead at Sierra Buttes. Ed is under water so the quiet smiling one from the night before decides to come along.

"That's Larry," Mike says. Larry looks at me and grins.

The jeep road to the Buttes is bad. The air is so hot and humid that our legs sticks to each other. The ride is long and exhausting.

The miners

We bounce over a rocky road, which soon narrows to a mere bull-dozer track. Wrong way. Mike glances at his gas tank, which is only a quarter full. Each road we take peters out, forcing us to turn around. All the while, Larry is drinking beer and getting bolder with each can. I feel his hand massage my shoulders; when I bend down to pick up the map, he sneaks a kiss on my back. I ask him to stop, but he just smiles. What Nancy and I wouldn't give to be walking now.

Suddenly the jeep road ends at a trail and the PCT sign. The guys want to come back that night but we decline.

"We'll probably hike a few miles yet, but thanks for the ride."

The truck lumbers away. Still wearing in-town clothes and sneakers, we hoist our packs and walk down the trail. But not far. Over the hill sits Oakland Pond, the only water source for miles.

We stop to camp. The guys won't find us here.

After supper, headlights slice through the night, and the music of the Marshall Tucker Band fills the darkness. Mike and Larry are back. We greet them coolly, but they surprise us by acting like gentlemen. Softening, we allow them to stay, and the four of us spend the evening sitting by the fire talking of life and dreams, listening to the music of Simon and Garfunkle. After a time, we hug and kiss good-bye. The guys drive back down the dark forest road, and we crawl into our sleeping bags. Tomorrow it's on to Belden.

Nancy is not the same woman I met on Deep Creek bridge three months ago. Her confidence and sense of self-worth have grown tremendously. This past week she's taken the guidebook and planned our days—the miles ahead, water sources, places to camp. She's also cooking, which she never did before. And mothering me. "You want to get thin, don't you?" she asks, closing the food bags when she thinks I've had enough. She makes me promise I'll be extra careful of snakes when the trail dips into hot canyons. All in all, we've become very comfortable with each other and our life in the outdoors.

We have made it to the Middle Fork of the Feather River, some

Nancy cooking

sixty miles north of the Sierra Buttes. There are no people in the woods, just an occasional truck on a logging road above the river. After washing up at night, we walk around camp nude, air drying. It's been so very warm, it feels good not to have clothes on. The Feather River entices us further.

I take out my braid. My blond hair, wavy from the days' old braid, blows in the wind, tumbles down my shoulders and breasts. I ease myself into the emerald pool. Ten feet away, the current moves swiftly. I swim over to a large boulder and wrap my limbs around it, hugging it, feeling the current trying to pull me away. I let go with my hands and my body extends straight out like a ribbon in the wind, or a piece of yarn on a sailboat mast. I feel in my element.

We sun ourselves on the smooth river rocks, fitting our bodies' bulges and depressions into the concave and convex areas of the rock. Sun warm. Breeze cool. Stretching out. We don't care if someone goes by up above and sees us. We've earned this luxury.

As good as yesterday was, today is miserable. The humidity and heat hit us like a brick wall on our seven-mile ascent out of the canyon. We've been doing over a hundred abdomen curls every morning, getting ready for our L.A. visit. The longer I climb, the more intense the pain in my stomach becomes. It only hurts when I breathe, which is pretty regularly when you're climbing uphill with a heavy pack laden with twenty sixteen-inch-long sugar pine cones. I've been carrying them since Sierra City to mail to my friends back East. I take Nancy's bandage and wrap it around my midriff. I feel better, but I can only take short, quick breaths. Soon the bandage bunches into a belt; I am not happy.

When we finally arrive at Lookout Rock, we collapse by the side trail leading to the viewpoint. Who cares about the view? We lay there with our shoes and socks off, airing our sweaty feet.

Nancy takes her shirt off and tries to dry it for the fourth time today. She says her feet hurt constantly, that she feels like she has stress fractures in all her toes. Our tempers are short and nerves are frayed as we look for a campsite. She wants to be near water; I want a flat tent site, even if that means having to walk to water.

In the middle of the night, I roll over and my nose comes within two inches of her bag's opening.

"My god! What's that smell?"

"Gas," she says. "I wanted to tell you not to turn this way, but I didn't want to wake you up."

Later in the night, I accidentally sneeze on her face. She wakes up startled.

"Is it raining? I thought I felt rain on my face."

Playing along, I look out to see if there are any stars.

"Don't think so, Nance. Go back to sleep."

Hurry, Belden! This living together is getting tough!

Jon and Ken, Todd's other partners, are pushing toward the end. We spot them cruising down the trail in the distance. "That's got to be them," I say. "They're walking like they mean business."

Six hundred miles remain for them to complete the entire Pacific Crest Trail. Like Steve, they fear October snows in the High Sierra. Jon says that Todd has been sending them care packages. Poor guy really misses the trail. I decide to look him up when I return home, for we live only eighty miles apart. We separate with thoughts of ending and home strong on my mind.

I'm finishing this year's hike at the same time I finished the Appalachian Trail—Labor Day weekend. The mountains here even look like the Appalachians, with rounded, forested crest lines. We are also ending in an environment more like that of southern California than the High Sierra. A land of manzanita and sagebrush, heat and drought, lizards and snakes, Belden and the North Fork of the Feather River lies below in the gorge. So does our friend Brian. On our last day on the trail, though, we're in no mood to hurry.

I look over at Nancy, who's trying to get the peanut butter out of its container. I won't miss that stuff. I shipped it from home and the oil floated to the top. We ate it oily the first days, never bothering to stir. Now you need a knife to pare off slices from the dry mound. The things you learn to live with out here.

Nancy's shirt is rolled up at the sleeves, revealing a felt-tip tattoo I drew on her arm in the tent last night. It's a heart with the word "Mom" inside it and an arrow piercing it. She has about twenty-five small holes all over the back of her shirt from her pack rubbing against her back. They look like rat bites.

I look down at myself. My hiking boots gave me blisters in the early days. As the miles went by, my heels toughened and my wool socks wore away. They all have gaping holes in the heels now.

My boots still rub, but my skin is like leather. I wouldn't even need to wear socks. The nails of my big toes are black, dead from pounding down hills.

Our last day wouldn't be complete without one more near crisis. As we cruise down the thirty-eight switchbacks into Belden, Nancy suddenly starts screaming and hopping down the trail.

"What's the matter?"

"I almost got bit by a rattlesnake! I stepped right next to it! It started to coil around my ankle, and I had to shake it off!"

I can't help it, I start to laugh.

"I don't think you understand how serious this could have been!" she complains. "What would you have done had it bitten me?"

"Cut and suck," I reply smiling.

"But the road is only half a mile away," she says. "Would you have gone for help? What would you have done?"

"Cut and suck," I tell her again.

"I don't think it's funny. It could have been very serious."

"I'm sorry. But nothing did happen. You really should have been an actress instead of a ski instructor."

Cindy (left) and Nancy

Belden is a booming town of eight. It used to have a population of seven, but one young woman recently gave birth. Inside the little store that houses the post office and bar, Brian sits on a stool, his back to us. We burst in the door. "We made it!" we scream. Hugs! Champagne! Guacamole! We sit talking loudly and attracting attention. We're so proud. I finished what I set out to do: hike nearly half of the Pacific Crest Trail. And Nancy, who the guys said would never make it, is right by my side.

Brian photographs me with the champagne bottle lifted to my lips. The bubbles burn. Feeling good, I call home to Mom and Dad, squeal another "I made it!" into the receiver. They're happy. They just wanted me safe.

I receive a card from Derreck, along with many other notes and letters from friends congratulating me. I hurry to open his first. It reads, "In answer to your question (which I asked as a joke), I am married of sorts. I've been living for two years with a man who is my lover."

I almost die. I give it to Nancy to read. Neither of us can believe it. I am so disappointed. He's what got me through some of the hardest times on the trail. Many a night was spent reading and rereading his letters, dreaming.

Before we drive to Brian's place in San Francisco, we take a side trip north to climb Lassen Peak, the southernmost Cascade volcano. Upon reaching the summit, we see Mount Shasta suddenly loom on the northern horizon. I didn't even know the mountain was there, hidden as it was by Lassen. The Cascade volcanoes, solitary snow-covered giants strung out one after another all the way to Canada. What an exciting thing to look forward to—the second half of the Pacific Crest Trail!

Brian's little Datsun flies across the Sacramento Valley. The Coast Range lies in the distance. On the other side is San Francisco. Behind us is the great barrier of the Sierra Nevada. We race away. The wind whips my hair. The setting sun shines on my tanned arm. The grasses are warm and honey colored. Oaks scatter the saffron land. Such wide open spaces! Will Pennsylvania satisfy me? Will Hawk Mountain's Appalachian views fulfill my need for space? Have California's mountains become such a part of my soul that they will haunt me forever? I remember that I felt like an alien when I came out here. Now I feel at home.

Nancy, too, will be snatched away from my side. Soon we'll be living three thousand miles apart. We've grown so much together, shared so many memories. Who knows when we'll be together again?

All those memories of miles of desert and deep Sierra snow will soon start to fade and get shoved into the back of my brain with all the other memories of my life. It seems sad. It's all so vivid now.

I sit back, relax, and look over at Nancy and smile. I know it's part of life—this coming together and then separating. We came out here to grow, to learn, to share, and to experience. It won't be lost. We have been added to. Made whole.

> *An acorn is not an oak tree when it is sprouted. It must go through long summers and fierce winters; it has to endure all that frost and snow and side-striking winds can bring before it's a full grown oak. These are rugged teachers; but rugged schoolmasters make rugged pupils. So a man is not a man when he is created; he is only begun.*
> —Henry Ward Beecher

I'd amend the quote to say: So a woman is not a woman when she is created; she is only begun.

PART
II

Cindy and Todd

11

Partners

June 15, 1984

I am in a time warp. I find myself in the exact same spot that I was in two years ago, above the village of Belden, California, and the Feather River Gorge. Being here is like going back in time, getting another chance, picking up where I left off. The heat and dizziness of the climb transport me back.

Nothing up here seems changed. The mountains look the

same. I gaze across to the dozens of switchbacks that Nancy and I charged down toward Brian, singing "happy" songs and dodging rattlesnakes. But Brian's truck is gone, and Nancy is nowhere to be found.

Across the gorge, to the south, I see the live oaks we walked among in the sticky heat and buzzing flies. The flies are still here and so is the beating sun. Beyond that mountain and the next and the next, a couple hundred miles to the south, lies Sonora Pass, the site of my fall. No doubt there's snow on the north slope now. The thought of it makes my blood curdle, as though my accident happened two weeks ago instead of two years.

In the natural world, change is so slow as to often seem imperceptible. My other life back home seemed so full, so complicated, so busy. Now I'm back and see no change around me. I wonder what occurred in those two years in my life that was so significant and important. This world certainly didn't miss me.

A figure with a backpack emerges from the oak scrub and startles me back to the present. He moves with a steady assurance but slowly and deliberately as though his load were heavy and the miles long. Soft dark curls frame his face and hang in ringlets on his perspiring brow. A beard and mustache forces my gaze upward to his intense dark eyes, which spill with emotion when the shy heart inside cannot find the words to speak. They twinkle when they see me. His lips turn up in a smile. It is the face of the man I love, my husband Todd. He is what has changed in my life over the last two years!

Todd was out here himself two years ago, hiking with his own group. He was one of the people who assembled at my house to exchange information prior to departure. Back then, we were just acquaintances. His dream of hiking the entire trail in one season was shattered that year. He was ahead of me and hit the Sierra even earlier than my group. What made it impassible for him was the incredibly high run-off from the snow melt. It made the stream fords dangerously deep and fast, so his group decided to leave the six-hundred-mile Sierra Nevada for last, after the snow had melted.

He and his partners took a bus to Belden and continued their trek northward to Canada. They planned to return later to pick up the Sierra section after the snow had melted. But here in northern California, they found a nightmare. The snow wasn't as deep as in the Sierra, but thick evergreen forests made navigation difficult. Just finding their way took all their energy. Their disappointment grew as the weeks dragged by and the snow remained.

One night, at their thirteen-hundred-mile halfway mark, they gathered around the fire in celebration. Nothing, they said, would stop them now. They'd been through the worst.

The very next day, they were traversing a steep slope that was like hundreds of others. Todd stopped to strap on his crampons before venturing out. Halfway across, the soft snow began balling under his spikes, leaving him no bite. He fell and slid down the slope into a tree. When his foot hit the tree, the teeth of the crampon bit in and held, while the rest of his body dropped and twisted into the melted tree well. Since his foot was planted firmly in the bark, the twisting broke his foot. Although it started to swell up immediately and the pain was severe, he insisted on walking the fourteen miles out to the road. Search and rescue fees are high and he hoped to "walk it off." It didn't work. His foot was put in a cast, but he still didn't give up. He hitchhiked ahead, town stop after town stop, waiting for his partners and hoping his foot would heal. It never did. He had to abandon his dream and return home. What made it so disheartening was that the trail left the snowy section the very day after he fell. That was their last traverse.

But because he returned home, events brought us together and he got a wife instead of a finished through-hike. His fall occurred in central Oregon, so he'll be repeating the eight hundred miles from Belden north. Knowing what lies around the next bend may sound like an advantage, but every mountain we approach brings haunting flashbacks for Todd.

That year, 1982, was a record year for snowfall. This winter has been normal, but the only thing he envisions are these slopes at their worst. He remembers nothing else and can imagine nothing less. We both watch the mountains ahead like hawks, looking for snow-covered peaks. He studies the guidebook, searching for places where the trail approaches seven thousand feet elevation. That's where snow may still linger, and he awaits it with anxiety and fear.

I'm carrying around my own scars. I spent two years away from the snow, two years telling people about my Sonora Pass fall and repeating the words, "I could have died." Enough time passed to distort the fall and make me as scared as Todd about the thought of traversing another steep snowslope. I was also nervous about returning to trail life. It still seems so uncertain. I feel so vulnerable. A lot of time passed between Sonora Pass and now. If I had gotten right back on snow and gotten used to it again, I probably wouldn't have built up the tremendous fears I now have. Sonora Pass didn't cripple my body. But I did allow it to cripple my self-confidence. I hike in fear that on a mountain ahead there will be a slope with my name on it and a fall that this time will kill me.

Back home, our families shared our fears. While we were around them, we had to behave as though we weren't even fazed by the approaching journey and dangers. Despite our feigned nonchalance, however, the truth came through.

Some people wondered how I could return to the trail after my serious fall. The truth is that I was excited to return even though frightened of the prospect of more snow. My two years away from the trail only exaggerated my fear. But it wasn't going to keep me home. The trail, I decided, is where I am happiest. My fear is just a handicap that I must learn to overcome.

I remember my father's eyes when I left for the trail last week. They lingered on mine at the car with a look that transcended time and place. They looked into my soul and said, "I made you. You are my child. Know I am with you." It was scary. It was as though he wanted this last gaze to last forever.

I wanted to go quickly, not to linger, not to think of when we would come back or of our friends and family changing in our absence. I brushed Mom a fast kiss as she got teary-eyed. I went quickly, as though it was all casual, all fun loving. "Of course we will be just fine," we assured them, but now, Todd and I wonder. So do those back home. Together we send up a prayer to keep us safe.

When we descend from the higher elevations, we forget our fears of snow for a while and very easily slip into the rhythm of our new life. A forest of white fir greets us. The sparkling white trunks of the young trees are slender and straight. Their branches are symmetrical and perfectly shaped. They are the well-dressed, exquisitely groomed ladies of the forest. Perfect posture, elegance, and grace.

A breath of wind passes overhead. At first I think a road is near and that I'm hearing the sound of a passing car. But we are miles from civilization. The sound turns out to be the wind moving through the firs! How long must one be in the wilderness before throwing off associations from the outside world?

As we descend lower into the narrow gorge, green moss appears thickly on the trees, though on one side only. The other side of each trunk is moss free. Even their lower branches look as though they were dipped in the stuff. In the low evening light, the moss glows as if it were fluorescent.

Once in camp, I lie on my foam pad, stirring macaroni. That's all I do to run this "household," cook macaroni. Normally, chores are divided equally out here, but I am exempt from all duties except cooking. Todd takes care of the rest. He sets up the tent, collects firewood, fetches water, does the dishes, and hangs the food. So I have all the sunlight and time I need to record in my journal. What is so amazing about it is that he does the chores cheerfully and by choice.

We have sought a distinctively different life style, beginning with our wedding and reception. It was a sort of pioneer wedding, with horse-drawn buggy and bluegrass band. We worked together, making all the food for two hundred and fifty guests — roasting a pig, baking sixty loaves of bread. The wedding party wore old-fashioned dresses, and I sewed them all. We knew that with a start like that, we'd have a wonderful life together, sharing, working on our dreams, following whatever paths our lives may take.

Hiking the present long-distance path is already much easier for me, thanks to a dedicated husband. For the first time, I don't have to carry an overly heavy pack, which enables me to keep up more easily. Todd is slightly bent over from the weight of his pack, however, and his hips have turned red and raw. He insists that this happens to all male backpackers. So the trail is not killing me and we are really doing quite well these first days.

The patches of gold sunlight in the woods are now warmer looking. Insects fly in fits in a spot of sun, ricocheting off one another. Are they attracted to the light, fighting for the energy and heat? I put down my pen and nestle closer to Todd, feeling the evening chill. We are very content in this new life together and look forward to a four-month hiking honeymoon.

We are now in the Cascade Range, which begins with Lassen Peak, about thirty-five air miles north of Belden. Four hundred miles remain in California. The Cascades are dominated by individual volcanoes, massive cones rising five thousand feet above the forest floor, thrusting up to more than fourteen thousand feet into the heavens. They are part of a great circle of volcanoes, called the "Ring of Fire," that encloses the Pacific Ocean. For us, the Cascade volcanoes are snow-covered beacons by which to gauge our progress. They march in a string, each volcano reigning over both the landscape and our thoughts.

Much of the Pacific Crest Trail through the Cascades lies at the seven-thousand-foot mark. Though not as high as the Sierra Nevada, these mountains lie farther north, where it is cooler and rainier and where the snows are heavier and the snow line much lower. In northern Washington, the North Cascades change to a jumbled, chaotic mass of peaks, saw-toothed and razor sharp, steep sided and avalanche prone. Seven hundred glaciers drape their sides

Lassen Peak, the southernmost volcano in the Cascade Range, is a plug dome, unlike the other major volcanoes. It was created when lava oozed rather than erupted from a vent in the earth. Too thick to flow far, the lava just piled higher.

Before Mount St. Helens, in southern Washington, erupted, Lassen Peak was North America's most recently active volcano. Its last eruption occurred in the second decade of the twentieth century. As we hike, we see many signs of that activity. The trail is strewn with pumice. I pick up one rock and am amazed at its slight weight. Then I notice that it is riddled with holes, which look like popped bubbles. And that's what they were—bubbles of gas trapped in the molten rock.

We climb to the top of a ridge and, suddenly, the massive volcano fills the sky. We've been in forests for days without realizing the mountain was so close. Now, thanks to the crystal-clear atmosphere, the great peak seems close enough for me almost to touch it.

Two years ago, Todd and his buddies spent a delightful afternoon soaking in the hot water baths of Terminal Geyser, in Lassen Volcanic National Park. Although we're not frozen and miserable, as they were, we still deserve some pampering after five hard days on the trail. Terminal Geyser is really a fumarole, an opening in the earth that emits steam, gases, and hot water. The water temperature, however, fluctuates. When Todd was last here, he was able to bathe within view of the fumarole. This year we must walk far down the valley, following the stream to a place where the unbearably hot water is diluted enough by cold springs to make it tolerable. A half mile down, we still can't tolerate the temperature and must let water sit out in pans to cool before we use it to wash.

While we're dressing, a middle-aged couple on the way to their bath stop to chat. They ask where we're going. When we tell them Canada, the woman says, "I met a woman in this park last year who was doing the whole trail. She's writing a book about it, too." My stomach drops. I am so afraid that someone will hike this trail and get a book on the market before I can.

We talk some more and exchange addresses, for her daughter lives by the trail in northern Washington and it's possible that they could pick us up for dinner. When she sees my name on the piece of paper, she questions me further. As it turns out, I was the woman she'd met, only it had been two years before, not one. She and her husband were climbing Lassen Peak and were on the summit the same day that Brian, Nancy, and I were. She remembers how Nancy and I were telling stories to a crowd of listeners, bubbling with pride that we had just finished our hike. What is so strange is that she hasn't been out hiking from that day to this.

Farther along the trail, Todd and I arrive at Boiling Lake. What a colorful sight! The water is a creamy mint green with orange and red earth surrounding it. Deep green conifers surround the lake and a brilliant blue sky shines overhead. We see that the lake is, indeed, boiling, farting, belching, and smelling like rotten eggs.

Mud pots along the shore spit and gurgle like bubbling porridge. We keep our distance. Downstream from the lake, the outlet stream is still hot. Green, stringy algae thrive in the warm water and wave with the stream's current.

There is something magic about Lassen Volcanic National Park. I've never seen the earth behave this way, as though it were an unstable, sleeping dragon. Its inner energy reminds me that this planet is unpredictable and makes me look at that snowy peak again and wonder if it wouldn't put on the biggest show of all and blow up before my very eyes. I know that it's possible.

North of the park, the trail leaves the higher, cooler forest and drops onto the Modoc Plateau, through which Hat Creek has cut its course. The opposite, west, side of the Hat Creek valley is lush, with many lakes and campgrounds. But the PCT is on the east side, on arid Hat Creek Rim. Hat Creek Rim is not inviting. The guidebook is full of suggestions for alternate routes. The trail register is full of entries from hikers who plan to skip this section.

We slowly climb the escarpment, packs laden with water for the dry stretch ahead. Our fear of snow is over for a while, but we must now confront heat, drought, and dust. There is no breeze, no bird sounds in the air. We hear only eerie sounds of insects rubbing their wings together in the trees. They make a clicking sound like an old roller coaster climbing its first hill or the crackling sound of high-tension wires.

My incentive to keep going is the thought of a candy bar. Todd isn't interested in finding it for me when we reach the top. The candy bars are buried in his pack, too much of an effort to locate. But I must have one and insist he look for them. He tosses things out of his pack angrily. "No candy bars!" he yells.

I quietly pick up the food and put it back in his pack, trying to hide my tears. Arms encircle me and kisses touch my head.

We've never fought before. He has never even raised his voice to me, nor argued. If I do make him angry, he just stares at me with those dark eyes icy and hard. I, on the other hand, yell and get what's bothering me out in the open. But my need for Todd's support is what drove me to his side two years ago. When I returned home from the trail in 1982, few people could understand me or what I had just experienced. I wasn't the same person, yet everyone expected me to be. I slept in the backyard in the open air, ignoring street lights. My parents murmured, "I don't under-

Hat Creek Rim

stand it. She has a perfectly good bed." I walked around sniffing a box of sage from my mother's herb shelf because the fragrance reminded me of my days in the desert. I was haunted by memories, smells, scenes, feelings.

I became sluggish from the lack of exercise, eating bad food, sleepless nights.

Since Todd had been on the trail himself in 1982 and lived close by, I went to visit him. The broken foot that had forced him home had made him melancholy. We shared our stories, our slides, but mostly the pain of how much we missed the mountains and the life on the trail. We shared a vision of returning and completing the trail and began to cling to one another—perhaps more tightly than most couples.

Even now, married and back on the trail, we need each other's support. We have no one else out here; nothing but our life together on the trail.

In the spring, the Hat Creek Rim is covered with wildflowers. But in July all have gone to seed, donning sharp little jabbers that stick to our socks and work their way into our skin. These seeds attract mice, which attract rattlesnakes, which we can't see because of the tall, dead grass that we're charging through.

Keeping our heads low to look for snakes makes us aware of other things that otherwise might have gone by unnoticed, things like ant lions. Todd points out that close to the ant hills that are scattered over the ground are tiny little funnels in the sand, each about one and a half inches deep. At the base of each funnel is an insect called an ant lion, which lies in wait for ants and other small insects.

"Watch this," Todd says, as he picks up a good-sized ant and deposits it in the funnel. The buried ant lion starts kicking up sand to knock the ant down into the hole. The walls of the funnel are steep and loose enough to give the ant quite a fight as it tries to climb out. Most ants make it out, but this one is grabbed by its leg, pulled underneath the sand, and disappears. We quickly try to scoop up the sand hoping to discover what this tiny insect looks like, but are always unsuccessful.

The day quickly becomes hotter as the sun rises in the sky. The trees begin to thin out. I can feel the sun bleaching my hair, burning my skin, blistering my lips. Sunscreen forms a caked circle around my mouth. My face is dried with salt and sweat. When I rub it with my bandanna, white grains fall off. We can't use our drinking water to rinse our skin, so I spit on my bandanna and apply it as a shoddy alternative.

The tread is easy and flat, so we're averaging better than two miles per hour, but the heat makes us long for the hour when, finally, we get to take a break. I look at my watch every five minutes, hoping to see some progress. It feels like an eternity. Before we make it to our sixty-minute goal we collapse under a rare tree, downing nacho chips and sipping precious water. I laugh out loud when I think of the care packages our health-food friends send—no salty snacks. They find it so hard to believe that we get weak and sick when we don't take in enough salt.

To our left is a mile drop-off to the valley below, to sweltering highway 89 and Hat Creek, the alternate route. To our right there are cows chomping, their bells ringing. Where in heaven's name do they drink? In front of us, the plateau stretches for God knows how far.

We're aiming for a reservoir that the guidebook suggests we camp by, where we can go for a delightful swim. The idea has been on our minds all day. When we spot the blue speck below, Todd takes off in a trot, hollering like a madman. He kicks up the chocolate-brown dust and chases all the cows, who run away in their own frightened cloud. I lag behind, giggling at the sight.

When we arrive, we stare in disbelief. The "lake" is four inches deep! It's a slime-covered mud hole! The water level is very low, so that rocks that no doubt normally lie submerged are exposed. We step on them to get out to the water. Muddy ooze squishes from the pressure of our weight, disturbing billions of mosquitoes breeding in the slime. Immediately they cover our ankles and begin sucking blood. Take a swim in this? Todd begins the laborious project of filtering water. He takes a sweaty bandanna and drapes it over a water bottle opening, putting a shallow dip in the cloth to help the liquid through. I swat bugs off him as he collects a gallon. We look at each other. "Let's get out of here!"

We spend hours following the curves of the escarpment, which runs predominantly westward, into the sun. Even in the

Filtering water

early evening, the sun is still robbing our bodies of precious moisture. We hope to go a few more miles yet. It will mean that much less rim to cover tomorrow. But Todd is feeling pretty sick and weak and is incredibly thirsty. Still, he says, "Let's keep going."

I get dizzy every now and then and when I stop to lower my head to prevent the world from spinning, I see his face, in pain and anguish.

"Let's stop, honey," I say.

"I can keep going," he answers. But it doesn't seem worth it.

Suddenly, a rattlesnake buzzes beside me! I jump off the trail, away from it, and the surge of adrenalin robs my body of all its remaining energy. "Let's camp, Todd. I've had enough."

It's nearly seven P.M. The sun is still high in the sky. Plenty of mileage in it, but none left in us. For me and Todd the day is over. We sit on the rim, naked, underneath a Coulter pine, where a breeze finally blows. We boil the infested water — not interested in food, only in a drink. We sip hot lemonade in the ninety-degree heat, too thirsty to wait until it cools. The strong iodine flavor shouts through.

Up here, we see what we have covered in the last days and what is to come. Lassen Peak is to our left, and the cone-shaped Mount Shasta, our next Cascade volcano, is to our right. A lot of heat in between.

We each have a quart of water for tonight and a quart for tomorrow. The next source is eight miles away. We plan to get up by five and get off the rim by noon. Coyotes howl all night long. They stand along the side of the rim and howl out to the valley below. We see the evidence — scat lies on many of the rocks along our path. Between their yipping and the prickers in our clothes, we sleep little and awake feeling worse than we had the night before. Burney Falls, a state park with showers and a store, is twenty-one miles away. Sounds heavenly, but we're not sure we have a twenty-mile day in us.

After we drop off the rim, our trail crosses two sets of young lava flows. From a distance, they look like parched yellow fields of dry grass, with sparse live oak struggling to grow here and there. Close up, however, large black volcanic rocks are revealed, hiding in the grass, turning our ankles, and forcing us to watch our step. It's hot and getting hotter. The bottle of cherry Kool-aid is down to four ounces. I'm sick of drinking so much sugar, but the iodine taste is too putrid without it.

The trail around Crystal Lake Fish Hatchery should have been easy, but the blasted cows used it when the ground was wet, making four-inch holes that have since hardened and are exhausting to walk on. Between this and the lava rocks, my feet are killing me. The cows make me so angry, I start to cry. I know I'm tired when I resort to tears to express my emotions. I do manage to compose myself when I see Todd.

We're really pushing ourselves. Yesterday we did seventeen miles. Today we're shooting for twenty-one. If we don't make it to Burney tonight, we need to save enough water for supper, the night, and breakfast. If we can walk the full twenty-one miles, all of what we carry we can consume this afternoon. That's the reason for the death march.

Ten miles remain after lunch. We have a half gallon of water each. Four pints in four stops, doing two and a half miles in between, and we'll be there. Simple. Each pint disappears in one big swallow, and we're faced with another hour of walking before our next drink.

In the early hours I can think of nothing but moving my feet along. No thoughts enter my head except making it to Burney. Todd walks at my heels, encouraging me to talk.

"Don't want to," I say. "Nothing I care to talk about." I just want to get there. There's a dull ache in my thigh and a sharp, piercing pain in my neck from looking down. His pounding boots sound like a stampede right at my tail and it drives me nuts. When I stop to itch my leg, he plows into me.

"Go ahead!" I snap.

He ignores my crankiness and goes by. He knows I'm frustrated. Now that he's ahead, he stops every two hundred yards to give me a kiss for encouragement. After the fourth time, I blow him a kiss and yell, "Keep going! If I stop, I'll never want to get up!"

When we do rest, we remove our boots and air out our feet. Our socks are black and smell awful. Our feet ache and are swollen. We're covered with filth. Everything has chocolate-brown dirt on it—our clothes, our gear, our bodies. Todd's hair is a few shades lighter brown from the dirt particles sticking to the oil. Our faces look like they're festered with blackheads. I have hard, pimple-like boils under my arms where my pack straps rub.

As the sun lowers, each segment of trail gets progressively cooler, making us less thirsty and more certain of our success. Just after eight, we fall into the park. A fifty-cent shower, beer, ice cream, and orange juice do a lot to make us happy. Todd clogs the drain in his shower, and my pimples clear up in just a few hours. In bed, we hug and kiss like new lovers discovering one another. It's a good ending to a bad day.

We are beginning to walk a wide arc around Mount Shasta, our second volcano. It will take more than three weeks to com-

Mount Shasta

plete this half-circle, and we'll see this magnificent, snow-covered cone from the south, the north, and the west.

It feels so good to be in the trees again, as we ascend into the forest and away from the Modoc Plateau. The shade and higher elevations guarantee cooler temperatures. The trees grow to magnificent heights in these dark, moist canyons. Mammoth Douglas firs obscure the sky. Their cones, which line the trail, succumb to the weight of our boots. Far off we hear the roar and clank of logging equipment. Timber sale signs are posted on the giant firs. We come into a clearing, see an old logging scar, and look up to a Caterpillar high on the next mountain. How did the operator make a road up that steep canyon? They've logged all the virgin timber that was easily accessible. Now they must plunge deeper into the wilderness to get the small amount of old-growth timber that remains.

We walk through many old scars. Hot sunlight pours in from the holes in the canopy, making the air warmer. In an hour or two, we hit very young clear-cuts. We must climb over ten downed firs in a twenty-foot stretch of trail. The air is sweet with their perfume.

Logging roads cross our trail all day, sometimes totally obliterating it. We discover yellow ribbons tied to the trees that are supposed to direct us through the destruction. I think of the miles of clear-cut walking ahead.

Later we meet a Forest Service man at a road crossing. "What's going on?" I ask.

"The lumber companies and the Forest Service are getting further away from selective cutting," he says, "even on National Forest land. The land isn't being replanted, because it takes too much time and the mountains are too steep for any trees to grow back. The rains wash the seedlings away and leave gullies in the soil."

"What about this destruction?" I say.

"Too much work," he says regretfully. But I think of the poor, exploited earth and what it must do to reclaim and rebuild itself. The scales don't seem balanced.

Mushroom Rock ranks high on the list of places to fear in the southern Cascades. Here, Todd and his buddies encountered terrible traverses and almost "had their candles blown out." Today we'll hit it. Our first steep traverse.

All day, images of what this place looks like form in my mind. On and off the words "Mushroom Rock, Mushroom Rock," play in my head, like a skipping record.

Our dry trail is suddenly blocked by a huge snow mound, higher than our heads. It starts at the summit and stretches steeply down the mountainside. There is no alternative but to climb onto it and go across. Okay. This is it! Do it girl!

Todd goes first and cuts steps. I hang back until he's safely across. When he's on dry ground, he plants the head of his ice ax in the edge of the snowbank, holds onto it with one hand and, with his other, gets ready to grab me when I come across.

"Okay, honey. Come on."

I hesitate, nervously look down and wonder if I could self-arrest if I had to, as if I had miraculously learned how to do it while living in Pennsylvania these last two years. He sees me staring down.

"If you fall, you won't go far," he tells me. I study the trees fifteen yards below, which would stop me all right . . . painfully.

I cautiously make my way across. I step into the last footholds and reach my hand out to Todd's outstretched arm. I did it!

"Were you scared?" I ask softly.

"A little," he replies, smiling, and lowering his eyes as if ashamed.

"Me too," I add, and pull his curly head down for a kiss.

From the looks of what lies ahead, the route won't be any picnic. We've been seeing a snow-covered range in the far distance and are unable to tell if it lies in the direction we are heading.

"We don't have to attempt anything dangerous," Todd tells me. "I know Sonora Pass continues to bother you. We'll try for the high, scenic route, but can bail out at any time to a lower route."

Over and over he says we don't have to cross anything steep, but I feel I have to. I don't want to let one range go by unwalked just because of my fear.

Most of our hike today consists of rounding gullies. We are crossing the mountains westward. The trail winds uphill half the day and then about two o'clock we reach a saddle, the high point, and spend the rest of the day winding downward toward a raging stream on the canyon's bottom and a campsite.

The south-facing side of each gulch has oaks on it and scattered sunlight. The small, dried leaves sound like corn flakes under our feet. The rocks amid them sound like glass tinkling when we knock them together. There are very strange yellow flies here, too, biting flies that alight on the strangest places, fingertips and such. The oaks have thick, curly lichen on them. It's very dry to the touch.

When we round the gulch to the north-facing slope, we find cool pines and firs. The walkway is smooth and needle-covered, and the shade is deep and cooling. Totally different environments just across a gully. Every gully!

As soon as our camp is set up at Squaw Creek, Todd runs around the banks of the river like a kid, with a piece of fishing line in his hand and a half-dead, but still crawling, grasshopper that he caught a few miles back and carried in an empty film container. He asked me to make supper late. His face is beaming as he hops off. I settle in to write in my journal.

Lately, I've been thinking about our life out here. We live such a simple existence. There are no other hikers around—just Todd and me. We don't do a lot of deep thinking. We don't have any divine thoughts or insights. Instead, we feel—the heat of the sun in a logged area, the wind on a rim walk, our aching feet in the middle of the night. We listen—for running brooks in a dry section, to the different voices of the wind blowing through a ponderosa pine or a white fir, to thrushes in the late evening and mosquitoes buzzing in our ears, and to hundreds of gray lizards scurrying through the oak leaves. Our senses are at work, our brains are on idle. Home and our past lives seem so far away. No people are here, so we live and move through these mountains, quietly working toward our goal.

Todd returns from the stream empty-handed, so it's macaroni and cheese tonight.

"Two weeks have passed," he says, as he settles in. "All we have to do is what we just did, six more times, and we'll be in Canada."

It doesn't seem so long—or lonely—when we look at it that way. It sure would be nice to see some other hikers though. Both of us have our roots in the Appalachians; we miss the camaraderie found on that very social trail.

I think back to my early trail days in southern California two years ago. I seriously contemplated going home while I was walking that road into Warner Springs. Now, I feel that it's time to rearrange my thinking, to begin getting more out of this hike. I was looking for some sort of mental stimulation, as though it was necessary in life. I thought that while I was here, I should be doing something remarkably constructive, as though hiking fourteen hundred miles isn't enough. My job is to be here now, to be as relaxed and open to my surroundings and my senses as possible, so that I can record them to share with others. I mustn't look for more. If it's done well, it will take up all my remaining energy.

It's a long, hot pound down to the town of Castella on the Sacramento River. We see our destination from high atop the ridge early in the day and figure that we'll be there in a few hours. But it takes most of the day to get down switchbacks that are so long and gradual we're not even aware that we're descending. These add numerous miles. Our descent is even interrupted at one point by a long ascent to a spring. By the time I finally get to the asphalt road, I am irritable and bitchy. Todd can't seem to remember how far it is to the first store, and I find that unbelievable. It's only been two years! He takes my foul mood with amusement and understanding. When Sam's Market appears on the horizon my problems suddenly vanish.

On the picnic table behind the store, I spoon Day-Glow pink

strawberry ice cream into a water bottle of milk and mix up a milkshake. The stuff tastes like chemicals and refuses to melt, but I'm happy, for I am nearly done for the day.

When we stumble into Castle Crags State Park, the ranger in the booth remarks, "You must be Cindy Ross. My dad has been waiting for you for two years. He helps all the hikers."

"How does he know me?"

"He heard about you from other hikers. He even knows you got married! He'll be up to your campsite later this evening."

The ranger tells us of the wonderful set-up the park has for hikers. Everyone else pays six dollars to camp, but the hiker's fee is fifty cents, showers included! Four picnic tables are provided, four campfire rings, and four wooden lockers to protect our food from animals. A side trail was even built leading from our campsite directly to the PCT!

When we return from our showers, an old '64 Chevy with dull green paint sits out front. A man in his early seventies, with baggy trousers and a tucked-in dress shirt, learns against the bumper.

"Pleased to meet you, Ma'am," and he takes off his hat. "I'm Milt Kenny." He reaches to shake our hands.

We spend some time talking about mutual hiking friends. He pulls out a stack of postcards and letters from past hikers, notes that tell of their progress after Castella and thanking him for the hospitality. Piles of Christmas cards come each year from hikers whose lives he has touched. We know many of them, for the long-distance hiking community is small.

Milt Kenny's wife died a few years back. He needed something to fill his life and his heart and make him feel needed. Hikers are needy people, so Milt became a hiker-liker.

The mosquitoes are very bad. Todd and I slam them on our skin and talk about what a pain they are. Either Milt is oblivious to the insects or he's too much of a gentleman to say or do anything, for they land right on his face and forehead and bite him while he talks.

"Milt! There's one on your eye!" I can't stand to watch them

Milt Kenny

bite him. As we part, he asks if we'd meet him at the dance tonight so that he can buy us a beer. All right, Milt!

Eleven P.M. The band is just now arriving. The beer Milt
bought us is putting us to sleep fast. Milt is a live wire, however,
dressed in a Caribbean print shirt and double-knit green slacks.
All the ladies love the sweet man and gather around him. He buys
each one a beer.

Most small towns have local color. The crowd looks like the
type of folks you'd expect to find at any Fire Hall club or American
Legion across America.

It's break time. The town people sit around on benches facing
the dance floor, chatting. Intermission entertainment arrives in
the persons of a tall, heavy woman in a skimpy black halter top
and jeans so tight they look painted on, and a skinny, scruffy,
drunken cowboy type. They sit on a bench up front. She sits on
his lap, facing him, her legs around his waist. He's got his hands
all over her, while she squeals with delight. Then they tumble to

the floor, where their bouncing reminds me of a rodeo event. Leering onlookers in the crowd egg them on. When her top falls down, cheers go up. Though Todd and I are wide awake at this, Milt doesn't notice the sideshow because he's deep in conversation with a woman nearby. Fortunately, the band returns before any more clothes are removed or children are added to the town's population.

Sunday is layover day. Milt arrives at eight A.M. to take us to Dunsmuir to do our laundry and go to Mass. Long-distance hikers carry only the minimal amount of clothing. Usually it is so filthy we must wear our rain gear while our clothes go through the cycles.

We stand in the back of a local church in our coated nylon and Gore-tex, trying to be inconspicuous. It's eighty degrees outside. Inside, the temperature is much higher. A visiting missionary is saying Mass and spends twenty-five minutes shouting his sermon in broken English. Meanwhile, as my body temperature soars inside the rain gear, I begin to feel faint. Todd's smiling dark eyes look at me sympathetically.

Milt takes most hikers out for a steak dinner, but Todd and I are in a mood for Chinese. We drive to the town of Mount Shasta, nestled in the shadow of its namesake, to have dinner. Over egg rolls, Milt tells us about the area.

Mount Shasta is the second highest mountain in the range, second only to Mount Rainier in Washington. Shasta towers fourteen thousand feet high, ten thousand feet above its foothills, and can be seen for one hundred miles in every direction. It is a most powerful sight, and many consider the mountain sacred. There are a variety of cults and sects living at its base. Some believe there are civilizations living within the mountain. One race is said to have a sense organ in the middle of their foreheads that provides them with ESP and enables them to disappear at will. Another group has magical bells that have supersonic sounds that can hollow out tunnels into the mountain.

Lava tunnels really do exist in and around the mountain. They were formed when the volcano erupted and molten lava flowed down its sides. The outer layer of lava cooled, hardening into a crust, like the skin on cooling pudding. This got so rigid it remained immobile, but the lava continued to flow underneath. When the volcano's eruptions were over, the lava left empty passageways with roofs. They can be followed for many miles. The Indians would never enter the lava tubes, for they believed that Sasquatch (i.e., Bigfoot, the legendary ape-man of the Pacific Northwest) lived in them. Mount Shasta is also believed to be a landing field for interplanetary travel. Numerous sightings of UFOs have been reported in the area.

When we leave Castella behind, Todd and I climb up to the Crags and look down to the village below. We cannot help but think of the people there in their little Monopoly-sized homes, living their lives so very different from our own. We think of Milt and feel grateful that there are people like him. We're fortunate that he touched our lives.

12

Trouble Ahead

July 2

Todd and I had an eagle's view of Castle Crags before we dropped into Castella, so we saw what lies ahead. Green and forested mountain ranges with light gray, triangular rock that looks like a colossal granite castle. The PCT won't go into the rocks. Too much blasting would have been necessary to cut a trail and it would have destroyed the rugged wildness. Instead, we'll climb to their bases, and circle them at tree line.

Todd and Castle Crags

The sun is hot and fierce as we climb up to the crags. My head feels like it's baking in an oven and ready to explode. The orange juice and beer from yesterday are gushing from my pores.

At our first trailside creek we strip down and immerse ourselves in a pool. Aaah! Our body temperature drops. Five minutes later we're dressed again and well into our snack when two hikers pass by.

Hikers! They're the first people we've seen on the trail so far. I'm so glad we're decent and acting decently. No more skinny dips or sex on lunch breaks. Those are luxuries enjoyed only by early-season hikers. It's July now. The weekenders are starting to enter the backcountry. The hikers say only a quick "Hello!" in passing.

The state park does a very good job of marking creeks within its boundaries. Every little freshet has been given a name. Creeks that aren't on the map or in the guidebook are named and flowing.

Ten miles from Castella, there's a "reliable" stream, where we plan to camp tonight. It will be our last sure water until tomorrow night's camp, fourteen miles farther.

Rounding so many gullies in our ascent makes it difficult to keep track of exactly where we are, especially when we hike slowly and stop often. Our natural, built-in clock gets thrown off.

About the time we figure we should be there, we cross a wide, dry creek bed with a few flat spots to camp, but no water. Todd doesn't think we've come far enough. Besides, we're down to one cup of water and need to find more. If intermittent streams are running, then a reliable one should be too.

About twenty minutes later, I see Todd sitting on the trail with a sorry look on his face. "That was it," he announces. Great. We can't even remember how far back the last water was. What do we do? Todd doesn't want to go back and talks of continuing.

"Fourteen more miles?" I ask.

"Maybe there will be some snowmelt before that."

It's eight o'clock now. I am starving and slowing down considerably. He is fired up with adrenalin and responsibility.

"I'll go on myself without a pack and come back when I find water."

"Oh no!" I cry. "We're not separating."

We've been ascending alongside a gorge, the same canyon the dry creekbed was in, only now we can hear water below. It could be the wind in the trees, for it's sometimes difficult to tell the two apart. On the map we see a short blue line indicating water in the upper reaches of the canyon. I know what will probably occur, however: Todd will drop into this steep gorge in search of water.

When the trail takes its first switchback away from the canyon wall, he drops his pack and instructs me to continue until I find a flat spot on the trail for the tent.

I peer over the edge of what looks like a cliff.

"Please don't do anything dangerous," I beg. "Turn back if it gets too difficult."

I hurry down the trail to find a camp spot, then race back to where I last saw him. It's already starting to get dark. When I arrive at his pack, I yell out, "Todd!" No answer. "TODD!" No answer. Fear fills me. On the third try, he answers me and stands in the open so I can see him. My God, he's a long way down! Just a tiny speck.

"How was it?"

"I almost didn't make it," he yells back. I panic. I knew it was crazy to go!

He's just starting to fill the water bag, so I have lots of time to get upset. I sit down on the trail and sob. As he stands down there with his green shirt on, tying the water bag around his waist and neck with the climbing rope, darkness descends. I memorize the spot I last see him.

"I can't find a way up!" he yells. "How does it look?"

"Like a cliff!"

He yells that he's going down the gorge to find a better way. My mind races. What if he's stuck down there all night? What if he can't get up and needs to be rescued? What if he falls?

Suddenly, I hear rocks fall. Then boulders roll and crash to the bottom of the dark gorge. My heart sinks! When there's finally silence, I call his name.

"Todd!" No answer. "Todd!" What if he's lying down there hurt?

"I'm okay!" he finally answers, sounding very out of breath. "I'm safe and am past the rocks!"

When I see his hand grab a tree and his head poke up over the edge, I start to cry again. I embrace him and the water bag saying, "Never again. I will go back ten miles for water. Go all the way back to the valley. Even quit and go home. It isn't worth it."

It takes until the tent is set up and the macaroni is cooking for me to compose myself. Our tent is staked right on the trail, hanging on the side of the mountain. Castle Crags rise like a wall behind us, the light granite reflecting the pink in the fading sky. Stars come out and the moon shines brightly. I hug my honey for the hundredth time.

There they are again, the snow-covered peaks that appeared on the horizon last week. They are probably the Trinity Alps. They terrify me. They lie in the direction we're traveling, directly west, and they're not that far away.

On a midafternoon break, Todd and I share a lemonade slushie at a lingering snow patch.

"What's wrong with me?" I ask. "We haven't had any snow problems yet. We've barely walked on the stuff."

Still I worry.

"You see trouble ahead," he replies. "I'm tired of the suspense too. Just because it's clear here, doesn't mean it will be clear tomorrow."

I'm worrying over something that might not even exist. I wish I were stronger.

The Klamath Mountains are made up of a number of smaller ranges, each individual and unique. These mountains were mostly formed from molten rock, or magma, that cooled and crystallized underneath the earth's surface. In contrast, the volcanic rocks of the Cascade Range formed after the magma erupted onto the earth's surface. In the Eddy Mountains, the

Trinity Alps

rocks contain a lot of iron, which gives them a ruddy complexion. In the Trinity Alps the rocks are mostly white granite.

The snows get very deep in the Eddy Mountains, and in winter the winds are often high, but there's no danger from either on this warm summer day. The country is open. Only a few trees grow on these slopes, leaving the rusty soil in full view. The only snow that exists forms high, thin lips on the summit's north-facing side. Town folk said this country was impassible two weeks ago. All the glacial tarns visible in the basin below were just recently ice bound. The snow melted rapidly in the intense heat of these last two weeks. At the seven thousand, six hundred foot point, the trail is open! We're elated!

Conditions could have been much worse here. Whitebark pine, a lover of fierce winds and harsh weather, grows on these high slopes. They have little competition this high. Their trunks lean out from the slope and then bend upward, a deformation caused by the downward creep of snow. We step over a lingering patch of snow and see a partially buried pine. Its base and tip are beneath the snowpack, while the middle section forms an arch above it. Avalanches mowed the trees down, covering them, and the snow hasn't melted enough to release their crowns. We pull on the captured tree and it breaks loose, bouncing and bowing up and down as though in recognition and thanks.

The other tree that grows this high is the mountain hemlock, which thrives where there's protection from the wind, where the snows are deep and lasting. Its dense cover barely lets the sunshine penetrate. Todd and his partners learned to hate the hemlock in 1982, for they knew they'd encounter harrowing traverses underneath its boughs. The snow barely got soft for them, unlike the open passes in the Sierra where we traveled through snow that made us sink to our hips. Only small patches of snow remain now.

Below us I catch a flick of movement. It takes a few seconds for my eyes to focus, sort out the activity, and suddenly a brown dirt patch is transformed into a deer! She's lying on her belly on the refrigerated ground, neck outstretched and head resting peacefully in the snow. Her tail swats to chase a bug.

In a few days the trail takes us into the Scott Mountains and the Salmon-Trinity Alps Wilderness. The trail stays high, winding above basins that glaciers carved. Grassy meadows nestle here and there in flat areas. Lakes sit on shelves, acting like brilliant mirrors, reflecting the color in the sky. Dark green evergreens are scattered along the shores, reflecting in the still water. This is what the High Sierra must look like when it's dry. When you look down on lakes and meadows, you almost feel as though you are walking in the sky. When you pick your head up, only the heavens are above; everything else is at your feet.

The scenery bursts into view with every corner we round. The tallest peaks in the Trinity Alps are more than nine thousand feet in height. We stand a few air miles away from these dreaded snow-covered monsters, with the gorgeous Tangle Blue drainage between us. Our trail goes up to meet this scene, displays it for us, then takes a sharp right. "We can be happy again!" Todd yells back.

Masterson Meadow is covered with tiny yellow flowers. Out

there are those exquisite mountains—hateful and wicked before, when they stood for fear and destruction. Now they are my friends. What better place to camp?

As the sun sinks lower, the meadow begins to glow. All the blades of grass and yellow flowers begin to radiate with light. Each single blade and petal has a golden halo around it. Todd walks through the meadow with outstretched arms and seems to float through the light. His entire body is surrounded by an electric glow, his curly hair is on fire with sunlight. I drink in this moment of magic. In a minute the sun is down and it all suddenly disappears.

July 7

Around seven P.M. we begin looking for a campsite. The ridge crest ahead looks like a good spot, affording a wide view of the mountains beyond. Todd walks on ahead, then looks back at me, sullen and serious.

"How long do you want to hike tonight?"

"What? What's wrong with the ridge?"

"You're not going to like it."

On the other side of the crest is a huge, vertical snowbank that buries whole trees and empties out onto boulders. My stomach drops. We try to decide what to do. Camp here and worry about what awaits us in the morning? Or get it over with now? The snow is somewhat soft at this late hour. Tomorrow it will be dangerously icy in the early morning hours, and we've no crampons.

We decide to go for it and choose the boulder route instead of the snow. When I take my pack off to lower it, my legs begin to shake uncontrollably. Past the rocks, we encounter steep snow under the hemlocks. Todd cuts good steps for me and we begin to look for a "small patch of heaven in the middle of hell," where we might camp. I didn't think I'd be sleeping in these conditions again, like so many nights in the High Sierra. Even so I can handle them. What worries me is what may lie ahead. The first thing tomorrow we traverse high above Russian Creek Canyon on a trail so steep that the route has been dynamited out of the granite.

Lingering patches of snow could remain until mid-July, the guidebook warns us. It's now July 7.

When we awake the next morning, the air is cold and damp from the evaporating snow that surrounds us. It makes our pace quicken. The town of Etna lies at the end of the day. No reason to dilly-dally.

The topo lines showing Russian Creek Canyon nearly touch on the map. It's so steep that we can't look down to the valley, only across to granite peaks still in shadow at this early hour. Snow lies on their summits and in long fingers in couloirs. This area looks so much like the Sierra I was not surprised to discover that it was indeed once a part of that range, a part that has shifted about a hundred miles northwestward as a result of fault movement.

Tears come this morning when I think of what could be ahead. When the trail takes a sharp bend away from the canyon, over to its sunny side, Todd waits for me. I sit on a rock with him and my tears flow freely. All morning my stomach has been in knots, but my tears calm me down. After this release, the day

Russian Canyon Traverse

moves along fine and I am able to relax for a while. The wind is refreshing, the miles effortless, and the town ever in mind.

Until Payne's Lake. In the midst of my sandwich, a hiker comes staggering into our lunch site. He looks like a long-distance hiker. That is pretty easy to tell. There are water bottles hanging outside of his pack with siphon tubes attached. When we talk to him, he seems a bit slow, like he's not all there. The crewcut and army greens make us conclude that he's just been released and is, perhaps, still a bit disoriented. There's a strange, far-away look in his eyes when he answers our regular questions, "Where are you coming from?" and "How far you going?" Not until we ask, "How was the snow?" do we begin to understand our friend.

"Pretty bad, it was," he murmurs.

"How bad?" I ask. "Where was it bad?"

"Cliff Lake was terrible. There's a few bad stretches in the Marble Mountains, but the worst is right before here."

My eyes widen. "Where?"

"Right before you get to the road into Etna."

"What's it like?" I ask. "How long is it? Can we go around it?"

"About one hundred yards long, and, no, I don't think you can go around it. You need crampons. I should have had mine on in the Marbles and Cliff Lake, too."

I hand Todd the rest of my sandwich. I can't get it down. Already I feel sick. As soon as we thank our soldier friend for his bad news and hike off, I begin to bawl. Todd stops me right on the trail and says, "Look, we'll try to go around it. If his steps aren't good enough, there's a side trail half a mile before the road that we can take." Todd has been so understanding about my irrational fear of snow. I feel like such a burden to him.

We know exactly where the snow will be, and the spot is just around the corner. As we traverse high above Smith Lake, we see what we've been dreading: snow mound after snow mound in the hemlocks. Every now and then stretches of trail are exposed. Below the trail, the mountain is steeper than the part we traverse. No, we won't be going around this section.

We left our crampons home this year. I didn't use mine once two years ago and Todd's caused his accident. Every item in our pack is weighed by its worth. The crampons got thrown out. We figured we'd just do our best with what we have. A mountain climber once asked us why we don't rope up across a steep traverse. To rope up, you need a serious rope. A serious rope means serious weight. We can make twenty traverses in a day. Roping up that many times would never get us to Canada. Once again, we have to do our best with what we have.

We take one mound at a time, looking for the best way across it. Sometimes the best way is the most direct: down into and up out of dry tree wells, fighting branches every step. At other times we go around these depressions where the heat reflected by the tree has made the snow at its base melt faster. We try to pick the easiest, safest route over each mound, unlike our army friend.

Though his exact routes are not always the best, his footsteps act as a general guide, telling us which direction the trail leads.

Soon the snow becomes solid. Todd stops every few yards ahead and waits with an extended hand, his ice ax—our anchor in case I fall—planted firmly in the snow with his other hand. We're making it through just fine. I must have used up my fright before I got here. Todd takes the time to cut deep, close steps for me. He instructs me to place my foot gently in the hold, and not push off, which could cause the step to slide out. I'm gaining confidence. I repeat over and over, "Be courageous and careful. Be courageous and careful" . . . self-brainwashing.

Before reaching the dry, snow-free trail twenty-five yards away, we must cross the worst section of all, a slope so steep that to touch it Todd merely has to extend his hand twelve inches from his chest. I stay close behind and wait for his steps. This can't be very easy for him either. After all, he has his own fearful memories to deal with. I talk to him every now and then to break the silence and let him know he's not alone.

"Take your time, Todd. You're doing a terrific job." I stand poised in my footholds, waiting to advance, and look down the mountain below me. White firs lie scattered, buried in the snow, with only their tips exposed. That's what I'd fall into should I slip. They'd stop me, and I wouldn't fly all the way down the mountain. This has a soothing effect on me.

As I cross the snow slope in Todd's footsteps, I look across to the dry trail ahead, which seems so far away.

"When I get to Etna, Todd, I may get a little drunk to celebrate. Maybe they'll have a pizza parlor in town."

"Don't count on it," he answers back.

Finally, we are both over the edge of the snowbank and back onto dry land. We hug and kiss. Etna finally seems within reach. As we race down the mountain to the winding dirt road, a ferocious hunger builds.

"Oh, wouldn't it be wonderful to have pizza and beer?"

"It's Sunday. What's the chance any place will be open in a small town like Etna? We'll be lucky if a store is open."

At the dirt road, we drop our packs. We can see the road wind way down the valley for miles. Not a vehicle in sight. No one probably uses this road.

"Get your taste buds ready for noodles and tuna," I tell Todd. "We may be staying here tonight."

My boots are off, my foam pad is out. A truck appears out of nowhere, speeding down the mountain. I run to the middle of the road, barefoot. It would be difficult to ignore me.

"Going to Etna?" I ask.

"Climb in!" the truck driver answers.

As we bounce down the ten miles of curves, I feel foolish for even asking, "Is there a pizza parlor in town?" The driver looks at his watch and yells back, "Opened five minutes ago!"

The pizza parlor not only offers whole wheat crust but their sauce is from tomatoes that the owner grew and canned himself! After we have eaten, the waitress calls a bed and breakfast up the street and finds a shower for us. "Hurry, though!" she says. "Showtime begins in twenty minutes."

After we clean up, we hurry to the near-deserted movie theater, still dazed from the recent rush of events. Ordering large root beers and popcorn, we take our seats, giggling like kids on a first date. As the room darkens and the image appears on the screen, we are swept through time and space on a ship called *Bounty*, sailing around the Horn in search of breadfruit. We forget the trail, the snow, our worries. We are on that dinghy floating in the ocean, fighting over seagull chunks and last sips of water. I can't remember ever being so involved in a film back home. Perhaps it has something to do with our life on the trail.

Our senses are so alert, we are so aware when we hike. Living so close to the natural world, we're tuned in to subtleties of smell, touch, and sight. In the city, you learn to block out the neighbor's barking dog, cars humming by, radios in the distance. Out here we function as though our hearing aids are turned up to high, and we have the nose of a dog, the sight of a hawk. In essence, we are more awake. Perhaps that is why something as ordinary as watching a film can seem profound and life-changing to a hiker on a long journey.

On our way back to the campground in town, Todd and I try to sort out all that has happened to us in the past few hours. We are still somewhat in a daze. Hours ago we were stuck on a traverse, barely advancing, time at a near standstill. Then, to a bleak road crossing, completely devoid of cars and any form of activity, only to be swept up in a vehicle, raced down the mountain, and deposited in front of a pizza parlor. In minutes, we're fed, clean, and are circumnavigating the globe on a ship!

Our idea of time is always distorted anyway when we come into town. It takes a very flexible hiker to handle this change, adapt to it, enjoy all the stimuli besides. Perhaps that is why most long-distance hikers shy away from towns. They are geared down so low that they cannot shift so quickly into high. Throughout my life, I've sought out change; it has always come easy for me. That's probably why I so enjoy my town visits, especially small, friendly towns like Etna.

The next morning we arise refreshed and walk down Main Street, which is lined with Victorian homes that the owners have renovated. Their flower gardens bloom with color and their mani-cured lawns are surrounded with brilliant white picket fences.

Everyone we pass greets us with a cheery hello. In some towns, people ignore us or think us strange, but not in Etna. The hardware store sells white gas by the bottle for our stoves and the drugstore is fixed up into an old-fashioned ice cream parlor. We indulge in fresh blueberry milkshakes. There is friendliness and peace here and it rubs off on me. I need a strong dose of it.

On our way back up the mountain, I worry about the snow slope near Cliff Lake, our next major obstacle on the trail. My cousin told me on the phone in Etna that I shouldn't be afraid, for there are angels all around us. I'd like to believe that.

I awake, anxious to have the day over before it even starts. I'm hungry for breakfast but shortly after it's down, I begin gagging and nearly throw up. What the fear of snow can do to my normal appetite.

From this moment on, Todd knows he has to use some psychological trickery to get me through the day and have it be somewhat enjoyable. He keeps me in front, following close at my heels and being unnaturally chatty. He picks topics that I'm interested in and asks me questions that make me ramble for hours, discussing and explaining. The miles fly by and I eat lunch with a hunger I've not experienced in the past few days. Every break we take, though, as we put on our socks and boots and hoist our packs, I get a little more anxious. Cliff Lake is closer every time I get up to hike.

A two-thousand-foot climb remains to the cliff. We walk along a granite bench, crossing wide patches of snow, while rushing water floods our path.

"Boy, I'm getting tired."

Oh no, honey! Not now!" Todd says frantically. Since he normally does not show such strong emotions his outburst now persuades me that I'd better muster up my strength and keep going. I remind myself over and over that angels will guide us over the cliff. It seems to be working.

The switchbacks climb very steeply up the last thousand feet and we finally see what we've been waiting for. The north-facing

Cliff Lake traverse

bowl above Cliff Lake appears vertical and is choked with snow.

Gray rock spires loom, a place where avalanches are born. Two small dry spots of trail are exposed, which will enable us to rest. Down below, the avalanched snow has cut off tree tops and buried others entirely. Before we venture out, we hold hands and face each other, then shout in unison, "Let's do it!"

When we get out to the snow we see that the crossing has been trampled down and widened! A team of horses crossed the cliff! Quite recently, too! What miracle is this? Where did they come from? We saw no tracks earlier. How did they do it? Horses can't traverse steep snow slopes, can they? The trail isn't even open to stock animals yet. I have a hard time believing their riders would lead them across anything so dangerous and steep as this, but their weight made four-inch hoof prints in the snow, which gives us wonderfully secure footholds. When we finally get across, we say a quick prayer of thanks and are off to hike the remaining mile to our campsite.

After a few steps on dry ground, the drama of the moment, the effort of the crossing, hit me. I call ahead to Todd and walk up to him crying, "Oh honey, there were angels with us on the cliff!

"Horse angels!"

Cliff Lake is now a memory. We are building our confidence on snow, building our trust in God. We made it through another day in this time of great uncertainty. Something tells us that our tomorrows are going to be a little bit easier.

The Marble Mountain Wilderness is a pleasure to walk through: very little snow, nothing at all dangerous, with fascinating mountains and canyons made of marble. Long-distance hikers walk so many miles, however, and we see so much, that sometimes the scenery blurs and runs together. Sometimes our minds are elsewhere, focusing perhaps on an acute pain in our body, causing us to miss everything that day. And sometimes the only reason we go to an area is because the trail runs through it and we can't avoid it. A week would probably not be enough time to soak up all the magic that is the Marble Mountain Wilderness. But in our solitary day's visit, we are mainly conscious of it as a place with no snow.

When we climb Big Ridge on the northern boundary of the wilderness, I am even more sure that life will get easier. From here, we look down the deep, V-shaped canyon of Grider Creek, which we'll descend to Seiad Valley. On the horizon sit the twin peaks of Kangaroo and Condry mountains. I am looking at the first convincing evidence that we will be all right. The range ahead is entirely snowless.

Seiad Valley is a scatter of houses, a store, a bar, a cafe, and a trailer court. Mostly a trailer court. The Klamath River winds lazily through this sleepy village, where locals come for groceries on a horse, and life in general seems to have hit a standstill. I can see why. It's one hundred fifteen degrees in the shade. We go into the store for our mail and something to drink, being careful not to move too much. We perspire profusely from doing nothing. With a half gallon of orange juice, we settle on the concrete slab under the store's roof and catch up on the news from back home.

A beat-up pickup pulls up. The door opens. Metal lunch pails come hurling out and hit the concrete with a crack. Caulked logging boots follow, then jackets, gloves, and chain saws get tossed in the dirt. Three grungy barefoot loggers fall out after the debris. Their clothes all look the same color from the ground-in earth. Their faces are streaked with dirt and sweat. They disappear into the store for a minute, come out with a cold six-pack, and take a seat farther down on the concrete slab.

Soon a plump, sweaty kid dressed in a camouflage T-shirt and shorts scuffs by. His hair is short, with long bangs cut straight across at his eyebrows. Two brown dirt circles ring his neck. The loggers stare, even more puzzled by this get-up than we are.

"Going to war?" asks one logger, as the kid reaches for the door handle.

"Nope."

"Coming back from war?" asks another.

"Nope," he says again and disappears into the store for an ice cream. It's forty degrees cooler in the store, so we take our time strolling the aisles, planning a supper menu. At the cash register, the owner invites us to camp on their grassy back lawn for the night. "There's a hose hooked up for water and an outdoor fridge you can keep your food in."

The woman who owns the trailer court has a weedy, overgrown field that she calls a campground. She charges three dollars fifty cents a night for you to roll out your sleeping bag and take a shower. We need her shower and laundry, however, so we go back. A sign on her spigot reads, "Water is not free—twenty-five cents a gallon." The showers are concrete block buildings painted a chartreuse green for the men, shocking pink for the women. Black mildew covers the floors and walls. There's no toilet paper in the stalls or doors on the hinges. We approach the trailer with a sign reading "Office," and a sassy, middle-aged woman holding a cigarette comes to the door. The overnight fee, she says, is three dollars. "How about just a shower?"

"Fifty cents."

We opt for the shower and the store owner's free backyard and take all of our dirty pots and pans in to bathe with us. As filthy as I am, I make a special effort to keep away from the walls.

We spend a lazy evening behind the store, eating homemade burritos, packing our food, and watching the life around us. The trailer court owner walks by a half dozen times and looks over at us.

In the morning, we pack up and enjoy a logger's breakfast at the cafe. Afterward, we discover that they make the best milkshakes on the entire Pacific Crest Trail, so rich and creamy that you have to eat them with a spoon.

"We'll take two!"

When we suck our glasses dry, we look at each other and say, "The Siskiyou Mountains are waiting. The sun is rising higher in the sky." This is our last stretch before dropping into Oregon. It was quite a struggle to get through California. It took a few attempts and a few years. We look ahead to the Siskiyous and the completion of the state with anticipation. But, it will have to wait until we drink another milkshake!

An enemy lurks in the Siskiyou Mountains. It stalks us in the morning and attacks us in the afternoon. We try to hide, but in these mountains there is little cover. Our enemy is the sun, and we battle it every day. Only after eight in the evening does the enemy begin to retreat.

Our only real weapons are our snow hats, which consist of about six scoops of lingering snow packed into our bandannas. We then fold the cloth over and roll the ends, securing them tightly under our chins. The snow hats sit right on top of our heads, where the sun's attacks are the fiercest.

Water drips off our noses and chins at a steady rate. As long as we keep moving and giving off heat, the melting snow regulates our body temperature beautifully. Perspiration comes to a near halt. All we have to do is stop walking for thirty seconds, however, and our brains begin to freeze. Each hat lasts around half an hour, long enough to get us up a climb. Now, unlike before, we eagerly search for lingering snow!

The Siskiyous are old mountains and boast a greater variety of flora and fauna than perhaps any other forest region west of the Mississippi. One of the more unusual of the fauna may be the Sasquatch. The dense forests and steep, remote canyons of the Siskiyous have been the site of more reported Sasquatch sightings than any other area of similar size in the region. Although there is no proof that the Sasquatch exists, every hiker who passes through these mountains must wonder, as we did, about whether there is any truth to the legend. I walked with sharp eyes, alert ears, and my camera at the ready . . . without results.

The area around the California-Oregon line has only a few scarce, spindly trees standing here and there. Otherwise, it has been totally clear-cut. In the middle of such an area, we share the magic moment of passing from one state into the next. A small wooden sign nailed to one of these stragglers simply states, "Oregon-California." Todd arrives first and welcomes me into the state like a member of Oregon's Chamber of Commerce. We sit in line with the single tree's long shadow, a very skinny strip of shade and, with cups of warm lemonade, toast the advent of a new state.

So it is done. For nearly half a year I've walked the length of California, discovering its mountains, meadows, towns, and people. The Pacific Crest Trail, a line of dirt in the earth, asks nothing of us. It is silent, immobile, indifferent, yet everything experienced along its course is intimately connected to life. I turn my head to the south. Follow the trail that way and it will take you to Mexico. Follow it the other way, and you'll climb into Canada. Just looking at this beaten foot trail gives no clue to what could happen along the way—education, physical fitness, spiritual renewal. It is so much more than a dirt path. Right now, it's our life.

In the town of Ashland, Oregon, the celebration of completing California continues. We toast our progress with margaritas in a Mexican restaurant and enjoy *A Winter's Tale* in the town's outdoor Shakespearean theater. The singing, dancing, and energy of the actors make us feel like all the world is celebrating with us.

We'll be taking three days off in Ashland to resupply for the entire length of the state ahead. Food boxes are usually mailed from back home, but they're heavy and cost a fair amount. For Oregon, we'll buy our food in Ashland, package it, and mail it ahead. This alone is a full day's work. In the grocery store we pile two carts high with food and the bill comes to three hundred and fifty dollars.

We're staying with Jinny and Butch Rigg, who have three of the most beautiful girls we have ever seen. White-blond hair that

Packing food in Ashland, Oregon

looks as though a halo should be above it. The girls take after their mother, whose blond curls and triathlon-trained body make her look ten years younger than she really is. This family is determined to make this town visit our most memorable yet.

When Jinny goes for a run, the two youngest girls put on a puppet show from behind the couch for me and Todd. The girls are wonderfully creative. Brianna, the youngest, can barely get her lines out for she's too small to speak well, but we clap and laugh at all the right times, so they're happy.

On the second night in town, the Riggs take us to the county fair, where we roam the aisles, looking at exhibits, while sales reps try to suck us in.

"How about a new telephone?"

"We don't need a phone where we're living right now, thanks."

"But everyone could use a second phone."

We walk on by, smiling. Another tries to interest us in a Jacuzzi. We approach a stand where two jolly, overweight women are selling dehydrated food called "Fantasia." The menu is extensive and extraordinary, with delicacies never before experienced on the trail. We stand there for quite some time figuring cost per pound and volume of food compared to freeze dried. Just as I'm ready to fill out a hefty order, I ask about the calorie content, to see how many miles we can get for our money, and discover that the stuff is diet food. Move on!

Doctor Hook, a rock band from the seventies, is playing for free on the grandstand. The musicians are bald and fat, look tired and burned out, but they sing the old songs just the same, and the crowd loves them. A new piece, a "love song" with the tender words that he will kill his girlfriend should she leave him, along with breaking her neck and cutting off her legs, drives the punk rockers in the audience wild. Todd and I look at each other. "What is happening here?"

On the way home in the car, the girls fall asleep on our laps. We pet their heads.

After a night like this, we're reminded that we've lost touch with a certain part of the world. By avoiding society for a few months, our life slows down, while change in this world continues at a phenomenal rate. A few years back, while on the Appalachian Trail, I came out of the mountains and discovered the pope had died. I was shocked. Then I was told that he replaced the pope that had died just a month before! Two popes had died since my last dose of news! Long-distance hikers live in a vacuum on the trail but in close intimacy with the natural world. The things that concern us and make up this life are amazingly different and separate from the life we left behind. Small villages like Seiad Valley, where life is slow to begin with, don't really affect us. But every time we leave the mountains and enter a town the size of Ashland, it's like going back and forth in a time machine. In many ways, Todd and I prefer the pace of the past. I guess that's why we've chosen to walk the length of this great country.

Mount McLoughlin and lava rock trail

13

Lake Country

July 22

"When I walk downhill," Todd exclaims, as we descend the lava rock trail, "my feet roll forward! When I walk uphill, they roll backward! And when I try to just walk flat, they roll from side to side!" His voice is barely audible above the noisy grating sound of the rock. We are walking around Brown Mountain, a shield volcano consisting of successive lava flows. Most of the larger peaks in the range are stratovolcanoes, which consist of lava flows alternating with layers of rock debris spewed out during explosive eruptions. This debris includes volcanic ash, cinders, and bombs. The Cascade stratovolcanoes grow to lofty heights and are covered with snow much of the year.

Measured in geological time, Brown Mountain is very young. Even now there is very little vegetation on its flanks. A few patches of evergreens dot the slopes, but for the most part, there is no color and very little life. Most of the mountain is a brownish black wasteland of lava. Even the sky overhead is gray and lifeless, but we don't want an intense sun during this crossing of our first lava field.

Our trail is by no means level. The flowing lava produced hundreds of miniature mountains and valleys. Climbing up and down these miniature knolls causes premature fatigue. Here and there a few trees have managed to root and drop enough needles to form soil so that other trees can take hold. This process of rebuilding the forest is slow. We look forward to the small patches of woods—not for their shade, but for the needles' soft cushioning under our aching feet.

Brown Mountain is a minor peak. Our first major Cascade volcano after Mount Shasta is Mount McLoughlin, a medium-sized stratovolcano that reaches a height of about nine thousand five hundred feet. Snow still lingers on its upper flanks, but there are no creeks here, no marshy or swampy areas, no ponds or lakes. The ground is just damp from melting snow.

Billions of mosquitoes have just hatched, and after lunch they come on us in swarms. We can't watch the trail in front of us, but must constantly turn an elbow over, look at a shoulder, swat a calf. We start to feel insects crawling everywhere—even places they're not. The bug dope we use is strong and deadly. If you hold a ballpoint pen after an application, the compound on your

Cindy with headnet; Todd

fingers will melt the plastic! I don't like to put it on my face or around my eyes. Todd hates to put it anywhere. If we do apply it, in those few seconds when our legs stop swinging and we're a still target, they catch up and cover our skin. So we usually run down the trail, waving our arms and swatting furiously. We were hoping this was just a short stretch, but they're not going away. Get the head nets out! We quickly tie the drawstrings around our necks, but at least one manages to get inside and buzzes in between my glasses and my eyes. I cross my eyes to spot it and trip over a rock.

Soon every place on my body itches, and I walk down the trail brushing my skin, slapping, and looking at every nervous twitch.

In camp, we must swat each other in order to perform even the simplest task. When Todd fills the stove, I swat for him, and when I clean the pots, he swats for me. When we brush our teeth or fill a water bottle, they immediately begin sucking any unclothed area. We already have about three layers of this potent, deadly dope on our hands.

Before retiring to our sleeping bags, we want to wash the bug dope off our sticky skin. We lift our head nets and quickly swab our faces. Next comes the top. One calf, then the other. The swatter takes care of the side that the bather is not washing.

With all our chores complete, we're ready to dive for the tent. Todd stands at the door waving a large piece of clothing like a maniac. When I open the zipper and dive in, a hundred mosquitoes join me in a matter of five seconds!

Dead, black mosquito carcasses cover the tent's inside walls as I kill them by smashing their bodies against the nylon. When Todd lunges in, he has four dozen of his own to kill. I comb my hair and dozens of little bodies and wings fall out. After every little pest is dead, we lie in the tent safe and naked, for it's very warm out. Thousands of insects hover around the mosquito netting.

They know we're in here, and they're thirsty. My head leans against the nylon tent wall and they bite me through it! The mosquitoes' high-pitched buzz is almost deafening and it makes us wonder how long we can take it. We couldn't stop for a break the entire afternoon or they would get us. We just stumbled along, exhausted from the extra energy of swatting. Still, we're not in danger. We're not walking on snow. We're just totally uncomfortable.

This is the Sky Lakes Wilderness, a wonderland of ponds and lakes, except when the great hatch occurs – then it's hell on earth. In bug season, you only enter these woods when you must. Anyone who chooses to deal with this insanity on their vacation is definitely touched. No wonder the wilderness area is devoid of people.

You can imagine how surprised we are to find a tent set up along the trail in the middle of this buzzing nightmare. We yell hello as we approach. A young man emerges from the zippered door, wearing black climbing tights, no shirt, eighty-dollar sunglasses, and a narrow braid of sandy hair, which is three inches longer than the rest of his crop. A gorgeous golden retriever follows.

"Hi," the guy says, "I'm Tre. This is my dog, Bradigan. We're hiking from Tahoe to Canada. More or less." Looks like less today; it's noon and he's still in his tent.

Tre is the first hiker we've run across in more than four hundred miles. We know of only one other guy on the trail, an old AT friend, who is ahead of us. He's been sending postcards back to us with snow reports. Thirty miles of near-solid snow await us at Crater Lake, our next stop. Tre has never enjoyed the delightful experience of traversing snow since he skipped the last section, so he thinks it's in his best interest to stick with us for the next few days.

Todd's group skirted Lucifer Peak and Devils Peak two years ago. They took the low route and remember looking up at the merciless, snow-choked slopes. I volunteer stories of my past fall and Todd's to justify any emotional instability I may exhibit. Tre tells of a time when he rammed a tree while skiing, fractured his skull in five places, leaking cervical fluid and narrowly escaping death. Suddenly, I feel like a baby.

Tre and Bradigan

The traverses aren't exactly fun, but Tre constantly asks how I'm doing and then winks when I say "okay." That gives me the determination to save my pride and cross like a courageous, seasoned hiker. From the high point of Devils Peak we can look ahead to Mount Thielsen, our next Cascade volcano, which rises like a spire in the distance. Sure enough, there is plenty of snow ahead.

Atrocious bugs put a quick end to any socializing we may have planned, and we all go to bed, still strangers.

The next day, we get to know a little bit more about our new companion. Tre is twenty-six and just recently divorced. His wife left him for her career, he sadly admits. Seems like our friend is on a healing journey.

But before we can learn more, a voice suddenly comes from behind, shouting, "Where ya'll heading?"

Quite startled, we turn around to see a flustered youngster, very sweaty and out of breath, carrying an orange fluorescent tube. He was hiking so fast that we didn't hear him come up behind us.

Bill Green is on his first solo backpacking trip. He's fresh out of high school, nervous and inexperienced. His brown eyes betray his fear. His inexpensive cowboy hat is pushed back from his perspiring brow and smooth, hairless face. Purple-striped white athletic socks are pulled high like knee socks out of his high tops sneakers. An old cut-off football shirt and a rolled, red bandanna complete his costume.

It's apparent that this lad is private about his inner feelings, but in relaying the last day's events, it's also pretty obvious that his initiation was intense.

On his first day out, Lucifer Peak gave the poor fellow quite a breaking in. He crossed the peak early in the morning, when the snow was hard and icy, wearing only sneakers for traction and using an orange fishing-rod tube to steady himself. Then he tried to follow our footsteps but lost the trail. Knowing there were hikers not too far ahead, Bill pushed his pace to a steady jog until he caught us. Welcome to the group, Bill! We've had no company

Bill

for over a month, and now two in two days! This, along with the
fact that we just surfaced out of mosquito hell, is cause for celebration. I've been carrying a nectarine since Ashland, waiting for a
special time to indulge. We'll make an instant cheesecake with
the fresh fruit for topping.

Just then, yet another hiker cruises into our campsite. This
guy has wire glasses and long, bushy red hair tied in a ponytail.
His legs are strong and muscular, and his clothes and pack are
soiled enough to have seen many miles of trail dust. He smiles.
There's something familiar about him—maybe the hair.

"Wait a minute!" he says, as he unshoulders his pack with
ease. "I know you guys!"

"Redman!" Todd yells. They hiked together on the AT four
years ago, and we ran into him on the Long Trail in Vermont just
last year. In fact, Redman's old AT partner is the guy who is ten
days ahead of us, writing postcards back. Neither knows the
other is in this part of the country, yet they're only a week and a
half apart!

Fellow long-distance hikers warned us that Crater Lake National Park would not welcome us with open arms. The only campground is on the perimeter of the park, miles from and well below the lake, store, and precious post office. It's a ridiculous waste of time just to walk back and forth to pick up supplies and use the facilities. The only place to stay nearby is the expensive lodge, which far exceeds a backpacker's budget. We understand that a close-by campground would disrupt the fragile ecological system around the lake. Todd, in a letter to park administration, asked if it were possible to sleep near the post office, roll out our bags behind a maintenance shed or on a strip of blacktop. We wanted to see the lake and needed to use the post office. We hoped they would help us. But their reply was curt and said that no special allowances could be made.

Redman, a pacifist by nature, does not care to deal with it all and cruises right through. We, on the other hand, must wait until the post office opens in the morning, because this is a scheduled mail drop for us.

Our first priority, however, is a shower. We leave our packs outside and enter the carpeted, air-conditioned information center. The little balding man behind the counter folds his arms across his chest as he sees us approach.

"Could you tell us if there is anywhere that we can get a shower?"

"No way can you get a shower here," he says, grinning, arms still crossed, rocking back and forth on his heels. "Maybe at the lodge?" Todd asks. "You can't buy a shower here," he insists. "There's no place you could buy a shower here."

We step aside to look at some postcards, for there's a heavy-set woman in her bedroom slippers next in line, and it's evident we've gotten as far as we can with this guy. She wants to know where the closest motel is and doesn't even seem interested in the magnificent lake up the road. Instantly, his tone is sugar sweet. He tells her about the lodge by the lake. I suddenly get very angry and stomp out of the information center.

Outside, we stop a ranger and ask him about the trail conditions ahead. He's pleasant and begins asking us how the trail has treated us so far. Then we bring up showers. He advises us to call the lodge and offer a price for a shower. But, the more we talk, the more he opens up and he finally tells us about a secret place, where there is a shower in the back of the laundry room building, back past the equipment sheds, garages, and private residences.

We take turns. Ladies first. I walk by numerous park service employees with my stuff sack under my arm full of clean clothes, shampoo, and soap. Some workers smile and nod. Sure enough, in the back of this little wooden building, in the dark, is a shower stall, complete with toiletries! There is even a sign-up sheet for the washing machine. I add my name to the list.

At the visitor center we meet Glenn Thompson, a naturalist who can't relate to the tourists or the park rangers. He's here releasing peregrine falcons into the wild. Away from his wife and children for a month, he lives in a cabin on the far side of the lake. We quickly become friends. Glenn works as a truck mechanic from eight to four and devotes his spare time to mountain search and rescue. He tells us stories taken from his years of experience, and we're most impressed with this very unassuming and humble man. We make plans to meet near his home in Washington. Our tents are set up in a secret campsite that we discovered, a stone's throw from the visitor center, and we take Glenn over to meet the rest of the group.

The next morning we make the long, twisting walk on the road up to the magical lake. We are winding up an ancient volcano that literally blew itself out seven thousand years ago and then filled with water and formed what is now known as Crater Lake. The Indians that witnessed its destruction, as well as their ancestors, tried to keep its presence a secret, believing that the lake was sacred and that anyone who gazed upon it would die. White men crossed the area for nearly fifty years without knowing about the lake. The Indians never said a word. Then gold seekers stumbled across the lake in the late 1800s.

I feel very much like those first adventurers as we climb to the rim and see before us this unbelievably beautiful lake. It is so huge, so blue! The lake is six miles wide, and its shoreline is twenty miles around. A small, solitary mountain called Wizard Island, which is really a volcano within a volcano, pokes through the water's surface. In this early morning light, it is a pale, shimmering blue. Cliffs and peaks surround the shore, the sides of what was the volcano called Mazama.

Mount Mazama was about twelve thousand feet tall before its final eruption. The explosion happened with a force forty-two times greater than that of Mount St. Helens' 1980 eruption. Twenty-five cubic miles of ash and pumice spread over what is now eight states and three Canadian provinces. The mountain collapsed in on itself, forming a caldera about four thousand feet deep. Following the eruption, the still active volcano began to rebuild itself, much as Mount St. Helens is today. Lava flows gradually filled up and sealed the floor of the caldera, which began to collect runoff from melting snow. Eventually, the caldera filled to form Crater Lake. No streams or rivers bring water in or drain it

Wizard Island and Crater Lake

out. As a result, the lake's level remains nearly constant.

We pull ourselves away for a while to take a look at what man has added to the area. Crater Lake Lodge was built in 1928 under the supervision of William Steel, the father of Crater Lake National Park. He dedicated his entire life to working for the protection of the lake, and when the park was established he had the road built to provide access for everyone.

In the concession building, we stroll down the aisles of souvenirs: rubber Indian tomahawks; seashell wind chimes; shiny, cedar-slab clocks; and plastic turquoise jewelry. Todd picks up an ashtray with the words "Crater Lake" printed on it, turns it over and says, "Look at this. 'Made in Taiwan.' " There are Crater Lake salt and pepper shakers, dish towels, and hundreds of T-shirts silk screened in tacky, unnatural colors. We grab a few postcards and make our way to the food aisle. Paper plates, charcoal, cigarettes. Can't eat any of that! A whole row of miniature whiskey and liquor bottles! Let's get out of here. Out to the lake to watch its ever-changing beauty.

It's high noon, when most landscape light is white and washed out. But now, Crater Lake's water is the bluest, the most intense, deep indigo that I've ever seen. This color is more than a reflection of the sky, for today the lake is far deeper in color than the Oregon sky. The water's intense color has something to do with its molecules absorbing short blue light waves, which can penetrate three hundred feet of water.

Toward the end of day, we pack up, bid good-bye to beautiful Crater Lake and head north to the Pumice Desert, our home for the night. Large rocks called lava bombs lie about, making it seem as if Mazama erupted within the last hundred years, instead of seven thousand years ago. Scattered lodgepole pines are the only trees in the area because they adapt well to harsh environments. The Pumice Desert gets a lot of snow in the winter, but most of it rapidly drains downward, leaving the upper soil layers dry. Very little precipitation falls in the summer. There aren't many nutrients in the ground either, for these too are leached out by the rapidly draining water.

This is our first night alone in well over a week. Redman left the area yesterday and Tre and Bill walked an extra five miles to get a better shot at climbing Mount Thielsen in the morning.

Actually, it was Tre's idea, but Bill was forced to follow for he depends on Tre's equipment. On the other hand, Tre is broke and depends on the funds that Bill receives from his mother. They need each other.

They come to us this morning, pumping us for trail information. They have no guidebooks or maps and have no idea where water is, how many miles there are to the next town, or how many days' food they'll need. We're amazed at how inexperienced and ill-prepared they are. Todd feels responsible for them like a father. We share what we know. Besides, they shouldn't be with us for long.

Clouds begin to move in early the next day and, as we approach Mount Thielsen, the heavens begin to rumble. Shaped like the Matterhorn, Thielsen is called the "Lightning Rod of the Cascades."

It is a plug, the remains of a very old, extinct volcano whose sides have been eroded away by weather and glaciers. Their grinding exposed the inner column of lava that hardened in the volcano's neck.

This rock, hard and resistant, forms a sharp point that pierces the dark, stormy sky. We search the peak, which disappears and reappears through the racing clouds, for the guys. Todd and I are the only people out here who know their whereabouts and plans. If they don't show up, we should go back and search for them. If they get hurt, we'll have to go for help or try to get them out of the mountains. Their decisions and actions greatly influence our plans and our trip. As it turns out, Tre and Bill were smart enough not to attempt a climb up Mount Thielsen in the midst of a lightning storm.

The next day we cross Tipsoo Pass, the highest point on the PCT in Oregon and Washington. There are miles of continuous snow. We spend a lot of time locating the trail and searching for old blazes on the trees, trail markings made in years gone by. As the only ones with a map and guidebook, we are forced to do all the scouting ourselves. It would be a great advantage to have two more sets of eyes and legs to discover which direction to travel in, but Tre and Bill are behind us. We haven't seen them for hours. They're probably taking their time and will merely follow our footsteps after all the work is done. We see Redman's tracks go off the trail. So far, he's gotten lost three times! Then another set of fresh, unmelted Nike bootprints appear, headed in the right direction. Looks like we're gaining on him.

The snow doesn't bother me at all, even the patches that are a little steep. I seem to be healing from my own fears. I think all the crying and upset stomachs are necessary to work it through.

Cliff Lake was a major breakthrough for me, because it was the most difficult traverse, the most anxiety ridden, the most feared. When I crossed it successfully, my confidence finally began to outweigh my fear. It amazes me how much time and energy it takes to push through your fears.

At lunch, Bill and Tre finally catch up to us. We discover that they got lost. They followed our footsteps, but these disappeared at a point where we cross a wide pumice flat that was free of snow. When Tre asks if he can carry our national forest map, Todd gives it up. We have the guidebook with us but the maps printed in it are so small in area that using them is like having tunnel vision. We prefer larger maps for their broader perspective.

I am irate! We told Tre and Bill to buy a guidebook at Crater Lake, but neither wanted to give up their treat money. We also discover that Bill has no rain gear, no sleeping pad, no tent, no pack cover, no maps, and now no money.

Todd says that the next time we come to a trash receptacle, he's going to fashion some rain gear and a pack cover for Bill out of dirty plastic bags! Without even realizing it, Todd and I are playing parents to our tag-alongs.

14

Company Arrives

July 31

When long-distance hikers get together, it's like a reunion of college roommates. We've had experiences that the rest of the world doesn't share and when we're reunited after a long period of separation, it's a celebration.

Images, smells, feelings, all the things associated with our memories emerge and we're able to live them once more. By reliv-

The group (left to right): Tre, Redman, Bill, Steve, Todd and Cindy

ing them, we get insights into our past, who we were, and how we've changed.

Todd's PCT partner, Steve Peck, is meeting us in the resort village of Cascade Summit to hike with us for a while. Todd and I fly down Trapper Creek like excited children. There is a rush of warmth in our bodies, an anticipation. We are going to be with a soul mate! We are going to sing with someone who knows all the words!

Steve and Todd stayed at Cascade Summit the year they came through. There's a campground, laundry, showers. That's where we'll meet Steve.

It will be a fine reunion! Redman fell out of the mountain this morning. On one of our breaks, the freckled elf suddenly appeared from behind. "You were supposed to be ahead!" we said. "I got lost!" Redman is not too adept with map and compass. His guardian angel works overtime. There will be four long-distance hikers, plus Tre and Bill, here tonight. A definite cause for celebration.

At the campground, we spot Steve's pack, a sun-faded, green Kelty with broken zippers and frayed-apart seams. Silver duct tape wrapped on the ice ax distinguishes it from any other. "He's here!" Todd says. "I'd know that pack anywhere!" We turn and see a bare-chested man approach us. He's tan and strong, with a sunburned nose and a bright red bandanna around his forehead to hold back his straight brown hair.

"Steve!"

We hardly recognize him. The last time we saw him, he was immersed in a computer problem and looked pale, sickly, hunched-over, and puny from lack of exercise. He walks towards us erect, arms and hairy chest pumped up from working out and climbing, his compass around his neck on a chain of knotted dental floss. The compass starts to sway as he breaks into a run. I stand back and wait my turn as he and Todd embrace. "God, it's good to see you," Steve says. Todd can say nothing. His big puppy-dog eyes fill with fluid. When their eyes meet, you can see memory after memory, shared experience after shared experience, rush through them at such a rate that all they feel is joy, absolute wordless joy.

We march into the resort store to find what facilities are available and buy some grub for dinner. As we mill around, checking out the aisles, I make small talk with the owner.

"Not many hikers on the trail this year. Hardly saw anyone out there. Any ideas why?"

"Working! They're all working!" he says in a loud voice, heavy with bitter resentment. "They all have jobs. They're being responsible!"

We take our sour cream onion chips outside.

The tent sites the store owner offers are just bulldozed scars in the woods with mounds of muddy dirt around. The site he picks for us is right up front in the open. The backhoe sits a few feet from the fire ring.

Todd and Steve remember a vacant boat-storage building on the other side of the resort. The atmosphere there sounds much more attractive. The structure is dry and spacious but full of broken glass, dirt, empty beer bottles. We sweep it clean using "brooms" of flattened six-pack containers. It'll be quite comfortable. Bill joins us, but Tre decides to stay at the campsite.

The stories and laughter flow as the candles burn into the night. Bill sits with wide eyes and perked ears as we relive incidents that almost got us into big trouble. Soon the conversation turns to long-distance hiking. Why we're here. Why we do it.

Long-distance hiking is not a vacation. It's too long for that. It's not recreation. Too much toil and pain involved. It is, we decide, a way of life. A very simplified, spartanlike way of living. Life on the move. The movement seems to speed up the experiences: different storms, mountains, people, predicaments, challenges. You must deal with situations, survival situations, that force you to think and take action. Lots of growth happens quickly. The hard times, the days of rain, miles of snow, heavy packs, sweating brow—they make you appreciate warm sunshine, companionship, cool water. The best way to appreciate those things that are precious and important in life is to take them away.

So we learn what really matters. Back in town, life is so fast and full of time-consuming chores that it's easy to forget. In essence, we come out here to gain a clearer vision.

We also come out here to learn about ourselves. The biggest prize of long-distance hiking is the gift of free time. Time to be by yourself. Time to look. Time to think. Time to feel. All those hours you spend with your thoughts. You don't solve all of your personal problems, but you come to understand and accept yourself.

So with this clear mind, you return home and try like hell to keep that magic in your everyday life. You come to discover that you don't need a lot to be happy. Not much money, but a whole lot of freedom and time to experience these moments of magic. You need peace of mind. You need the calmness and beauty of the natural world. The fast-paced, goal-oriented, money-making society that makes our country tick no longer feels natural. Everywhere, you see values that seem empty, goals that seem selfish and greedy.

Returning home is the most difficult part of long-distance hiking. You have grown outside the puzzle and your piece no longer fits. So you go about changing it to make it as close to the life you had on the trail as you can. So that the needs you created can be met. It's very hard to divorce yourself entirely from modern society, and most of us don't even want that. We only want to keep our vision clear, our hearts from getting hard, and our spirits from dying.

Everyone, after a certain amount of time, begins to yearn for the trail again, begins to actually feel pain for it. When life feels like a sprint on a treadmill, it's time to head for the mountains. In the spring, when the sap rises, that's when you feel it in your blood. Some of us have to wait until the kids grow up, or money is available, or retirement. But the worst part is marrying someone who doesn't share your yearning and won't let you go. Anyone who has ever been out there for any length of time wants and waits and dreams for the day when he or she can return.

The boat shelter is dark, except for the solitary candle. Its soft light flickers and dances on the wooden boards. The hour is very late. Conversation has slowed and now stopped. I look around at the group. All faces glow with joy and contentment. Steve's is the brightest. Here, on the trail, with fellow long-distance hikers, in this dirty, dingy boat shelter, he has come home.

The next morning we hold water races on the slanted wood floor of the boat shelter as we wait for our wash to dry. Beads of water poured from a bottle race another team's. Todd gets creative and makes tributaries with his finger, hoping to move the water faster. While an expensive motorboat speeds by on the lake, we entertain ourselves with a bottle of water and an incline.

We dress Steve up and make him pose for a future slide show. He wears his bandanna, glacier goggles, and a chain wrapped around his neck, fastening him to his pack. His teeth glare, and spit foams from his mouth, illustrating what too many miles can do to a healthy young brain.

Tre is having a hard time relating to our fun. When we leave Cascade Summit, he will be going with us, if somewhat reluctantly. His supply box arrived, but again without maps or guidebook.

Seventeen-year-old Bill Green is staying behind and will have to catch up. None of his supplies arrived, but how could they? He only told his support team to mail them yesterday! These two don't learn very quickly.

Back on the trail, we spend entire days laughing and joking. We walk together in a tight line, one right behind another. I'm up front, setting a slow, easy pace. This way we can all converse, and no one has to miss anything. Bill caught up and sticks to us like glue. Tre is always ahead, hiking his three-miles-per-hour pace and then waiting for us when he hasn't seen anyone for a while.

We're not sure why he hangs around. It's clear that he doesn't really like us.

The problem is that we cannot get away from him. On the trail, you're sometimes forced to travel and live with people you don't care for. It's not your choice. If this happened back home,

Steve chained to his pack

you would simply not be in that person's company. Out here, it's not always possible.

We call ourselves the country of "Crest." A country on the move, self-contained. Everything we need is with us. Redman is our Mayor, for he wears wide, flashy neckties over his bare chest. The mayoral tie. Steve is the oldest, the most experienced, and has the slickest tongue, so he is the Mayoral Advisor. Young Bill is the working class and Tre (although he doesn't know it) is our health club instructor. Todd and me represent family life in Crest. The guys want our Mayor to give a speech on hiker immorality tonight. They want to populate our country but first need mates.

Whether our destination is seven miles or twenty, we take the entire day to get there. The guys are always ready to take a break and "five minutes" ends up being an hour. There is a time when one must hike seriously. But not now. On our first day together we go swimming. Steve decides to test the floatability of foam pads. We cheer him as he musters the courage to dive into the chilling waters of Dumbbell Lake. "Go for it, Steve!"

Steve diving into Dumbbell Lake with foam pad

He does a belly flop on his pad and stays up! It works! Then we all dive in and splash in the refreshing liquid. We form a circle with our bodies in the shallow water. Someone picks up a large stone with his feet and we twirl it in circles like seals, complete with seal sound effects. Then we do water ballet. Everyone extends one hairy leg with pointed toe into the circle, bends it, and goes underwater. Everyone except Tre, who sits on shore, not wanting to get wet.

Tonight's festivities at Charlton Lake include fireworks shot off across the expansive water. They were sent to Todd and me in a friend's care package to "put a spark" into our marriage.

After the ceremonial fire is lit, Steve does a wonderful job reciting Shakespeare's "Soliloquy on Death" and builds our excitement for the Mayor's speech. The community is called to assemble. The Mayor is announced and appears smiling at his podium (a large backpack with its rain cover over it). Applause and cheers! He gives the peace sign, says a few nervous words, and that is it. He's a shy Mayor.

Shortly after we enter the Three Sisters Wilderness, we come upon an older man and woman, and a teen-aged boy who looks too young to be their son, camping right by the trail, on a dry flat. We wonder why they've chosen to camp here since beautiful, secluded lakes abound in this area, supplying breath-taking views and a ready water supply. We don't wonder long. When we see their campsite up close, it is evident that they're beginners. They have so much paraphernalia set up around their site that it looks like the cover of an outdoor catalog—to be specific, one of those family camping catalogs, like that of the Don Gleason Company. So we dub them "the Gleasons." We yell hello and approach to talk. "Don" comes right over, tucking his light yellow dress shirt into his trousers and running a comb rapidly through his white, wavy hair.

"Hi, kids. Where you heading for the night?"

"Up the trail a way," we answer, "to some lake."

"How far from here?" he asks.

"We don't exactly know," we say. "A few miles."

"It's a little late for hiking, isn't it? Seven o'clock?"

"We still have two more hours of daylight," Steve answers.

"I'm doing the whole PCT," Don says, "in sections."

"Great!" we reply. "Where have you hiked so far?"

"Around Crater Lake. Actually, that was our first trip, four days." He goes to fetch something in his tent, and returns with his hiking staff, which has six big topographical maps rolled around it and rubber-banded to the stick.

"Good maps are important to have," he says. "You can't get along without them. I always keep these here on my staff, handy for use."

(Topo maps, we have found, are next to useless out here because most of them are too old. They show trails that no longer exist. And the PCT very often isn't even drawn in.)

The maps are unruly as he unrolls each of the six. None wants to stay open and flat. The guys help hold them down. Don struggles to find the trail and when that fails, asks what the name of the lake is that we're looking for.

"Nebbish Lake," Steve says, inventing a name. They pore over the map, straight-faced, looking for the nonexistent lake. I am watching them from off to the side, bending down to tie my boot.

When I hear Steve, I start to laugh and fall backward on my pack. "Come help me, guys!" I yell, feeling like a turtle on its back. The rescue stops them from searching for the bogus lake any further. We go on our way.

The next day we meet up again and the Missus is all worked up over some sunglasses. "Don" wasn't expecting snow and we've been hearing reports from south-bounders that the trail could be buried ahead. His wife is upset with him for not planning for this.

"I wear contacts," the wife says, dressed in a floppy hat and double knit slacks, "and I must have sunglasses in the snow. Do you have an extra pair?"

At thirty dollars a shot for glacier goggles, no one has an extra pair. And no one is particularly anxious to give them to a stranger that we may never see again. Don then asks us to walk ahead, detour to Elk Lake Resort, buy a pair there, return and wait for them along the trail. We aren't too excited about the plan.

We help them out by telling them how to improvise should there be snow. "Make sunglasses out of stiff paper or cardboard. Cut a narrow slit to see where you're going. It works well in a pinch." We also tell them about a low route they can take, perhaps avoiding some snow. We mention that tomorrow our group plans to stay in a lean-to along the trail. Then we say our good-byes and go on to make camp.

Throughout our encounters with the Gleasons, the boy has remained silent. Who is this strange young fellow, and why is he with them? We call him Sherpa. "Perhaps he's along to bridge wide streams or counter-balance their food bags," the guys joke.

The next day our trail crosses expansive Wickiup Plain, where we get our first close view of the Three Sisters volcanoes and all the other peaks crowded together in this wilderness. A wide flow of lava called Rock Mesa flowed down South Sister's

Wickiup Plain chase

slopes and stopped just short of the plain, freezing in its tracks and forming a forty-foot-high wall. The long plain runs along its side and consists of pumice fall-out from the volcanoes.

The sky is cloudy and gray. A chilly breeze blows, damp with evaporating snow. From afar we see the Gleasons and Sherpa hoofing down the plain, full rain gear on, "just in case." They stop and turn around, they see us and point, talk for a while, then begin moving down the trail even faster. They're heading for the shelter that we told them about. They're trying to beat us there!

One by one, each member of our group passes by the Gleasons.

"Looks like rain," Don says, as he wipes his sweaty brow and ventilates his neck. The Missus has had enough and tears her jacket off. No one mentions the word shelter, but we all know what is happening.

The six of us have made ourselves quite at home in the shelter by the time the Gleasons arrive. The Missus comes by, laden with pack, and says, "If you snooze, you lose. If we wouldn't have overslept and gotten lost on top of it, we would have beaten you to the shelter."

"It wouldn't have done you much good," I reply. "We would have just moved in with you."

Young Bill Green is a damn good hunter for his age. When our dinner is just about over, he comes running up to the shelter. "Hey, guys! I know where a herd of elk is grazing!" Todd, Steve, and I follow. We run down the hill behind the shelter and there, across a boggy meadow, stand the long-legged golden animals. Big. Much bigger than deer. We sneak along the edge of the trees, still a good distance away, trying for a closer view. Oh, to run with them, be wild with them! We feel like children of nature and the mountainside, akin to the elk.

The wind must have changed. A bull raises its massive rack and looks our way with stern, dark eyes. In a matter of seconds, the whole herd thunders away, and we're left staring at an empty spot in the meadow, wondering if we even saw them.

> *The great hurrah about wild animals is that they exist at all, and the even greater hurrah is the actual moment of seeing them. . . They show me by their wariness what a prize it is simply to open my eyes and behold.*
> —Annie Dillard

Tonight, Sherpa comes over to our campfire and finally begins to speak. His name is Ricky and he's traveling with his aunt and uncle, whom he doesn't see very often or know very well. "Aunt Billy and Uncle Agnes," he calls them. "You mean Uncle Billy and Aunt Agnes?" we ask. "No," he says, "at least I don't think so." We shake our heads.

He hints that he's not enjoying their company and wishes he could hike with our group. We have plans to take the day off tomorrow and climb South Sister, a ten-thousand-footer. Ricky wants to come along. Can his aunt and uncle come along too? Sorry, Ricky. Even if we wanted their company, I doubt they'd attempt such a feat.

After everyone has stared at the dying embers as long as they can without totally succumbing to sleep, we say our good-nights and turn in. Bill politely plays host and tells Ricky that he'll escort him back with his flashlight.

"No, I'm not ready yet," he says, surprisingly assertive. Todd and I chuckle quietly as we zip our bags, and Bill reluctantly sits down with the lad for another hour's vigil.

I roll over on my side, face Todd, and think of the last day's events. It is no crime to be inexperienced. Everyone is a beginner sometime. But people like "Don" and the Missus come out here with a set of rules to follow, a protocol from that other life that doesn't allow for any deviation. If there is any rule at all out here it is to be ready for anything, for any change.

The scenery along the Cascade Crest portion of the Pacific Crest Trail is usually dominated by only a single volcano at a time—except in the Three Sisters Wilderness, where three cones more than ten thousand feet tall sit side by side. This volcanic playground consists of forty alpine lakes and a half-dozen major peaks in one small area. In addition to the Three Sisters, an entire family of volcanoes resides here—the Husband, the Wife, the Little Brother, Bachelor Butte, and many others. South Sister, the youngest of the three, is a redhead, from the ruddy-colored pumice on her summit, and sports a nearly perfect, rounded summit. The climb up is the easiest of the three and involves no technical rope work. "A walk-up." I have my doubts about its ease from the beginning, but Steve is the one who encourages us to take the day off to climb and approaches the whole thing as a carefree jaunt. Tre's comment, "You're only as fast as your slowest member," adds little to my buckling self-confidence.

We climb, following the side of Rock Mesa until we surface above the trees. The men shift into their competitive paces. I relax into my own. For the lower part of the climb, I'm alone. Todd is up with the boys. Except for the privacy of our tent and zipped-together sleeping bags, Todd and I have not felt like a couple lately, but rather have dissolved into the group. We try to leave early in the morning, before the others get moving. It gives me a head start, plus keeps Todd and me tuned into each other. While I miss his constant company, I am enjoying the group very much.

We follow dry creekbeds, crossing ridges, until we join the backbone route recommended by the guidebook. The trail is loose scree and for every three feet you gain, you slide back one. You can't grasp anything, for it's all so unstable. Even large boulders slide from under you. When I approach nine thousand feet, the elevation begins to affect me and I really slow down. Glaciers drape both sides of the narrow trail. Where the glacier pulls away from the rock, huge chunks of ice still adhere. Deep crevasses plunge to terrifying depths. I hear sounds like thunder rumbling through the alpine air. Low, close to the earth, the living glacier moves.

Todd joins me. He stays close at my heels and says he wants to be with me, but I think he's trying to push me along. I don't speak to him because I can hardly find the air to breathe. The rusty dome looms before us. Its size makes the distance deceiving. It looks much closer than it actually is. Our friends' tiny bodies on the trail above us provide the only visual clues to the mountain's true mass. A glacial pool appears. Its creamy mint-green water is full of rock flour (silt) that the glacier has ground from the rock. I pause and wonder what it tastes like.

"Do you want to turn around?" Todd suddenly asks when I stop.

"I may not be as strong as you guys, but I'm strong enough to make it to the top." Perhaps he thinks he's being supportive, but I resent his insinuation.

On the summit climbers are clustered in the rocks like barnacles. Our clan cheers me when I top the peak. It makes me feel

The view from South Sister

good but I can't help but wonder why they don't greet each other like that. I want to be accepted, to fit in, but I'm not one of the guys. I can't always keep up with them. Sometimes I long for another woman's company.

The view is impressive from up here. Middle and North Sister are separated by only a deep gash. We have a bird's eye view of a glacier: deep cracks and flowing ice. To the north, "the Cascades rise inspiringly" – a long string of peaks that gets fainter and fainter in the distance – each one paler blue than the one before it.

There are quite a few other climbing parties on the summit. One man wears a three-piece suit that he packed up for the occasion. He changed clothes on the summit and wears yellow lichen in his lapel. It's his long-ago honeymoon suit, saved for important events. This climb qualified. Mayor Redman – in his tie – is disappointed. He had hoped to be the most formally dressed hiker above ten thousand feet. After toasts are made and celebration fireworks are shot off across the glacier, we begin our run down the mountain, glissading down the permanent snowfields. If we lean back and dig our heels in we can gain control and slow down. Once on the steep pumice slopes, the red rocks fill our gaping boots and after every few steps we must scoop out a painful handful of rocks.

When we arrive at the Rock Mesa, we see a forty-foot snow wall dropping off the lip of the lava flow. It has a long, snowy, rock-free run. "Go ahead, Bill," the guys dare, never expecting him to actually do it. "Go slide down that!" The mesa wall is steep. He climbs it like a ladder, shoving his hands and feet into its side for holds. Bill lets out such a scream when he flies down that Steve has to try it. We all have to try it. Todd takes off his nylon hiking shirt, puts his legs in the sleeves, and pulls it up to his armpits, so he doesn't get a raw back. When I climb up and look down, it is so steep that I can't see the bottom! The Mayor goes down head first and gets quite a rush. We all follow, while Tre watches with binoculars from a short distance away.

Back at the shelter, we all devour our supper and lie on the wooden floor, watching the setting sun turn South Sister to a dark, rusty color. Bill is so tired that he can't speak in full sentences and calls everyone by the wrong name. Tre's announced that he's going ahead for a few days to climb Mount Jefferson. Tonight, though, we all feel like one big, happy family. We've forgotten our differences and dwell on the one thing that we all share—a wonderful, successful climb to the top of the Cascade sky.

It's three-thirty in the afternoon. I haven't seen Todd since lunchtime. He said he'd "be right there" when I left. The boys were busy chopping pieces of a snow bridge off to throw over Obsidian Falls. Three and a half hours at my slow pace, and they haven't caught me yet! I'm sitting at this trail intersection with no idea which way to go. The trail isn't even called the PCT in the wilderness area, and there are no white diamonds or hatchet marks on the trees to point the way. I have no guidebook or maps, and I feel like a fool. I'm afraid to go too far ahead because I'm uncertain about this trail.

That settles it! After today I'm taking the guidebook and I'll see them at the end of each day. I understand Todd wants to play with the boys, but sometimes I feel like a third wheel. I try to push away my anger and move onto new country, hoping I'm heading in the right direction.

I've been walking a circle around the Three Sisters volcanoes. Glaciers sweep down their sides, with creases and folds in the ice like wrinkles on the faces of old, weathered people. Below the snowline pasque flowers bloom in the dry patches. The snow is going rapidly now. It does strange things in these mountains. I see rushing whitewater pour off the snowpack right above me, turn into a gentle, meandering, twelve-inch-wide creeklet at my feet, and disappear totally into the porous volcanic soil a few feet below me. All within twenty yards!

The landscape looks devastated — like Mars, the moon, or the earth after a nuclear holocaust. Cinder cones made up of dark, soft-looking ash, each sporting a sparse skirt of trees at its base, litter the area. The cones look like the coal-dirt mountains in Pennsylvania. Even the trail here is dusty from the ash, and it feels like I'm walking in sand.

As I start to climb up Yapaho Crater, I see the guys' little bodies coming behind me, moving very fast. Jerks! I pretend I don't see them and keep going. When Todd finally catches up, he is apologetic and humble.

"What were you doing all this time?"

"We were working," he says.

"I don't think that's funny."

"I'm sorry, honey. We got carried away. It started when we decided to break the snow bridge across the creek and open the stream for navigational purposes," he says, smiling. "I raked the hard snow with my ice ax head, while Steve ran from the stream with buckets of water that he dumped on the spot. Redman jumped up and down until the piece broke off. We got very dedicated and involved, working away. One time a group of weekenders came cruising through and looked at us strangely. We quickly sat down on the snow on our hands, concealed our work tools and smiled. Then someone yelled, 'We have work to do!' and we jumped up and kept scraping. The next time someone came by, we didn't stop. Before we knew it, three hours had passed and we had to crank out a four-mile-per-hour pace to catch you."

The boys continue playing at tonight's camp on South Matthew Lake. After dinner we entertain ourselves by watching Bill light his farts. He throws his legs in the air and spreads them open, then sticks a lighter flame almost too close to his pants. When the gas explodes, an orange-blue tongue of fire flares in a V-shape, six inches long.

Todd and I walk side by side, holding hands. This morning, he's hiking with a long face. It's incredibly difficult to learn what his problem is when there are other people around. It takes patience and hours of private coaxing. When that isn't possible, I encourage him, even push him, to communicate, which makes it worse. His sour mood makes me unhappy. I resent the fact that we are both miserable and I don't even know why! Because of his German upbringing, he learned to keep his problems to himself. Because of my Polish-Italian upbringing, I learned to share everything, openly, immediately. One more minute spent being unhappy in life is too long, in my eyes. Todd, on the other hand, seems to get into it. We are beginners at marriage communication, and being with the group sometimes complicates things.

When we arrive at Lava Lake, I see him gulp water like a madman, then he comes over and hugs and kisses me.

"Is that what your problem was, thirst?" I ask, recalling that good water was scarce all morning.

"I hate to drink iodized water," he explains.

"So you'd rather go without, risk dehydration, be miserable, and make me miserable?" I ask.

"That's right," he says, smiling, for he knows how ridiculous it sounds. I shake my head and smile back, knowing it's hopeless.

McKenzie Pass Highway is a winding ribbon of black asphalt over a chaotic jumble, the largest lava field in the state. The road is a series of tight curves, but it's lightning quick compared to what the route was like before.

Paralleling the highway is a remnant of a lava-rock road built by one man for ox-drawn wagons, the original route over the mountains. Lava rocks were turned with their flat sides up and laid like a cobblestone or brick. The eight-foot-wide road must have taken years to build, and travelers were charged a toll to use the highway. Although the road looks lumpy and bumpy, it would have been a cinch compared to the nearly impossible task of trying to walk over the lava.

The lava blocks making up this eighty-five-square-mile field oozed out of the nearby Belknap volcanoes. An observatory sits atop the lava field, made from the same black rock that it sits upon.

Even close up, it's difficult for the eye to make out the structure, for the observatory blends in with its surroundings. Inside the empty building are little windows that the mason built. Each one reveals a different Cascade volcano, framed like a picture.

It was good to take a break and do a little sight-seeing, for our route ahead is a hot and dirty one. We have to cross this destruction in the heat of the day. So desolate is this area that astronauts visited it to experience a moonlike environment. The lava seems endless. Black valleys and mountains look like a sea of broken macadam. It beats heat onto our bodies. The few trees scattered over the lifeless wasteland are dead skeletons, their naked limbs bleached white from the sun. Lava rocks litter the trail with stumbling obstacles.

We wind up between two forested knolls that somehow kept their "heads" above the hot, black lava. We can see clearly how the waves of lava curved around the land. On the far end of the knoll, we regroup and tell our friends about some noteworthy ammunition, snow hats. Even in this intense heat, small patches of snow remain in the deepest lava trenches. Todd and I show them how to fashion the hats out of bandannas. Redman scoops six cups of snow and pounds it into a ball before rolling it up and tying it over his bright red ponytail. He's quite a sight, our Mayor, with his bare chest, wide, shiny blue tie and a snow hat worn so that it looks like he has a toothache. In a line we march across the lava,

Todd (left), Steve (middle), and Redman in snow hats

keeping remarkably cool thanks to the dripping turbans. Half-way across, we step aside to let a long string of young boys pass. They stare at us with puzzled looks. We stare back. Each of them is chubby and wears a long-sleeved shirt, buttoned at the wrist and tightly around his chubby neck! Their flushed faces, dripping with sweat, look like red balloons bobbing around their throats.

"Why don't you guys unbutton your shirts and roll up your sleeves?"

"Naw. We're okay."

We watch as they stumble into the sun, as though in a trance. Could this be someone's idea of weight reduction?

In Sisters, Oregon, we put Steve on a bus and send him back to Wisconsin. This morning he became depressed. Leaving the trail, going back to that "other life," seems like death to him.

Steve can't extract the same life and energy out of a mass of computers and microchips that he can from his spirited fool friends in this wilderness playground. Our life on the trail comes to an end far too soon for any of us, but Steve is faced with it long before the trail tired him out or beat him up.

We have been following the melt. We are walking northward along the Cascade Range at exactly the same rate that the snowpack is moving vertically up the mountains. What timing! All along, the postcards we've been getting from our hiker friend, Redman's old partner, who's ten days ahead of us, speak of the miles of buried trail waiting for us. But when we arrive, the snow is always gone.

We've heard from many locals that the backcountry just opened up. "Last week, you couldn't have gotten through," they said repeatedly.

Here in central Oregon, the ground on the trail bed is soft and mushy, saturated with water, as though it just rained for days. But it hasn't. Grasses recently released from the snowpack are dry, yellow, starved for sunlight, and matted to the ground. Often, the snowline has crawled just above the trail, recently revealing the way. Two feet below the trail bed there is a series of traversing prints. Hikers tried to walk right below the snow on dry ground, so the snow must have been two feet lower only a few days ago. It looks like the snow creeps up the mountainside a few feet every day.

So far, we have timed this trip perfectly. Had we left Belden, California, only two weeks earlier than we did, we would be walking on solid snow. Now, there's none at all.

The spot where Todd took his fall in 1982 is only a few miles ahead. Back then, this area was fairly clear, too, but when the guys rounded that slope of South Cinder Butte, they were suddenly blocked by a wall of snow.

Suddenly Todd, in a grave voice, says "This is it!" We creep around the sharp corner and scream, "It's clear!" The land drops off like a cliff to our left. Trees forest the steep slope, and just above us there's a wall of snow. We imagine it reaching the trail and can feel the panic Todd must have felt when he saw it back then. He points to the tree that he believes was the culprit.

There are even scars on its bark.

Todd has been saving up a good supply of urine for the occasion. We all cheer and snap photos as he climbs down and waters the tree.

From here on north, it's new country for Todd. Most of the last eight hundred miles have been a repeat for him, albeit one that has brought him—and me—great pleasure. We're starting to feel worthy of such pleasures. After all, we paid our dues back in 1982. May our luck continue all the way to Canada!

Jefferson Park

15

The Volcanoes

August 12

When you first see a Cascade volcano from the Pacific Crest Trail, it is usually from a point miles away, when the cone appears as a distant white shape on the horizon. From such a vantage point the great mountains all look more or less alike. Only when you get closer, do they take on unique personalities and characteristics.

Every day, as you walk closer, more detail begins to emerge. You can see rock slides on the face of the peak. Fingers of ice become evident on its flanks. The greenery marching up to the foot of the glaciers separates itself into individual trees. When you get on the mountain, walking through the meadows, skirting the lava flows and rivers of ice, crossing the glacier-fed streams, a personal relationship with the peak begins to develop.

If you spend the night on its lower slopes, you can watch the mountain's face change, its complexion reflect the sun's glow and setting warmth. Its silhouette outlines the dark, star-studded sky. Breezes pour down from its upper slopes. It may display its anger and fickleness in a storm, expose its temper in the winds. Or it may smile upon you and flaunt its beauty in the bright skies of warm, flower-meadow days.

As you pass the volcano and begin to leave it behind, one last look at the peak causes all your memories of and feelings about it to flood back. But as you bid your sentimental farewell, it stands there in splendor — strong, powerful, indifferent. Even so, memories of its deep forests, rushing streams, and carpets of wildflowers will continue to enrich your life for years to come. There is an energy generated by great mountains that is unlike any other force in nature. Something magical happens up there, something spooky. You form a unique bond with each mountain, one that may well cause you to walk away from the encounter as a better human being.

The first time Mount Jefferson made an impression on me was back at McKenzie Pass, as I stood on the Belknap lava beds. The white giant rose out of the black wasteland, looming above and beyond Three Fingered Jack and Mount Washington, two older, smaller, more deeply eroded volcanoes. Jefferson's snow-covered flanks held out a promise of a cool, moist paradise that provided comfort while we crawled through that black hell.

But not until now, as we cross Jefferson's shoulder and drop

into beautiful Jefferson Park, an area dotted with lakes and meadows, wildflower gardens, and clusters of evergreens, do we really
come to love this peak. The park is an extensive plain stretching
directly from the volcano's base. The mountain rises abruptly, as
though it grew out of the plain, which indeed it did. The earth in
the park is marshy and springy because it has only recently been
free of snow. Tender flower shoots push through in a scream of
color: purple lupines, deep pink penstemons, flame red Indian
paintbrush, yellow daisylike sneezeweed, and orchid-colored
phlox. The blooms grow in clusters, as in a tended garden, as
though a Park Keeper designed it that way.

There are almost as many hikers in the park as wildflowers.
Being only a few miles from a road, this gorgeous area is easily
accessible for short trips. Trails lead to secluded lakes and campsites in scattered pine groves, for tenting isn't allowed on the lake
shores.

Tre left the group a little less than a week ago to climb Mount
Jefferson. We meet him again at Scout Lake in Jefferson Park. He
tells us about his adventures but does not ask about ours.

The Mayor gets cozy on his foam pad, listening to "Prairie
Home Companion" on his tiny radio. Bill lies next to him and puts
assorted nuts on their legs and bellies, trying to attract birds.

They keep very still. Soon, Steller's jays, the "camp robbers,"
land on them and pick the nuts off. When the nuts are gone, one
bird picks at the scab on Bill's shin, which is brown and in the
perfect shape of an almond.

As we climb up to Park Ridge, we stop frequently to look back
at this impressive peak and its park. White robed, it looks like a
king standing stately, the park at its feet like a courtyard full of
cheering, banner-waving admirers.

On the ridgetop our eyes travel down a long, semipermanent
snowfield, race across forty miles of thick forests and feast upon
Mount Hood, our next Cascade volcano. It beckons us forward.
The fickle hikers quickly forget their love affair with Mount Jefferson and bound down the snow, heading for an iced-over alpine

lake. Bill jumps in, naked, cracking the surface with the plunge of his feet. A deafening scream bellows out of his lungs when he surfaces. No guts, no glory.

We now begin a quiet interim between Mount Hood and Mount Adams. The forest is dense and virgin. Olallie Lake is our stop for the night. I'm not in the mood to be with the guys tonight, so Todd and I place our tent far away from the others. Been a long time since we had an evening to ourselves. While Todd sets the tent up, I position myself on my foam pad in "the kitchen."

Everything I need to prepare a meal sits around me. The water bag, food, the stove, our spoons, the spice bag. While I cook, I write in my journal. Todd sits close to me, head in my lap while I write. It's so much easier for him to be openly affectionate when the other men aren't around.

We found an envelope with our names on it nailed to a tree today. Inside was an invitation from an old AT friend who lives in the next town, Government Camp, below Mount Hood. He learned we were on the trail and invited us home! We don't think it would be too cool to bring everyone along with us, so we keep our plans to ourselves. No long-distance hiker wants to miss an opportunity for food, showers and accommodations in town. So, to avoid hurting anyone's feelings, Todd and I get an early start, ahead of the rest. We'll catch them in a few days.

Our climb up to Mount Hood is exhausting. Todd hikes right behind me anytime we ascend. I hate to feel pushed! Can't even bend over to tie my boot or stoop to scratch without fear of his ice ax going into my pack or head. He says he wants to be with me, but suddenly I realize, he's trying to make me go faster! No way! I'll go at my own pace and get there in plenty of time. "Go by me, please. We'll get to Mount Hood in plenty of time."

If you don't lift your head to see Mount Hood's bulk rising in the sky, and if you ignore the fact that you're climbing, you would think that you were transported to a beach somewhere. Grasses grow long and wild and wave in the wind on Mount Hood's south side. Your boots sink three inches into the soft, gray sand, and you're tempted to go barefoot. Heavy leather boots don't seem right for this surface.

We're walking on a dried-up mud flow that spewed out of Hood's south side two thousand years ago. The pasty flow melted snow and ice and mixed with blown-out ash. Tremendous volumes of this mud flowed down the canyon and buried an ancient forest. The mud dried up and left a sandy sediment that we must laboriously cross on our way toward Mount Hood.

To our left the land dives down to Whitewater Canyon and the Buried Forest. We stare up the fan-shaped canyon, searching for the point where it gets shallow enough to cross, for on its far side sits the famous Timberline Lodge, a wonderful building constructed in the 1930s by the WPA. It was fashioned out of native materials by artists and craftsmen, decorated in Indian and nature designs and is a registered national landmark. What catches your eye though, as you hike closer, is not the structure but the

Mount Hood's Buried Forest

ski run on this mighty peak. The lower glacier is marked off in lanes, like a pool set up for races. Ski camps for rich kids rent all the lanes but one, which is set aside for the general public. It would cost us eighty to a hundred dollars a day to ski. The drop is only seven hundred feet, but this is the only place in the United States that has year-round skiing. Two tons of salt are dumped on it daily to keep the melting down! By noon, the snow is too slushy to ski on, so all this effort is for just a few hours of morning fun. For four years they've been dumping salt, claiming it does nothing to alter the environment or affect the fish life in the streams below. How can they know this?

When we enter the lodge, we forget our anger. Animal heads adorn the outside walls, which are weathered gray and checked. Inside, the banister posts are carved into animal figures. A pelican rests under folded wings. Ornate, black iron gates guard the entrance to the main dining room. A magnificent stone fireplace commands your attention. Hand-wrought iron decorates every door latch and stair rail. Handmade rugs set off the hand-pegged wooden floors. Draperies of hand-woven linen grace the windows. There are paintings of deer, mosaics of bear, inlaid wooden pictures of the forest. A tribute to the arts, built at seven thousand feet next to this world of natural beauty. Now, if we could only get rid of the ski run.

Mail and a visit with our friend await us in Government Camp. Todd and I walk down the curving road. A shiny, red Corvette convertible nearly runs us off the road. "Watch it!" we yell. The car is packed with young skiers, girls crammed in the back seat, drinking beer and yelling. One throws an empty can over her shoulder. It rolls across the asphalt and stops at my feet.

As Todd and I eat our ice cream on the store's concrete steps, we watch the cars pull up. Expensive ski gear sticks out of the windows. Teenagers with pumped-up pectorals and muscle shirts cut off at their midriffs step out. Glacier goggles on brightly colored nylon cords hang around their necks.

An old motorcycle pulls up beside the cars. Its rider wears brown corduroys with the nap worn off and a stretched-out

T-shirt. When the helmet comes off, we see the familiar face of our friend, Bob Phearson.

"Trail treating you okay?" he asks. "I'll take you back to the house whenever you're ready. Oh! Someone else will be staying tonight, too. I just met him on the road. He says he's a good friend of yours." We look at him puzzled. Who could that be? We turn and see a backpacker walking toward us with a golden retriever by his side. A big smile covers the guy's face. Tre!

We have a really nice night, despite our unexpected guest. Bob shows us his wonderful slides of the AT all evening long. We lose Tre early, either to fatigue or boredom. For hours, we look at the less spectacular, but beautiful—and home to us—Appalachian Mountains.

Unlike the populated south side of Hood, its west and north are just the opposite, remote, serene, what we are here for. There is a side trail climbing high into the alpine meadows that is not part of the PCT. The trail is called Paradise and that's exactly what we find up there. Hills of wildflowers. Not patches here and there, but rolling fields smothered with brilliant color. I look up and see a bald eagle soaring overhead. Behind these fields, the mountain is kicking up clouds, moving them over its face like a teasing, veiled woman; one minutes she's covered, the next she's revealed.

We're all back together again. . . more or less. The group does not walk heel to toe, but is strung out along the trail. Smaller groups form and break up and re-form as this person or that surges ahead or drops back. But we are all more together than apart, and rarely does more than a half day of walking separate the first and last persons in the line.

Todd and I switchback along the side of the Sandy River Canyon. Looking over the edge sends my head reeling. Deep gashes of canyon plunge down the sides of Hood. Their walls are totally eroded away. No trees can cling to the sides, just sliding sand.

After our descent, we enter a lush, deep forest with gigantic rhododendrons and massive columns of evergreens. Rays of golden diffused light filter through the hemlock needles and light up enchanted pieces of forest. A Douglas fir sapling is spotlighted. A lit patch of fern performs next as it dances and waves fitfully in a forest-floor breeze. Where the light is not present, the forest blends in uneventfully. With a beam of setting sun, there is magic and wonder.

The rivers in the California's High Sierra are most dangerous during early spring runoff, when winter finally breaks and the great melt occurs. Crossings in the glacier-laden Cascades, however, are worse in the searing months of summer, at the hottest time of the day when the greatest of glacial melting occurs. The guidebook warns, "Do not cross after eleven A.M." So when Todd and I arrive at the Sandy River at seven P.M., we decide to camp and hold off until morning.

During the night, we are awakened by boisterous voices, heavy footsteps, and blinding lights piercing the privacy of our tent home. I look at my watch. Four A.M. What the hell is going on?

Our entire tent is lit up like there's an electric light on inside.

Someone yells, "Boy, was that deep!" Group after group passes by.

Sleep is impossible. Todd and I lie there, side by side, wide awake. I use our time together to ask Todd about a conflict we seem to be nurturing.

"I get frustrated from not being able to hike fast," he says. "When I'm thirsty and want to get good water, I want to do it quickly. When the guys brag about doing big miles, I want to prove that I can do it too."

"I know you can do it," I tell him. "You know you can do it. Isn't that enough?"

"I need to show them," he says.

"Unfortunately," I say, "you're married."

I wish he didn't feel the need to prove something. "I'm hiking faster on this trip than I ever did before. And I'm doing bigger days. We're ahead of our schedule."

"I guess I sometimes resent you for the pace you walk," Todd says. "I'd love to breeze by Tre and leave him behind in the dust, so we don't have to deal with him anymore."

"I'm sorry I slow you down."

"It's just when we get to a lake and swim. They stay for hours because they hike fast and make their miles. We have to pack up and leave early."

"You know, you've got some pleasures that those guys don't have," I remind him. "The pleasure of crawling into a zipped-together sleeping bag every night with warm, loving arms to hold you after a hard day's work. None of them have that."

And with those words, he reaches over and pulls me to his chest. Suddenly, a bright flashlight slices through our tent wall.

Finally, my curiosity gets the best of me and I yell, "What are you all doing out there?"

"We're hiking around Hood in one day. Forty miles. Beginning at three A.M."

"Who are you?" I ask.

"The Mazamas." The mountaineering club founded years ago by the "father of Crater Lake." I ask one how the ford was and he replies, in a strong English accent, "Bloody terrible!" Great. Something to look forward to come morning.

At dawn, Todd and I go down to encounter the raging monster pouring from the glaciers above. The gorge is filled with fog and mist, getting thicker up above and totally concealing the brooding peak. The rushing glacial water is white, as though someone poured jugs of milk out upstream. We cross boulders on the river bed for many yards before even reaching water and realize how terribly wide this ford would be during high water. Thirty yards! Now, it's only five yards wide and it's up to our thighs. Still, we give it respect and are aware of how dangerous a crossing like this could be.

On the open slopes of Indian Mountain, we see before us two new Cascade volcanoes: Mount Adams and what I assume is Mount St. Helens. St. Helens looks a little smaller and is cut off at the top as if the summit were a plateau. But when I put my telephoto lens up and adjust the polarizing lens, I learn the amazing truth: The flat-topped peak is not St. Helens at all but Mount Rainier! Its giant head is concealed in clouds, so that only its snowy base is in sight. Although it is forty miles farther north than Adams, it looks practically the same size! The mountain must be huge! Off to the west the real Mount St. Helens comes into view. It's bluish gray and dry. No peak, no snow. When I lower my camera, it melts away from view and I have to imagine to see it floating in the sky. The PCT doesn't go over Mount St. Helens, because the peak sits too far west. But we will walk on Mount Adams' powerful shoulders and around the base of Rainier.

We turn and begin a long descent into Eagle Creek Gorge, which funnels us down to the mighty Columbia River, the lowest point on the PCT and the dividing line between Oregon and Washington.

Eagle Creek Gorge is an alternative route that takes us through country far too beautiful to pass by. The first part of our descent is through an old forest fire burn from the early 1900s. Massive stumps stand like giant tombstones—a reminder of what used to be. They make us wonder how much larger they'd be if they'd continued growing these past eighty years.

We hear the creek roaring many feet below us long before we actually see it. Our trail, which was dynamited out of the sheer cliff, is high above Eagle Creek. There are cables along the inner side for the faint-hearted and weak-kneed. We round the corner and see one-hundred-fifty-foot Tunnel Falls crashing off the cliff and pounding into the gorge below. The mist from the thundering falls sprays everything. The moss-covered land drips with moisture. The rocks on the trail under our feet are slick, and we find ourselves groping for the cable, even though the trail is a safe three feet wide. The trail leads right to the falls and ducks behind the water in a hollowed-out passageway. It's like being inside a mountain's skin—hearing the deafening roar, seeing the water fall like a sheet just a few inches away. Redman and I, taking turns using my tripod, photograph the falls for nearly half an hour.

High Bridge spans the creek ninety feet above the water.

Tunnel Falls

Here, the creek is a narrow, cool green canal, looking like still backwater. Movement is hardly discernible. Cliffs rise straight up from its sides; roots cling to the rock precipice; sunlight dances on the water like shimmering diamonds. We decide we're thirsty, so Redman ties all of our parachute cords together to lower his dirty, plastic Lorraine's Drive-In cup into the creek for a drink. It comes up half full and we all take sips. That's why he's our mayor!

We pass more falls and imagine that this must be what Hawaii is like. Everywhere the land is blanketed with soft, green moss. Every rock, every branch, every tree, standing or fallen, is covered. Objects on the forest floor can be made out only by their shapes, for every square inch is blanketed by moss. Since we walked through the old burn, the live trees have reappeared, looking no taller or broader than their dead relatives farther up the gorge. Eighty years of growth doesn't seem too evident.

The lower we descend, the less treacherous the footing, the wider the trail, and the greater the number of people. Finally, the dirt beneath our feet turns to blacktop.

This is the end of Bill's trip. He's arranged for me, Todd, and Redman to go home with him in Portland for some R and R. Tre went ahead again, and we hope he keeps going. Bill has been sulky and quiet all day. When he does speak, it's to remind us how many hours remain until he goes "into prison."

At the trailhead, there's no sign of Tre, so we slip into Bill's father's car and head for Portland.

We always assume we smell bad when we come back into society, even though we can't smell ourselves. In the outdoors, in the open air, we rarely notice body odor. In a vehicle, it's intensified, especially to a daily bather's nose. We apologize profusely as Bill's dad rapidly rolls his window down.

Fine china and crystal sets the table for "the author" and her husband and friend. I find myself wrestling with the chicken leg and knife, waiting for it to sail across my plate or fall into my lap. Enough of this! I pick it up with my hands.

When we start repacking and making plans to resupply, Bill gets an empty look in his eyes, for he won't be returning. Since both of his parents' cars broke down after we arrived, Todd and I must shop for food to resupply for the entire state of Washington and carry it back to their house in our packs and in our arms. Maneuvering our tremendously heavy carts in the crowded store is a skill that seems to elude us. The metal frame backpack is shoved underneath the cart, but sticks out two extra feet. When we try to turn around in an aisle, we wipe out the bottom row of cans, so we abandon the cart where it is and run off to retrieve the spilled cans.

When we return from the store, blue Bill has suddenly turned happy. He's returning to the trail to hike with us! His parents think this is a great opportunity and he can benefit from our presence and influence. I go off to ensure that he brings the proper clothing this time. "Any wool in this boy's wardrobe?" The best I can find is a wool blend shirt that I toss on the growing pile of gear, along with the rain suit we insist he bring along. So far, we've been lucky with the weather. But we doubt very much that Washington will cooperate.

The mighty Columbia rolls wide and curving, breaking through the steep walls of the Cascade range on its way to the Pacific Ocean. In the town of Cascade Locks the river features a set of locks built in 1896. The locks allowed shipping to continue up the river past the twenty-foot falls that the Cascade Range is probably named for. The falls are now gone, buried under the Bonneville Dam. All that remain are the old locks and a museum built to tell you how it once was.

We are at the lowest point on the Pacific Crest Trail—one hundred fifty-five feet. Two thousand feet seemed like hell in the scorching Whitewater Canyon of southern California, so far south of here. At this altitude, with the moist, cool river and the never-ceasing wind, it's not hot. From this lowest point, we'll climb to the highest point along the PCT—the Goat Rocks at seven thousand eighty feet.

Located right on the water, Marine Park has large, roofed pavilions and free showers. The railroad passes twenty-five yards away so it's a favorite hopping-off point for hobos who ride the rails. One is wandering around tonight with a blanket over his head, asking for money and aspirin for his sore tooth.

Two years ago, Todd stayed here for four days, waiting for his foot to heal and saw many people get ripped off. The wind is so loud and strong you couldn't hear if someone crept up and stole your pack by your head while you slept. We set up tents to store our gear in and sleep outside by the door. But with the tent flapping like a sail, shock cords beating the nylon, sleeping bag filling with wind, the bright park lights, trains thundering by, and the roar of the wind, we sleep very little.

Bridge across the Columbia River

As we cross the Columbia on a narrow metal monster of a bridge, I scan the water below. The water is choppy as the wind gusts to fifty miles per hour. There is no pedestrian walkway. We flatten our bodies against the rail, avoiding the truck tires passing only inches from our feet. We must push against the wind in our struggle to remain upright. When we pass by a steel girder, the wind is momentarily blocked and we're thrown off balance. Our hands tighten around our carved walking sticks. We don't want to lose them down the square metal holes dropping down to the wild river below. "Welcome to Washington!" greets the sign, as we pick our heads up to see, fighting the never-ceasing wind.

The sign says: "Berries behind this sign reserved for Indians."
"Is this some sort of joke?" I ask. Here, on one side of the road, the general public can pick huckleberries; on the other side, only Indians. They come here as they have for centuries, to the Sawtooth Huckleberry Fields, where, according to an old agreement with the United States Forest Service, certain portions are re-

served for the Indians' exclusive picking. Some still set up tepees for the duration of their stay, but all travel in twentieth century cars, trailers, and motor homes. These fields are perhaps the largest huckleberry fields in the world. The Pacific Crest Trail cuts right through the middle.

The Indians believe that huckleberry, salmon, and venison are sacred foods and for years spent their summers picking and drying the berries. The tribes came from as far as Montana—with as much of their property as they could haul. This was also the time for sport, for horse racing, the Indian Olympics. Each tribe would bring their fastest pony to race those from other tribes. A half mile from the PCT is the Indian racetrack, where remarkable evidence of the race is still visible. A groove ten feet wide and several inches deep remains in the earth, for a stretch of two thousand feet. The braves would line the length of the track and bet all their possessions, even their squaws, on their pony. The last race was in 1920. The roadless backcountry became known as Indian Heaven in their honor.

Mount Adams is the third highest volcano in the Cascade Range. At 12,286 feet, it is surpassed only by Mount Rainier, the king, and Mount Shasta. Adams has remained largely unappreciated and delightfully undeveloped. According to Indian legend Mount Adams and Mount Hood are brothers who both courted the once-lovely Mount St. Helens. She favored Adams over Hood, who became so angry that he struck his brother with such force that he flattened his head. Ashamed and embarrassed, Adams never lifted his head again.

This unsung mountain is one of my favorites in all the Cascades. Ridges extend down all sides of the mountain. Our trail crosses dozens of these ribs as it contours around the volcano. In between are exquisite little valleys carved by fingers of ice in the last ice age. Each one is totally different, with its own mosaic of wildflower gardens and stands of conifers. Flat little meadows nestle on ledges. They were once glacier-carved lakes and then dried up and filled in with grass and flowers. In one wash a young doe stands. I walk into the next and find a tree full of baby grouse. In the next, a fat golden marmot whistles to me. Each wash reveals delightful variety. The Adams glacier hangs on the mountain like a frozen, suspended waterfall, one you'd expect to hear come thundering down. Because of its steepness, there are many enormous chunks of ice, called seracs, that break apart the glacier and make the "falls" look like it's throwing foam into the air.

With so much to photograph, I've been distracted. Todd has left me alone with my filming. I hope he doesn't feel like I'd rather be with my camera than him.

At lunch I learn otherwise. I interrupt my journal writing to replenish my water bottle and leave my book unattended. When I return and pick up my pen to continue, I find a note:

"Cindy, I love you a whole bunch. Thanks for being such a fine wife. This trip has been the best trip I've been on, thanks to you. You are worth all those beautiful flowers we saw on Paradise Loop."

Mount Adams

Right here, we're about the closest we'll get to Mount St. Helens on the PCT. Although the sky is cloudless and clear, there is a haze around the explosive peak. Four years after the big eruption it's still smoking, quietly building a summit cone. Its ridges are an ash-covered gray, the same substance that lines our trail, some thirty miles to the east. For about one hundred miles we've been walking in her soot. It's piled nearly two inches deep on the trail and is easily stirred into choking clouds when we walk. Our bodies and possessions are covered with the fine dirt. Black lines form in the crook of our arms, behind our knees, around our necks. We wipe our sweat and streak black across our faces.

It begins to rain, and the smell of sulfur fills the air as the drops wet the ash. When you dig in the forest, underneath the pine needles, there are a few inches of ash, then brown soil beneath that. Even logs and fallen trees are still coated.

This is the first rain we've encountered this summer. It's a bone-chilling, season-changing rain, and it worries us. Rain comes to the Pacific Northwest as autumn advances and the year winds down. Rain means it's getting late.

Since we left the Columbia River six days ago, we've been slowly gaining elevation. We're heading for the Goat Rocks Wilderness. I've been very excited about hiking through this dramatic place. The trail runs along a knife-edged ridge, the remains of a volcano that has been extinct for two million years. The way is narrow and precipitous as it winds high above glacier-carved canyons. We'd much rather hike it in fair weather, both for safety reasons and the view. We eagerly await dawn to see if the storm has passed.

The Mayor's bright red head pokes out of his equally brilliant yellow tent. "Is that sky cloudy or cloudless?" The lack of light and color at this hour makes it difficult to determine. "Blue sky! All right!" But the temperature has dropped. Yesterday's soaked socks are frozen hard. Our wet boots are stiff, too, and we struggle to cram our feet in. The moisture in the ash trail froze last night, hardening all the little bumps and depressions. It takes a good, fast mile before the boot leather is supple, and our toes stop aching. August 27. Summer must be over.

A frozen world glitters in the sunshine. Crystallized water droplets cling to each leaf and petal. In a matter of a few warm seconds, we see the frost melt into a drop and roll to the center of the leaf. As we climb higher, the views open up. The slopes we cross glow a rusty red color from the turning berry bushes. The older plants are cranberry purple and their fruit has already begun to dry up. The cream-colored flowers of pearly everlasting are turning to straw. Since the storm moved through, there is a definite taste of fall in the air, a sharpness and crispness. Mother Earth is putting on her autumn gown.

We climb farther and traverse high, open, grassy slopes. Waterfalls cascade right above us and splash over our chiseled trail. Across the deep green canyons, we can see our trail snake around the basins, like a line drawn on a map. The heart of the Goat Rocks, Old Snowy, sparkles above us.

In a land of talus and scree and lingering snow, we climb up to find the Dana Yelverton shelter, a stone lean-to built on the brink of a rocky ridge. A seventeen-year-old girl died up here.

When she fell ill with hypothermia, her friends left her alone in her sleeping bag and went for help. When they returned, they found her dead. The shelter was built in her memory to provide a haven from inclement weather and perhaps spare others' lives.

Mount Adams, Mount Rainier, and Mount St. Helens all stand guard in the heavens tonight. Massive Rainier has a lenticular cloud over its head, like a cap. The cloud moves constantly and one side looks as though it's dripping. As the sun sets behind the mountain, Rainier's tremendous bulk turns to an inky black shadow with rosy sky all around it. Adams' countenance faces the spot where the sun went down and the peak throws on a pink-orange evening robe. St. Helens fades in the background, a darker and bluer gray.

Because I am photographing the mountain show, making dinner—my chore—has to wait until after dark. In the darkness, I spill cream of chicken soup all over our gear. Todd is angry. "It doesn't seem worth it," Todd grumbles. "Getting into camp late, cooking in the dark."

I disagree. Days are becoming shorter and the same amount of miles need to be covered. Spending so much time photographing this spectacular scenery doesn't take that much time away from our day. To me, recording this important trip is essential. To Todd, getting into camp at a decent hour and doing our chores by daylight is more important. It's a conflict of priorities that comes up again and again.

First thing this morning we cross the upper slopes of the Packwood Glacier on Old Snowy's west side. At seven thousand eighty feet, it is the highest point on the Washington PCT. The trail leads us onto a harrowing, knife-edged ridge where mountaineer and mountain goat are equally at home. On the rocky backbone the scenery spreads out for miles on either side. We feel once again like we're scraping the heavens, walking in the sky. The trail is so narrow and the slopes so steep that there are signs warning you to look ahead, to send out scouts to see if there are any teams of pack horses coming across. If you encounter one, you'd have to turn around and go back to the last lookout point, for there are no other places to step off the trail.

The Camel cigarette man in the ads is a joke. The rugged, macho man with the curly, bleached blonde hair is supposed to symbolize mountaineers, but he looks more like a lifeguard or surfer.

They helicopter him in to remote places, dress him in designer outdoor clothes, and equip him with what would probably prove fatally inadequate.

On the Goat Rocks knife-edge we decide as a lark to stage our own Camel man ad. We dress Todd in a big pile jacket, Gore-tex pants, red kerchief and Bill's cowboy hat pulled low over his brow.

A green climbing rope is draped around his chest with a carabiner on it. An ice ax lies by his side. A Camel pack that we found on a road walk and carried for miles, sits in a chalk bag on a nearby rock. With Rainier looming in the background, Todd poses on the edge of the backbone, one leg extended, one knee bent. He raises

The "Camel Man"

his hands to light the cigarette that we bummed from a weekender in Eagle Creek Gorge and carried for this purpose. With the morning sun lighting his face better than studio lights ever could, he's perfect! The Camel man lives in the Goat Rocks!

White Pass is the next gap in the range. There, Bill will leave for good. I watch him as he tends the fire. He looks so much older now. His face is tan and rugged. His serious, dark eyes reflect the miles and the growth that he has gone through, yet they dance at the first suggestion of fun. I look at his wool shirt that he insisted he didn't need and laugh to myself at how stubborn he was.

"You're glad you brought your warm shirt, aren't you, Bill?"

He rips it off his back.

A few minutes pass and he forgets himself, for he huddles by the fire, his hands trying to cover as much skin on his arms as possible.

"Cold, Bill?" I ask.

With that, he whips off his T-shirt and sits bare chested.

"What's wrong with your pants?"

He jumps up and gets completely naked.

"If you're so hot, why don't you pour water on yourself?" and he takes a quart of cold spring water and dumps it over his head and naked body. We nearly die laughing. We're sure going to miss this entertainer.

Down at the highway store, we loiter all day, waiting for Bill's dad to pick him up. In his bashful way, he lets us know that he's going to miss us. He secretly ties all of Todd's pack straps together in knots. Every time I pass him, he taps me or nudges me or acts like he's going to trip me. As I sit reading, he shoves little stones between my toes. I put my book down and say, "What is it, Bill?"

"Nothing."

"Maybe I'll come back," he yells, as the car pulls away. We stand waving by the fuel pumps. "Maybe you'll find me at one of your town stops."

"We'll look for you, Bill," we call, as the vehicle disappears over the rise.

His trip is over but ours goes on. Three hundred fifty miles remain to the border, and September begins in a day. That freezing cold front that just passed through made us all think. As we walk back to our packs, Redman wonders how long he will last, and Todd and I wonder how long Washington's good weather will last.

16

The Big Push

August 30

I'm not sure if it's the way the area around Leech Lake looks—misty, foggy, with vapors rising off the water—or the fact that I am bending over to pick up a heavy piece of firewood, but when I stand up quickly, straining from the weight, my eyes cannot focus. I am not quite sure what I am seeing. A packer mounted on a horse appears out of the mist.

"Looks like the kind of night when a man ought to have a fire," he says.

Rider from the past

His voice startles me, as though he should be a ghost and incapable of speaking. The log I'm holding slides out of my grip. He dismounts, sliding one high, laced riding boot off the mare. His wool shirt is speckled with moisture; his Stetson is pulled low; a silk kerchief is tied around his neck.

"I remember when we built that shelter. It was back in 1913 and I was seventeen years old. Used to bring supplies and dynamite up from the valley. Carried it on mules for the men building the shelter and the trail." As he talks, he sits down on the log I dropped, peels back his deerskin gloves and proceeds to take off his boot. "A horseman can live with a creased sock, but not a backpacker."

When the sock is stretched into place, he laces his boot with incredible speed, grabbing both laces in one hand, with a finger separating the two at the exact same distance that the eyelets on the boot are spaced apart. With the twist of his wrist, the boot is laced. I stare in disbelief. When he speaks of the trail I have just come over, the far-away look in his eye makes him look like he's not really here — at least not in spirit.

"Where it climbs out of the timber," he goes on, "just south of here, in the Goat Rocks section, it was all built by hand with picks and mules. Lost a couple of men up there, too. Back then, the Mexico-to-Canada dream was already taking form. We were building the first steps. Good walking to you," he says and with that, turns and rides into the mist. I stand staring for a long time, caught up in the magic of the moment, in this visitor from another time. I gather my wood and head back to the shelter.

Redman lies curled in a heap in the corner of the shelter, like a New York City bum in the subway entrance on a cold night. His thin sleeping bag is pulled tightly around his body. The nylon coat that he found hanging in a tree is too small for him. The stretched cuffs go halfway up his forearms, and the quilting threads fall out and hang in strings. He clutches the bag more tightly.

Dozens of empty bread bags containing small amounts of food and crumbled, stale bread slices, lay scattered around his sleeping bag. Redman Breadman, who carries three loaves of bread out of town but compresses them into one single bag, could find nothing that interested him to eat tonight. Our Mayor is quite sick.

The shelter is a blessing for our sick comrade. He rolls over, moans, and adjusts his "pillow," which is an empty two-liter non-returnable, plastic Cola bottle. His water bottle doubles as a head support. He stares up at the log rafters.

We have our individual theories to explain why our Mayor is ill. He says "bad water," for he never purifies even the most disgusting, standing slime holes. But I think it's his pots and pans.

The state official here is not the cleanest person I've ever met. In all the weeks we traveled together, I don't think he cleaned his pot once, which isn't so unusual for male Through-hikers. He just has one meal on top of the last. The macaroni has a little oatmeal from breakfast left in and a little rice from the night before, and so on. Occasionally, things begin to grow on the layers of old food. I theorize that those growths are responsible for our Mayor's severe case of gut rot.

Cleaning isn't important to Redman. He's more likely to spend hours watching and photographing sunlight on bugs or disregarding the cold, wet mud he's crawling through to get a closer look at a beautiful flower. His days are filled with wonder. He marvels at the beauty of the natural world. And he is one of the most cheerful, pleasant, kind people I've ever hiked with.

We will, unfortunately, have to leave him behind. We hope that he'll get better and can continue. If not, the highway is close by and he can always get a quick hitch into town. Redman and Tre will be spending the next few days together in the shelter. Tre, as usual, must wait for a package. I look at the two men and wonder.

Tre is fashion conscious, trendy, impeccably clean, and seems to feel a need to impress others. Redman shops for his clothes in a Salvation Army dumpster, has dirty toenails, is carefree, childlike, lacking in inhibitions, and feels no need to prove anything to anybody. Todd and I wonder which will be worse: the predicted storm raging outside or the one that will almost certainly occur within the shelter walls.

When we pull out of the Leech Lake shelter, which is one-half mile from White Pass, the wind is blowing, clouds are low, and the air is saturated with mist. I almost envy those left behind. Not a good day to hike, but we must save our layover days for the most miserable of times. It's not pouring rain, so today doesn't qualify. This is just how I expected Washington to be. The woods are damp and lush. Moisture clings to the giant evergreen boughs and, as the wind rakes the upper branches, they throw water down, making it pour underneath. Big, cold drops hit my scalp with a plop.

In a normal rain, trees are the place to retreat to. In a mist, they are the wettest.

We circle around many lakes and tarns, as we make a wide arc around Mount Rainier. White, gauzy fog floats above the surface of the water. Light green sedges grow and bend in the shallows. Jutting black rocks pierce the water. The tiniest ponds are dark brown, full of tannic acid from the evergreens. "Wildflowers abound around these lakes," says the guidebook, "and mosquitoes."

Neither can be found. The season is changing.

There has been a remarkable change in the mountains since we left Mount Adams behind. We seem to be on the actual Cascade crest now, not hopping from the shoulders of one large volcano to the next, with low, lake country in between. We are nearing the wild North Cascades and the last leg of our journey.

This area is horse country, and the deeply rutted and widened footpath is proof. Horses are generally terrified of backpackers and panic at our sight. No matter how sweetly we talk to let them know we are humans and not monsters, they prance and rear and nearly run off the cliff with their riders. So horsemen ask us to step below, which sometimes is not too easy, for we're traversing high on steep slopes.

We ask all the horsemen what September's weather is usually like. We ask everyone we meet, for that matter. We're taking a poll and won't stop asking until all forecasts are positive. We have a friend who left Mexico some years ago to hike the entire PCT in one year. He got within ninety miles of Monument 78 and the Canadian border when the snow started to fly. He was forced to return home without reaching his goal. That was in mid-September. It's now September 2, and three hundred miles remain to the border. We don't want the same thing to happen to us. The more positive forecasts we gather, the more secure we feel, even if it is false security.

When we were in Crater Lake National Park so many weeks ago, Glenn, the guy who was working to introduce peregrine falcons into the area, told us to give him a call when we got near his Yakima home. He said then that he'd take some vacation time and

Glenn Thompson

meet us to hike. A few miles from Chinook Pass, we meet him laden with turkey breasts for barbecuing, fresh crab salad, crusty French bread with sweet butter, white wine, and tons of fruit for dessert. The thirty-three-year-old mechanic is tan and sturdy. His long ponytail is tucked entirely under his baseball hat so that the people who might be prejudiced against "long hairs" treat him with respect. And he does deserve respect. Glenn is a member of Yakima's Search and Rescue Team and frequently goes out to practice crevasse rescues, helicopter pick-ups, and river fords. He is on constant call. He tells us, "If you should get in trouble farther north and if you have any say in the matter, contact Yakima's team, for they rescue free of charge. The professionals that make up other teams charge regular hourly rates while searching in the bush!"

Near Chinook Pass we also meet three prime specimens of the Yahoo. They look like they're dressed for a scene in a slapstick comedy act. One guy has a huge duffel bag on his back instead of a frame pack. His big arms barely fit through the carrying handles. A faded pink homemade comforter rolled into a giant tube hang underneath the bag, almost touching the ground, swinging back and forth, hitting his calves as he walks. His flannel shirt is buttoned unevenly and is much too short to cover an expanding beer belly. One of his buddies—obviously the group's cook—carries a Coleman two-burner stove, like a green metal suitcase, in one hand and a six-pack in the other. From his red-and-white-striped canvas pack hang oversized pots and pans that clang and clink together, along with a sixteen-inch cast-iron frying pan. The third man carries a large kerosene lantern, a monster double-bitted ax that hangs precariously with no shield, and many, many yards of brand new, sparkling clean, three-quarter-inch white nylon rope. I stare in disbelief as they file by.

Dozens of people have found their way into the backcountry this weekend. And why not! It's Labor Day! And we're on the fringes of Mount Rainier National Park. Besides the hikers, many teams of pack horses are also stomping the trails. Although some

Yahoos

hikers complain bitterly that the animals rut the trail, deposit manure for thousands of miles, erode shelter and campsite areas with
their hoofs, and pollute streams, horse people, according to
Glenn, feel about the wilderness much as backpackers do. In fact,
the PCT is their trail too. It was designed with their needs in
mind—a steady ten-percent grade throughout its twenty-six hundred miles.

We've never been asked "Where are you heading?" so frequently by so many people. A big, dusty cowboy on a black horse
gives us the thumbs-up sign when we answer "Canada!" Our goal
is starting to feel close, but we keep a constant watch on the western sky. Every day, high wispy cirrus clouds streak the sky. Back
East, they mean a front will be moving in within twenty-four
hours. But out here, it clears up after a day full of racing,

thickening clouds. Always looking west gives us frequent glimpses of massive Mount Rainier, with its forty-two glaciers, one of which reaches three miles into the valley below and measures a full mile wide. We can even see the Olympic Mountains far to the west, rising like a pale, blue wall in the sky.

The animals that live near the PCT use the trail as a travel corridor. The terrain is often steep and the flat trail is a welcome advantage to many large animals. No matter how many hikers or horsemen are in the southern Washington Cascades, there are still more elk tracks than boot soles or hoofprints. The animals use the trail at night, and by the time we begin hiking, which is early, the trail is covered with hundreds of tracks.

Once, back in northern California, we camped right on the trail because there was no other flat place to sleep. That night a deer walked right up to our tent and stamped and snorted at the foreign obstruction. Not until we yelled "Go around!" did the doe stop her commotion and climb around the tent.

It makes us happy to see that a man-made addition to the wilderness, like a trail, can be a welcome addition to a wild animal's life.

> *The trails you travel through these lands*
> *Were made with Big Mike's mortal hands*
> *And still his spirit rides the breeze*
> *To punish those who mar his trees.*

The sign hangs on two dead trees so riddled with bullet holes it can hardly by read anymore. Many of the other trees in the area have already been cut, and pink flags mark the ones destined for future timber sales. A muddy road with deep gullies, used frequently by dirt bikes, all-terrain vehicles, and logging trucks, runs alongside. The drone of machines can be heard in the still afternoon air. A few yards farther is Mike Urich's cabin. A dedication sign hangs over the entrance.

Camp Mike Urich
Dedicated to the memory of Mike Urich (1888-1957)

The mountain Gods from seats on high
Rejoiced to see Mike Urich die,
And at his death gave his decree
To all that pass here know that we
Entrust to big Mike Urich's hands
These camps, these trails, these forest lands
To rule, protect, to love and scan
Well as he did while mortal man,
And deal out sentence stern and just
To those who violate his trust.
Stranger beware, leave not a fire —
Foul not Mike's camp, rise not his ire.

There is no floor left in the shelter. Either someone wanted to burn it and ripped it up for firewood or it was left to neglect and rotted. The dirt floor is littered with wood scraps and junk.

Rusty, metal couches with filthy, plastic-covered foam cushions lie about. Someone sat inside the cabin and fired a twenty-two pistol repeatedly at the closed door. The wood is splintered on the outside, where the bullets exited. No windows are left in the camp, just gaping holes with fragments of old plastic blowing in the breeze. Todd and I take some cushions and go outside to make supper among the glass chips and faded beer cans. The place makes me heartsick.

It's just as well that we see this place first as a way of preparing ourselves for what lies ahead. We are about to experience what for many through-hikers is the most dreaded stretch of Pacific Crest Trail. Worse than the heat of the Mojave or the endless snows of the Sierra. The experience of this section of the trail goes deeper than mere physical pain. Ahead lie sixty miles of clear-cut devastation.

Before we even leave the protection of the forest, we're affected by the logging. Machines move above us on the ridge, tearing up the earth, building a road. The noise is echoed in the valley below

Blocked trail

and sounds like the roar of a city or factory. Suddenly, boulders start rolling down the slope toward our heads! Then small trees are flung over the side! Run for it! They are supposed to reroute the trail until the clear-cutting is complete. Then move the trail back and erect guiding posts, which will be the tallest things standing in the area.

Our quick pace comes to an immediate halt. Three huge hemlocks piled high like giant matchsticks block our trail. The air smells sweet from the kill. This cut is really recent, this afternoon!

We can't go under the trees, there's barely enough room to slide an arm under. Going around is definitely out of the question, for branching limbs and other felled trees are on top of their ends.

We'll have to climb over.

Using our hiking sticks for balance, we pull ourselves up and lower ourselves down, twisting between branches, getting twanged by boughs. We're high off the ground, trying to maneuver with unsteady, top-heavy packs. Tears fill my eyes as fatigue from the end of the day wears me down.

Clouds form overnight and push a thick mantle overhead. The thought of crossing clear-cuts in wind-driven rain makes me depressed. No sense trying to follow the guidebook—the trail through here changes weekly along with the logging activity.

On the north side of Blowout Mountain, we come face to face with our first clear-cut. All the trees have been felled and removed, their branches and needles burned. An immense stump graveyard is all that remains. We hesitate on the edge of the forest, apprehensive about leaving the safe seclusion of the trees for the exposure of the clear-cut. We feel vulnerable, naked, and we find ourselves hurrying, as though the death and destruction all around could touch us, too.

All day we hurry, only to find absolutely no place to camp come evening. No shady spot by a refreshing spring. The water is gone. So are the trees. All we can find is a gravel pull-off alongside a logging road. A pink-gray haze fills the sky as the sun goes down and the smell of smoke hangs in the air from a slash burn. By burning the debris from logging, there is less competition for the young seedlings.

At dawn we awaken at the sound of pickup truck tires rolling over our fire ring a few feet away. The driver's look says, "What are you doing here?" We feel likewise. Soon, earth movers and tractor trailers hauling equipment inch up the road, climbing higher up the scarred slopes. We watch the whole scene over a bowl of cereal, until the thought hits me: "Todd, they could be heading for this very spot, right where our tent is set up!" The area around our campsite is a fresh cut. Many logs haven't even been hauled away yet. Frantically, we run around and gather our gear. Stuff the bags! Roll the tent! When we realize that our pull-off is not their destination, we relax and watch the operation.

A machine with a big, horizontal saw goes through the woods, slicing everything in its path, thick and thin, mature and sapling. Then a crane with a hydraulic arm picks up the logs like

Clear-cuts

they're twigs and loads them onto the trucks. Empty tractor trailers roar up the narrow road, loaded ones screech down. Both travel at amazing speeds. Time is money. But how are they going to pass? The roadbed is only wide enough for one truck. We see one traveling down quickly pull into a turn-off, seconds before another screams by on its way up. They must be communicating with CBs.

The demand for wood is extraordinary. They cut so much, so quickly. Forests are a renewable resource if care is given to balancing out the cutting and planting and allowing time for the growth of young seedlings. But in many cases, it seems, seedlings aren't getting planted. Little thought is given to the future, to making sure that there is something left for those who come after.

The Great Chief in Washington sends word that he wants to buy our land. The earth does not belong to man; man belongs to the earth. All things are connected like the blood which unites one family. Man did not weave the web of life, he is merely a strand in it. Whatever he does to the web, he does to

himself. We know that the white man does not understand our
ways. One portion of land is the same to him as the next, for he
is a stranger who comes in the night and takes from the land
whatever he needs. The earth is not his brother, but his enemy,
and when he has conquered it, he moves on. He treats his
Mother the earth and his Brother the sky as things to be
bought, plundered, sold like sheep or bright beads. His appetite
will devour the earth.
—Chief Seattle

What we had feared earlier becomes reality late this morning. Rain. Cold, forceful, driving rain. The kind that makes you batten down the hatches, zip zippers high, pull the drawstring around your face and walk. Walk to protection. Walk to the few surviving trees. Walk to get warm. I carry the the water bottle up front in a waist pack, along with some high-energy food and the guidebook in a plastic bag. We'll hike until we can't hike anymore. I shove dried pineapple chunks into Todd's mouth while he walks. Up ahead is the roof of Stampede Pass's weather station. There has to be a porch or an old shack that we can crawl into to rest and cook a hot lunch.

The weatherman invites us into the round, metal snow tunnel that connects his house and the station. After we make room by the mop and bucket on the concrete floor, it feels like heaven. The rain is deafening on the corrugated tin.

"How long is this supposed to last?" we ask the expert.

"A few more days. Then maybe a break for a day, and then more rain."

We both make sour faces.

"Get used to it," he adds. "This is September weather in Washington. This weather station was mostly built for small aircraft warnings," he says. "The clouds coming in from the west reach the crest and are pushed up on an angle by the drier, eastern air. Pilots fly just below this cloud mantle. As they approach the mountains from the east, they begin flying downward, find themselves in a canyon and smash into a mountain. We try to prevent that from. . . ."

"Look!" I blurt out. "Blue sky!" Sunshine streams from a small gap in the clouds, but in a matter of seconds, it's gone.

"That's a sucker hole," the weatherman says. "Makes you think the storm is clearing and makes a sucker out of you."

So, it's out into the weather again. The rain comes down even harder. Water coats my thighs with every forward step. Our feet are soaked. Every inch of us is soaked. Our goal is a few more miles to a campsite, but when I struggle for a full five minutes to get the cellophane off a fudge candy and am still unsuccessful, and my hiking stick continually falls from my hand, and my body shakes with uncontrollable shivers, it's time to change plans. Hypothermia is persuasive.

We stumble along deliriously, looking for a place to camp. All we find is a wide piece of trail that needs landscaping before a tent can fit—a job that's turning into a daily chore. Putting up a tent in weather like this requires practiced coordination, for the tent body shouldn't be rained on for long before the fly is attached. I drop my end four times, can't seem to grip it. It's a good thing we stopped when we did.

Into our small tent we dive, along with pads, bags, clothes, stove, cook gear, food, candles, guidebook, toilet paper, and flashlight. Basically, the entire contents of our packs. We stash very heavy, wet boots under the vestibule. Smelly, saturated socks are stuffed inside. Bundled-up rain gear is laid on top of the mess. Just to put on dry clothes feels wonderful. Immediately, we begin to get warm. A hot meal makes us new people. We lie in our bags, warm and full, staring into each other's smiling eyes, while the rain massacres the world outside.

"How much of this can we take?" I ask Todd. "Will we have to live this way for the remaining three weeks to Canada?"

"It could always be worse," he answers, smiling.

"Yeah, all this rain could be snow."

The time could either pass by in a flash or be a total, living hell. It's a good thing Bill went home when he did. He wouldn't have liked this part.

We lie awake nearly all night long. The rain goes from torrential downpours to drips off the trees, sounding like hundreds of popcorn kernels exploding as they hit our drum-tight tent. When the drops hit our dirty pots outside, they make loud metallic pings, ringing six inches from our ears.

In the morning, we do as much as we can to get ready from inside the tent. Todd produces two bread-bag gloves for me. My hands stay warm and only a bit moist, and as long as they hang limp and keep away from the plastic sides, they don't even feel sticky. The only drawback is that one hand smells like fish from the sardine can that was in it and the other smells like Italian spices and garlic.

Thirteen miles to the resort at Snoqualmie Pass. While descending the ski slopes to the pass, we notice the clouds finally begin to break up. We watch them blow away and reveal the jagged mountains ahead. Our eyes widen. Snow! All that rain down here fell as snow up there!

As we walk up to the store, we are still in shock from the snow, thinking how it will change our lives. Then we're hit with another jolt: leaning against the store's outside wall is Bill's pack!

17

The Return of Bill

September 5

It's not the same hike anymore. Gone are the warm, sunny carefree days. Gone are the fun-filled afternoons. Tre and Redman never caught up to us. But Bill is looking for the Mayor. Looking for a good time. Looking very disappointed when he realizes how drastically it's all changed.

The lady at the rock shop-grocery store offers to take our wet, smelly clothes home with her for a fresh laundering. She also checks with the local police for a suitable shelter, and the officer

PCT sign

generously offers "the station." He doesn't normally do this, he says, but with the rain, he makes an exception. Bill will come with us. We expect some vacant, cinder-block building and are overjoyed to see a mobile home with a complete kitchen, beds, running water, and a phone for calling home.

Come morning, strange things begin to occur in Todd's body and mine. We're lightheaded, dizzy, weak. Probably from the lack of food, we decide. We've been up for hours and haven't eaten yet. Our systems are used to having immediate calories. We consume half a loaf of toasted bread and hope it takes care of the problem.

Back in town we perform our usual in-town tasks and prepare for the next stretch. In the grocery store, Todd comes up to me and hands over the items he's carrying. "I've got to go sit down," he says and slumps against the wall in a corner.

"What's the matter, Todd?"

"I'm so tired. My head is killing me and my legs are so weak I can't stand up."

"You sound like you're getting the flu." A few miles too many in wet socks and drenching rain.

Outside, the sucker holes in the sky have closed up.

Rain is pouring down. We must stay another night. Todd can't hike. He can't even stand up! I've got to find that cop!

"I have a big favor to ask you," I begin. "We have a problem. Todd is really sick and we were wondering if we could stay another night."

The uniformed man hesitates, lights a cigarette, and looks deep into my eyes.

I think he doesn't believe me! He's trying to see if I'm lying! I almost tell him to forget it, but it's too important. Todd's health is at stake. This trip is at stake!

Slowly, he says, "I think that will be okay."

I put Todd to bed in our warmest sleeping bag but still he shivers! I pump liquids down his throat, vitamins, penicillin. He usually fights me over taking a single aspirin, but these he swallows without so much as a disapproving look.

Todd's other PCT partner, Jon, lives in Seattle. I call to see if he's around. As soon as he hears where we are, he offers to come get us immediately. We know time is getting short to travel safely in the mountains. Winter is coming and the snow has already started to fly. We've been pushing this last week, for the burden of getting through hangs heavy on our shoulders. I give the phone to Todd.

"You make the decision."

"Okay, come get us."

When he hangs up I deliver a short lecture on how he must promise to rest and not tire himself out while we're there. There will be time for sight-seeing when the trip is over.

A few minutes later, he calls me away from Bill, into the bathroom. To talk in private, I suppose. When I shut the door behind me, I see that he's crying!

"I feel so guilty," he sobs. "I don't know if we should take time off."

"Of course we should." I take him in my arms. "It was the right thing to do."

"When I get better, I'm going to take much more weight so we can go fast and make up for lost time."

"Don't be silly, honey. We'll be fine. Things have always worked out before."

While Bill waited for us these last days, his food supply dwindled, as did his meager funds. We don't feel comfortable asking Todd's friend to take on Bill, too. So I encourage him to visit his sister, who lives close by, figuring he'd be more comfortable there than with strangers.

"You're just trying to get rid of me!" he says abruptly.

"That's not true, Bill," I try to reassure him. I sigh. This is too much to deal with. A sick husband. Rain. A teenager with hurt feelings. Todd and I go off to Jon's; Bill goes to his sister's. We plan to regroup in a few days, hoping that both illness and hurt feelings are healed.

A long ascent out of Snoqualmie Pass up to the Alpine Lakes Wilderness awaits us. We've had no exercise for three days and don't want to overdo it—especially with Todd still not fully recovered and carrying his usual, out-of-town heavy pack. We take it slowly.

The clouds are on the move. They sail at top speed into the mountain, hit it, and then travel straight up its slope and rush over the top. So low. So very quick. It starts to pour a half mile from the road. The three of us struggle to get our packs off

Bill and Todd in Washington's "official uniform"

and our rain gear on. Bill looks terribly unhappy. He pulls on his pants and his shoe gets stuck broadside in the pants leg.

Todd looks at me with sad eyes beneath his green nylon hood. I can see Snoqualmie Pass and the road below him. It's going to be a long week. "Sixty miles to Skykomish!" he says with sarcastic enthusiasm.

We now live to get to the next town or, more realistically, to get through the day. We no longer expect to see blue, sunny skies and doubt if we'll ever see a cloudless day again in Washington.

September 10

The trail through the Alpine Lakes Wilderness goes through rugged, high country. Chiseled out of granite cliffs, it winds among jewel-like tarns and meadows. We, of course, see nothing of the sort. Not even a lake twenty yards away. For the last eight days it has rained, and our existence is hurried, damp, and depressing. The days are getting shorter and with the decreasing light come colder temperatures on top of the never-ending rain. When we're not moving and producing heat, we must be inside our tents, inside our bags. One or the other. Our meals are prepared and eaten within the tent, either lying on our bellies in our bags or sitting in a line. Todd sits up front, where the ceiling is higher. I sit directly behind him, hunched over with my head scraping the roof, which is wet with condensation. All chores must be done from inside the tent and a tent isn't the best place for every chore. Todd shakes up hot gelatin in a plastic bottle. It explodes, splattering scorching liquid and red sugar crystals all over the interior. Mildew is growing on everything. Small, dark blue spots cover my extra clothes, my pad, the tent walls. It all smells musty. We haven't washed for days, nor do we plan to do so until the rain stops. There's no room in the tent to bathe, or even brush out my hair. Each morning I just divide it into three dirty sections and rebraid it. Many mornings I sit up, feeling dizzy and light-headed from lying down for so many hours.

The only happy times we have are spent zipped together in our bags, which are tucked securely around our necks to keep in

Alpine Lakes trail

heat. Our legs intertwine. We hold hands, looking at each other lovingly. Such comfort. Such warmth. The only warmth and comfort present in this life. No matter how bad the day is, we always know we have this to look forward to at the end of the day.

Poor Bill doesn't even have that. He shivers under his tarp and the wind blows rain right in. His head isn't visible. It's pushed way down to the interior of his cheap, thin bag. Curled up in a tight ball, the green lump vibrates pathetically from the cold. He's a lonely, sad boy these days. This life isn't what he expected. Todd and I worry about getting sick, but we worry even more about Bill getting hypothermia.

We take lunch and rest stops in the sucker holes. Sometimes they only last a few minutes. Entire days can go by without ever taking our packs off for a decent break. This is one such day.

"I wish my pack would break so I could go home," says the unhappy lad, stumbling along in his camouflage rain suit.

"You know, Bill, sometimes it takes more courage and personal strength to go home than remain in a situation where you really don't wish to be." No comment. Bill is giving in to depression, which can break a person.

Quitting is difficult to do. No one feels good about it. It's like divorce. Once the break is made, most people usually don't go back. So we stick with it, through the hard times, hoping it will get better. As long as there's a glimmer of hope and an ounce of energy, we must keep trying.

These are hard times. Todd and I have been trying to stay chipper, singing songs about rain when it pours and Christmas carols on the snow-swept summits. Trying to maintain our sense of humor. We crack sometimes. This morning I cried in my cereal. I'd had enough and didn't want to go out there and do it all again.

Todd says, "We're not in danger, only discomfort. We can get through. Come on." My smile encourages him. "Get psyched! Canada is within reach."

This is where the passion comes in, the quest for the higher goal. Every day we manage to get through brings us one step closer to reaching our dream. Nothing else can carry us through times like this, for our day-to-day existence leaves a lot to be desired.

The weather give us glimpses every now and then of what the dramatic country around Lemah Mountain looks like. Cloud curtains are raised and lowered throughout the day, and every act features five-star performers. Icy cliffs, jagged pinnacles, cascading waterfalls, razor-backed ridges — all float in and out of a sea of low, overhanging clouds. It's all very alluring and mysterious, for you never know when a magnificent view will appear and then disappear seconds later. I tend to trip when these shows are held and am so amazed at what beauty is out there. I sometimes think I like these tantalizing glimpses even more than a constant diet of clear views — minus the rain, of course. They are so infrequent, so special that no matter how short-lived each one is a prize.

The sun is no longer our enemy, but a fond, long-lost friend. We cheer and root for it when it gets high in the afternoon sky and kicks into full force, trying to evaporate the clouds. It often looks like it may be winning, but the clouds always prevail. A few times

a day it breaks through, just to let us know it's still there and trying with all its might, telling us not to give up or lose hope.

Today it's finally won. The sun comes out for five minutes, ten
minutes, then fifteen minutes! The temperature rises quickly inside our official Washington uniform (coated nylon and Gore-
tex), but we still don't trust it. After half an hour, we finally take
off our rain pants. We let the rays warm our skin for the first time
in over a week. In the heavens tonight, billions of stars come out.
The long, hard war may be over.

The sun looks so incredibly beautiful this morning. It's as
though I've never seen the early dawn. I want to look everywhere
at the same time—every piece of moss, every plant, every rock
glows with a warmth and color I'd forgotten existed in this uni-
verse. I want to photograph everything. The meadows in the Alpine Lakes Wilderness are ablaze with crimson. The cold front
made the foliage take on a breath-taking brilliance. Oh, the rain
was worth it if that was what we had to experience in order to
have this. My eyes have become unclouded. My spirit is sharp,
quickened, excited, like the crisp, clean air after a storm. Todd
walks toward me on the trail, without his pack.

"Oh, no! Have I been taking too long again?" I ask.

"No," he answers. "I came back so that I could see you. Besides, I want to be with you when you see Deep Lake. It's so
green! And Cathedral Rock towers right over it!" We hold hands
and walk to the lake.

This is no ordinary high, alpine lake. This one has deep, emerald waters and diamonds of sunlight dancing on its surface. We
haven't seen the likes of it in weeks! I will live these days in the
sun as though they are my last, for they very well could be. Thank
you, for even a taste. We've been thirsty for this for so long.

You'd think nothing could mar my feelings of wonderment
and joy on a day like this, but Bill is working on my nerves. He
hikes right at Todd's heels, pushing Todd smack up against me. I
feel like a locomotive with runaway cattle cars behind. When
Todd and I talk, we have to yell so that Bill can hear too and not
feel left out. If we discuss someone or something that he's not fa-

miliar with, we must explain everything so he understands the conversation. He wants to be with us all the time and, frankly, I'd like to be alone with Todd sometimes.

During our week alone, Todd and I experienced an intimacy of minds and hearts that we didn't have when hiking with the group. We shared the kind of communication that goes beyond words. We've begun to function as one again and experience the unbelievable closeness that this life can bring to a couple in love. We don't want to lose it.

In camp tonight, I say to Bill, "If we get behind, don't worry. We'll be along. We just enjoy being alone sometimes."

"I got the hint," he says.

Todd and Cindy

"You have to understand, we're still newlyweds."

"It's okay," he tries to assure me, but I know it's not. He looks all choked up. I hate to hurt his feelings, but like a lot of seventeen-year-olds, he's not yet sensitive to others' need for space. He goes on ahead.

At lunch, Todd is very unhappy. "I'm sick of this gross potted meat," he says, throwing the tin out of the lunch sack. "Not only do I have to eat the crap, but I have to taste it the rest of the day when I belch! I hate this sickening sweet drink mix," he snaps, throwing down the heavy envelope. "And I hate to carry all this weight!"

I watch his performance, which is quite unusual for him, and smile to myself. I've been saving chocolate pudding mix. When he realizes what I'm making, he flings me down on his lap, nearly knocking the bottle over, kisses me all over my face, and refuses to let me up.

Bill's new independence only lasts for the early part of the afternoon. Later in the day, we drop into Stevens Pass and must hitch a ride into the town of Skykomish to resupply. We encourage Bill to continue, instead of waiting by the road for hours. At this particular rare moment, it's not raining. He'd be smart to get some dry miles down while he can. Tomorrow we'll catch him.

Nope, he's going into town, too.

"Well, we better hitch separately," Todd says. "Three people with three large packs take up the space of six in a car. We'll never get a ride together."

Todd and I walk about fifty yards away from him. Town! A visit to town! And it's not even raining. Todd and I get a ride quickly and our good luck adds to our growing cheery mood.

Skykomish, which is a few miles west of Stevens Pass and the PCT, is having a celebration. "A Diamond in the Sky—75th Birthday." The whole village is out on the main street. While young men struggle up the greased pole, firemen battle with water hoses, and kids try their luck at throwing darts at balloons. A country band plays on the platform. A yellow-haired cowgirl in tight jeans, fringed glitter shirt, cowboy hat, and boots, serenades a bunch of goo-goo-eyed old-timers. Her band is a group of unusually clean-cut, short-haired musicians. When I see "U.S. Air Force" stamped in white on their black equipment cases, it becomes clear.

The restaurant in town was once a red-light retreat for hungry loggers and railroaders building the tracks over the Cascade pass. After quieting our stomachs with a great meal, we look for the cheapest shower in town. The hotel at the far end of town (two blocks away) has a community washroom, one tub for an entire floor of roomers. We get the key and walk up the narrow, dark stairway, wooden steps creaking under our loads, to the bathroom at the end of the hall. The door swings open and we see the longest, widest, deepest claw-foot bathtub we've ever seen! Let's hop in together!

While the tub fills, we look around the room. Cracked, old-fashioned linoleum is pieced together on the floor. Over the sink, a mirror is stuck to the wall with wide masking tape. An old bureau sits in the corner. The small window by the toilet is open and doesn't have a screen. Dingy lace curtains blow in from the breeze. You can see out past the tarred roof and crooked brick chimney down to the street, where Bill stands, listening to the cowgirl belt out an old Tom Jones favorite, "Release Me." That's exactly how we feel, as we rip off our filthy trail clothes and climb into the warm, incredibly deep bath water. Todd takes the side with the faucets—one very hot metal knob against his back, one very cold metal knob. We settle in, bodies completely submerged to our necks and forget all about the rainy trail, the heavy packs, and Bill.

The last volcano that we'll personally encounter on our long trek north is Glacier Peak, named for the abundance of snow and ice covering its flanks. In our traverse around its base, we cannot stay at a constant six thousand feet. There's too much snow and the avalanche danger is too great. The canyons radiating from its summit are so deep, so glaciated, that the PCT has no choice but to dive down to the depths of the rain-forested canyons and then labor up to exposed, wind-swept passes. Hundreds of switchbacks cut into one wall and they look like giant zigzags stitched to the forested slopes. We spend an entire morning climbing three thousand feet to the pass. That entire afternoon is spent braking down and losing three thousand feet, while covering only two air miles!

With the exception of the High Sierra, we find the most rugged and difficult hiking in this section of the North Cascades.

The rugged terrain is really taking its toll on Bill. He hasn't been too spunky these last days as we struggled over White Pass, Red Pass, Fire Creek Pass. He says absolutely nothing on breaks, keeps to himself, and collapses as soon as we stop. There he lies, not moving a muscle, until Todd and I get up to hike. He says he feels exhausted. The sun has been out and we've been sweating profusely since we entered the rugged Glacier Peak Wilderness. I stop him at a creek crossing and don't allow him to go by.

"Eat salt, Bill."

"Yes, Ma'am," he replies.

Mushrooms

He hasn't been eating or drinking much lately. Just seems obsessed with how much trail remains until the end.

The trail is extremely rugged and has been hard on me, too. All this way, all these miles, and I don't feel strong yet. We are all so tired at the end of the day that we don't even notice the strange fog rolling in as we traverse around a high ridge. Not until it gets so thick that we can barely see twenty feet in front of us, do we snap out of our delirium.

"What's going on here?" says Todd, stopping on the trail. "It's six o'clock in the evening. The sun is so obscured that it looks like night is falling."

"Do you smell smoke?" I ask. "It smells like smoke."

"Look up," says Bill. "The sky overhead is blue. This is coming from down in the valley."

Six to eight marmots stand up and whistle their shrill warning. The animals always know when something is not right. We hike on, hoping to hike out of this basin and into a clear one. What if it's a forest fire? I think. What would we do? There are tons of trails in this wilderness. What if we're walking down into a fire? I turn around and see Todd. His brow is deeply furrowed and tensed. "I don't like this at all," he admits.

Supper is tense. We watch the smoke rolling in overhead.

"I'm not very hungry," says my normally starving husband, and he dumps his meal back into the pot. In our tent, Todd says he plans to stay awake most of the night and check to see if it gets worse. He sniffs occasionally. But exhaustion overcomes us and we all sleep soundly, despite our fear of a forest fire.

Come morning, all traces of the smoky mystery are gone. When we come across the trail ranger later in the day, he explains: "They were burning down in the valley. The Forest Service does this from time to time to rid the forest floor of underbrush. It prevents disastrous forest fires from occurring." Mystery solved: a controlled burn had gotten out of control.

We are actually sweating as we traverse around Glacier Peak. Day after day we awake to cloudless, brilliant days, warming sun, and a riot of autumn color. I would never believe, coming from the East, that so much color could be present in a dark green conifer forest, but it's the forest floor, the meadows, not the trees, that vibrate with dazzling hues. It looks as though a scotch-plaid blanket has been thrown over the land—reds, oranges, yellows, greens. The late evening sun has taken on a much warmer quality. During the day, huckleberry bushes look dark purple. But with the setting sun behind them, they flame!

The forested canyons are the most lush and dense I've seen. Moss covers everything. Objects lose their identity and become part of the bumpy, forested floor. One long-dead, fallen hemlock has dozens of tiny seedlings sprouting out of its mossy top, almost as though it's growing a thick head of hair. The mushrooms have risen to the occasion. Bright orange, miniature toadstools march along the green carpet. Cream-colored coral lichen look like large sponges. Two white mushrooms push their heads above the pine needles. The whole earth seems to be erupting with life and color.

The expected change in the weather doesn't make us slow our pace nor relax our mileage. How long can Indian summer last? One week? Two? Thanks to the rain, we've developed a hiking style that we can't seem to shake. We hike fast in the morning because in the afternoon we could well be slogging through rain. A hunter in the mountains asked us if we were in some sort of race, this hike from Mexico to Canada. Yes, a race with the weather. My endurance seems to have peaked from the prolonged stretches of hiking in the rain with no rests. It's either genuine stamina or fear-produced adrenalin that keeps us pushing.

Bill is keeping up, but he's like the walking dead, moving as though in a coma. He asks the same questions every day: "How far are we going? Where are we having lunch? Where are we camping tonight?" His biggest obsession though is "How many miles are left to Canada?"

Today I take the guidebook and throw it at him. "Here, check it out yourself." He discovers that our last stretch—from Stehekin north—is quite high and that scares him.

"We could get caught on a ridge in a snowstorm and get two to three feet dumped on us and not be able to get down!"

"That's right," we answer. "It's something to get scared about."

Before, Bill didn't believe that snow would be a problem. Now, his all-encompassing fear forces him to attach himself to us like a parasite, in rain and in shine. When we sit, he sits. When we get up to walk, he gets up to walk, without speaking a word. It's been grating on me for days and has caused friction between Todd and me.

For some time I've wanted to talk with Bill, to frankly but gently ask him to give me some much-needed space. Todd rejects the whole idea. He doesn't think it's right to tell someone how to hike, fast or slow, just because we want to be alone. But tonight, when I have to explain to Bill that I'm moving our tent ten yards away from his, so my husband and I can make love for the first time in weeks. . . it's more than I can handle. In the privacy of our tent, my frustration and anger spew out like hot lava.

"Bill has the freedom to do as he chooses," I shout. "He sticks to us like glue. We have absolutely none, no choice whatsoever. It's not fair!"

The next morning, we awake to soft rain beating on our tent. It adds to my already gloomy mood. I ask Todd to go ahead. "I want to talk to Bill."

"Please try to say the right things," he pleads.

"I will."

Calling Bill aside, I begin by telling him that I'd like us to feel closer.

"If there has been any time lately that you've felt us pulling away from you," I explain, "or if we've hurt you, it's only because it's been exceptionally difficult for the three of us to be constantly living so close together. Before, in the group, there were enough other people for you to hike with, so that Todd and I could be alone sometimes. When we invited you to come back, we imagined a different set-up. We expected you to function as a separate unit, sometimes to go off on your own. We thought we'd be together much of the time, but not every day, all day."

"I figured I was with you two," he says, "so I'd do and go wherever you went. I like company."

"I know how you feel," I assure him. "I've never enjoyed hiking alone either, but there's a certain amount of space that long-distance hikers need—especially couples—and we're not getting it."

"Lots of times," he says, "I felt like you were giving me the shaft, like Tre."

"That's not true!" I say, hurrying to his side and hugging him. "We just need some time alone every now and then."

"I understand. I'll go on ahead now," he says, as we catch up to Todd, who's waiting by the trail. "I'll see you two later."

"You don't have to leave now, Bill," I say. But he's gone, probably feeling hurt. Todd looks at me questioningly. "Well, how did it go?"

"Okay. He says he understands."

On the way up to Suiattle Pass, we notice that the bushes all have slushy, frozen water lying in their leaves. Climbing higher, we watch helplessly as the rain changes to sleet, then snow. On top of the pass, where we enter North Cascades National Park, we're in a blizzard. We walk with our heads low, our parka hoods pulled over our faces. We look up only on occasion and only to see where the trail goes next.

Our route descends along Agnes Creek to a National Park Service road connecting the town of Stehekin to walk-in campsites in the heart of the North Cascades. At dusk we still haven't caught up with Bill, so we make camp. On our way into town the next day, Todd and I speculate how he'll act when we see him. Will he mention our little talk, or say anything to us at all?

Lady of the Lake, *Stehekin*

18

The Last Skies

September 22

Stehekin, "the way through." Sitting on the edge of North Cascades National Park, Stehekin is the last resupply point on the Pacific Crest Trail. It pierces the North Cascades and is the way through to the very heart of the wilderness. No road connects this town to the outside world. Most people get there by seaplane or boat. A few walk. Every day, the *Lady of the Lake* leaves

293

the town of Chelan on the lake's southernmost tip and heads for Stehekin. Travelers begin their voyage in a dry, irrigated landscape and watch the mountains grow and close in around them, until they're surrounded by rugged, steep-sided, glacier-mantled peaks.

If no roads lead to this mountain-locked village, then why are there cars and trucks driving around the one-street town? All the automobiles were brought in on the barge, which comes every Thursday of the week. For that matter, nearly everything in this town came on the barge: horses, lumber, washing machines. The town folk send grocery lists and blank checks to Chelan, and their groceries are picked out, packed, and arrive in boxes.

The people who reside in Stehekin year-round live a simple, spartan lifestyle. There are only a few radio phones, although the National Park Service, a dominant presence in the town, has a solar phone. There's a camera store and outdoor shop, a rustic resort lodge, a restaurant, a bakery, and a family-run lodge that offers horse pack trips and down-home dinners. That's about it. Many residents make crafts, artwork, cookbooks—anything and everything to sell to the tourists. They are a close-knit group, a town in which folks visit, hold quilting parties, and winter book swaps.

Summer is the busy time of the year, as the *Lady of the Lake* brings fishermen, backpackers, and tourists deep into the North Cascades. Park Service shuttle vans transport hikers, campers, and sightseers up and down the dirt road that starts in Stehekin and dead-ends in the heart of the mountains. Todd and I pile into one of the shuttle vans on a damp and drizzly day in late September.

Our last adventure in a trail town.

As the big metal door rolls sideways, a half dozen smiles greet us. Our soaking wet Washington uniforms are dripping. The heat is on high and most everyone else looks like drowned rats too.

Little, four-inch peep holes are wiped away on the foggy windows so the boarders can see the scenery going by. We just think about town. We ask the park ranger driving the van about accommodations.

"Except for the lodge, Purple Point Campground offers rustic tent sites," she answers. We've been chilled for days and our gear can't get much wetter, so we cruise into town convinced that there is an alternative shelter somewhere with our names on it. We spot a few and file them away for future reference.

When we get into town, there's no sign of Bill. By asking around we learn that he left on the last boat out the day before.

Public showers cost a quarter for only a few minutes. The same six-foot by twelve-foot building houses the public laundry. After picking up supplies, we head for the heated haven, promising the town new people when we emerge.

An older couple comes in and they frown at us. I smile and say "Hi." My hair is wet and stringy, and all I'm wearing is my rain jacket. All other clothes are being washed. They spy our piles of dirty laundry, the smell of which is intensified by the heat, and make a face. It smells like the garments are cooking. In an effort to organize, we've dumped our packs' contents and supplies all over the floor, for the rain falls madly outside. I scurry around, consolidating the mess and being extremely careful not to bend over. "Sorry, folks, there's nowhere else to go."

Next a couple much like ourselves enters. The guy looks at me and says, "I know you from somewhere."

"Oh, yeah?"

"From the Appalachian Trail. In Maine, in 1979. I spent the night with you in the last shelter."

All these years later and we both happen to be in this tiny, mountain-locked town and come into the laundry room to take a shower at the exact same time! Strangely enough, his name is Todd, too, and his girlfriend's name is Cindy! We decide to spend the evening together over dinner at the Courtney Ranch.

The owner's son shuttles dinner-goers back and forth to the ranch. He reminds me of Hoss on the TV show *Bonanza*. After a wonderful meal, he takes us back and directs us to the campground, which is where the other Todd and Cindy are staying and where he assumes we'll be spending the night. As soon as the van's headlights vanish, leaving only inky darkness, Todd and I turn around and head in another direction.

We first saw the cabin early this afternoon, when we came in on the Park Service shuttle. When we asked the ranger about it, she said, "It's for tourists, so they can see the type of home the settlers lived in." The cabin is so close to the ranger's house that we can't just stroll up the walk at this time of night. We decide to go around and go in from the other side, through a dark patch of woods. Her lights are on inside and it looks like she has company. Good! Distractions. We turn our flashlights off and carry our boots and sticks. Todd walks much too fast for me and, in my haste, I slip on a wet rock and fall. Her dog starts to bark! The outside light is thrown on! I lay there and wait, breathless. Todd freezes in his steps, hiding behind a tree. Soon everything quiets down and we make our way to the porch, through the front door and into the back room. The room is separated from the main room by a makeshift door of fabric, stretched meagerly across the opening, leaving three-inch gaps on either side and a full foot gap off the floor. The place is filthy. We move cobwebs and mouse droppings away and lay out our pads and bags. It's dry!

Very early in the morning, we're awakened by footsteps on the gravel path leading to the cabin. Oh, no! We stayed in bed too long! Don't move and don't breathe! Two white-haired ladies in orthopedic shoes and rain hats enter the main room. Oh, God! What if it's a tour and the ranger is accompanying them! The two sets of shoes chatter nonstop about the one's sick cousin, and we pray they don't become interested in what's behind the curtain. The shoes move closer, only inches from our bags. They stop, but the talking doesn't. They turn and move on, and we breathe a sigh of relief.

We pack up in haste and run to the road before there are any more close calls.

We meet two end-to-enders in Stehekin, guys who walked straight through from south to north. Their buddies from Alaska joined them to hike this last stretch. While listening to their traveling adventures, we learn that they saw a pathetic-looking hiker in the Seattle bus station. He wore a plastic garbage bag for a rain jacket. He sat, soaked and shivering, waiting for the bus to take him home. He seemed totally disoriented.

"What did he look like?" we ask.

"He had long red hair tied back in a ponytail and wore wire-rim glasses."

"Redman! That's our poor Mayor!"

The outdoor store has just posted their "New Winter Hours." Last week, they had summer hours up. What happened to fall? When we hear the weather report at the park headquarters and learn that there is an "unseasonal snowstorm" on its way, adding to the eighteen inches already up there, we know what has happened to fall. It was skipped! The postmistress says that as fast as packages arrive, she's returning them. No hikers that we know of are coming up from behind. Bill went home. Tre probably did too by now. And Redman. The four guys we just met aren't too concerned about the present conditions or the bad forecast. We know how bad it can get. Canada seems close, but the last seventy miles could be hell. No matter if it's PCT, alternate route, or road, we're getting to that Canadian border!

After saying our good-byes to the other Todd and Cindy, who are heading home, we make our way up to Stehekin Valley. There, we meet a trail crew, who warn us that it could get very bad up there and to be aware of serious traverses around Cutthroat Pass. They throw another log on our growing fire of fear.

September 24

Glacier-carved Stehekin Valley is U-shaped. It's open and brushy down below and gives clear views to the towering peaks above. There is snow up there, lots of it. Ice coats the branches of the trees on this twenty-degree morning. The sky started out blue and cloudless, but high cirrus clouds are moving in. The front they talked about is arriving.

Friends of friends live down the road from Rainy Pass on the North Cascades Highway. Normally, we wouldn't feel that a rest stop is in order only one day from town, but as the clouds crowd the sky for space and the temperature drops, we feel the need for advice. Alternate routes, bail-out points, places of extraordinary danger. Ron works for the Forest Service and knows these mountains better than most.

His girlfriend, Mary Ann, greets us with open arms and invites us into their simple home, as though we're kin. An antique wood cookstove glows in the corner, bouquets of dried flowers hang from the rafters, a spinning wheel sits in the corner, holding yarn made from their Samoyed's hair. Shabby, comfortable furniture, a patchwork quilt on the wall, dinner with warm cups of tea and tongue-loosening wine sets the mood. We pore over maps with Ron as he points out side trails and the advantages and disadvantages of each. He stars the places we can expect trouble and makes countless phone calls for a true weather forecast. We get a good, solid snow report from foresters who have

Mary Ann and Ron

just come out of the mountains. I call home and find that my family and all my relatives have been glued to the eleven o'clock weather, connected to us by that face on the screen.

September 25

The next morning, Ron and Mary Ann cannot bear to leave us on the road alone, so they both call in sick and accompany us the five miles up to Cutthroat Pass. Moral support. We pile into their junker pickup and head up into the mountains.

"Look, that peak isn't even covered," Ron announces. "You guys will be okay." Todd and I say nothing. We saw the trees on the pass, shrouded in wet, white snow. It hangs on them like cloaks, so thick that their green boughs are barely visible. Nobody's positive wishes can convince us that we will be all right. We just don't know. Nobody knows.

The sky is congested with low, dark, snow-packed clouds. What could it do to us? Strand us? Freeze us? Drive us home before we reach our goal? My mind turns the same thoughts and same fears over and over. Once again, I feel unsure, unstable, uncomfortable, so downright scared.

Chatter slows down to a few brief comments as the four of us climb higher toward Cutthroat Pass. The snow grows deeper and deeper: six inches, twelve inches, eighteen inches. We are placing our feet in boot-holes made by the previous four hikers. Petite Mary Ann sinks in to her upper thighs.

At the top of the pass, we all stop and stare in silence. I've never seen a more hostile looking world. Jagged, gray peaks are drowned in snow. Darker gray clouds rumble with thunder in the heavens. They're warning us. Go down! You don't belong up here! Can't you see the season has changed?

I look over at Ron and Mary Ann. They seem so forlorn, as though they're somehow responsible. We all know it's not going to be okay. Mary Ann shivers in her parka, and I shiver with fear. We embrace and look into each other's eyes. I want them to take me back, but we turn and walk away quickly, not knowing how much time remains before we aren't able to move. Ten miles to our first bail-out route. Ten miles! It looks like it's ready to storm any second. I race along the snow-covered traverse, trying to put the miles behind as fast as I possibly can.

Todd notices my abnormal pace and asks, "Are you scared, honey?"

"Yes."

"You can cry if you want to."

"Don't worry," I answer, as tears fill my eyes.

Cutthroat Pass. How I hate the place. The snow drifts across the traverse. Still I push through, quickly. I am afraid of a white-out. Afraid of getting stuck up here in blowing, piling up snow with no place to camp, for who knows how many days. Fear is pushing me through this.

Camp tonight is low, back in the season of autumn. The colorful, changing leaves are a comfort. With only four days to go, we find that getting to the border is an all-engrossing task. It's all I think about. It's our pot of gold at the end of the rainbow. Walking to Monument 78 at the Canadian border means more to me than anything I've ever done in my life. It has certainly been my most eagerly and persistently sought-after goal, the most difficult, the most energy consuming. Four days. Only four days. But four days are an eternity if they're crowded with fear and uncertainty.

September 26

We awake to falling snow. Today's bail-out point is memorized—as is every day's. The four guys camped near us last night and left about an hour ago. I watch how fast their prints fill with rapidly falling crystals.

On our ascent to Glacier Pass, I walk up switchbacks that are so tight that I feel like the steel ball in a pinball machine. We keep our heads low to guard against the driving snow. To keep my mind occupied, I repeat catechism prayers that I learned in grade school, but I get stuck on one Hail Mary for fifteen minutes. My thoughts drift to steep traverses, buried trail. A good title for the book flashes in my mind. How about *Death March—A Walk From Mexico to Canada*. Oh, I'm tired. We're pushing to get somewhere,

Cutthroat Pass

farther, and we are wearing ourselves out trying.

Breaks are even shorter now than when it rained, for there is no place that's dry. Snow is everywhere above the treeline. Our feet have never been colder. The snow lies on top of our leathered toes and melts. When we take breaks, our feet just hang in there, freezing, as soon as the motion stops. The only color in this winter landscape is provided by the golden alpine larches. Their ocher color is striking, even in driving snow. If not for them, this entire scene would look like a black and white photograph.

On a knife-edged ridge, a three-foot cornice has blown into shape and already hardened for the winter. Thick fog and blowing snow conceal any stomach-dropping sights we may have seen. It's just as well. These mountains are far too rugged and inhospitable to look at under these conditions.

Harts Pass tonight. Halfway in. We're in as deep as we can get from the North Cascade highway. The end is just as far ahead as the road is behind us. In camp, the snow turns to hail and then finally stops. Soon a few stars poke out, but we're not fooled. Should it clear, unbelievably low temperatures will follow. Even now we sleep with all our clothes and rain gear on. Once again, we memorize our bail-out route for tomorrow. These advance plans add a fragment of strength.

September 27

Is twelve degrees cold enough to be considered winter camping? I want to go south this winter! The snow cracks under our feet. Boots, bottles, rain fly — all freeze solid. Oatmeal cools off in the time it takes to lift my spoon and carry it the short distance to my lips. The pain in our feet is severe as we shove them into frozen socks and boots. They hurt even more when we put pressure on them, force them to bend and carry us up the mountain.

The sun has come out, but it doesn't make the cold any more bearable. We're wearing all our clothes. I put my gloved hand up to shield my face from the blustery, blowing wind and look back to see the wild North Cascades that we just walked through. It

The Pasayten Wilderness

makes me shudder. Since crossing Harts Pass, we've noticed a definite change in the mountains. They are gentler, not nearly so craggy and forbidding. We have entered the Pasayten Wilderness. The actual Cascade crest continued straight, but the PCT has veered to the east. Mount Baker and the horrendous Picket Range shield us a bit from the storm. Our mountains look like waves high in the sky, swelling and getting ready to curl and break.

Todd lies by my side, sleeping, while I write. His eyes and mouth are part open and through his mouth comes a soft snore, the way he always sleeps when he's extremely tired. His rust-colored wool balaclava is pulled around his forehead, cheeks, and neck. It's as familiar to me as his hair used to be, for I rarely see his bare head anymore. Our clothes are falling apart. Todd's shorts are downright indecent. My underpants have holes in them almost as big as the leg openings. Our sleeping bags' interiors have completely changed from a medium blue to dirt brown. It's time to go home.

Today is the first day we've considered life after Monument 78. We are a little more confident that we may make it. Only six end-to-enders have made it so far. Everyone we hiked with bailed out when they reached their personal limits. The ones who will make it are the ones who have the passion, the dream to reach the end. No one else in his right mind would put himself through it.

September 28

Early this morning, we begin our climb up to Rocky Pass. We walk on two-inch-thick hoarfrost. The frozen, upward-reaching crystals have lifted small stones away from the ground. The frozen strings are solid and support our weight. Deer and marten tracks are deep and well preserved in the now-frozen ground, like star handprints on the sidewalks of Hollywood.

We have been following the footprints of those four guys ever since Stehekin and have been most grateful for their guiding steps. They show the way, reassuring us that they got through and continued on. We follow them from Rocky Pass toward Woody Pass and become so accustomed to being led that we pay little attention to where the trail is actually going. Two of these guys are almost twenty-six-hundred milers, their footprints are to be trusted.

I don't think much of it when I step across the three small fallen trees across the trail. Strange for trees to be lying here, almost obstructing the way. Still, I ignore it and continue after the boot prints. Todd ignores it, too, follows me and makes no mention of it. The trail degenerates as we traverse around the precipitous slopes of Powder Mountain. Before we even reach snow, the danger becomes great. Our feet walk on a wildly angling trail, forcing our worn-down boot cleats to grip beyond their capabilities. Loose scree and rocks clutter the trail. Something seems wrong.

We never saw the trail this eroded. It's not safe anymore.

"I don't like this, Todd. The trail is really in bad shape. Barely any bed."

"I don't think this is the trail."

We look it up in the guidebook and sure enough it's been abandoned. We very cautiously turn around and see the PCT switchback down an avalanche bowl. A faint indentation still comes through on the slope, pristine and unmarred. No boots went that way.

Todd is upset with me for refusing to go across this rotten, abandoned trail, which is considerably shorter than the actual PCT. We will add miles to our day by going back and retracing our steps. I know the other guys made it but it doesn't seem worth it to me. Not on the last day of our hike. But mostly Todd is upset with himself, for not listening to his own intuition when he saw the logs across the trail.

I lead the way across the bowl until the snow gets deeper and the slope steeper. We are at the head of an avalanche area and can look down and trace its regular path for miles. Thousands of trees have been wiped out in a funnel-shaped design when avalanches have roared down the mountain in previous winters. My fear begins to grow. I let Todd go first. Footprints aren't enough. He acts

Todd plowing a trail

as a plow – dragging his outside foot horizontally as his inner leg cuts deep into the bowl's side, making the bed wide enough for me to walk on. His bare thighs are scraped raw from the cold and cutting crust.

Where would I be were it not for him? All the crying he put up with, my slow pace, my endless picture taking, doing so many of the chores so I could be free to record this trip. He is the very reason I am going to reach Canada.

If something had happened to him along the way, say, if he'd fallen again and had to return home, I would not have continued on alone. Nor would he have gone on without me. Reaching the end would not have mattered anymore. We're partners. We're a team. Getting to Canada for one of us is important only if the other is by our side.

After we get across the bowl, we examine the map for more north-facing slopes. Devil's Staircase is a narrow segment of trail that makes tight switchbacks down a knife-edged, north-facing point.

That is it. After this it will all be over. We'll head downhill into less and less snow. We'll be on our way to the border and safety. But Devil's Staircase is the highest point on the route since Dana Yelverton shelter back in the Goat Rocks Wilderness.

"DAMMIT!" shouts Todd, as he peers over the edge. "It's drifted shut!" He very cautiously swims through the waist-deep snow, slipping a few times and going dangerously close to the edge. Even now, on our last day, we have to work so hard. I grit my teeth and follow. This is the last time I have to do this shit!

As soon as we get down the staircase, we race. We can see the border swath in the forest on the mountain across from us, the dividing line between the two countries. We race toward it—no lingering, no holding back, no attempt to stall.

At last we arrive at the pointed metal monument, breathless. We have made it!

Stepping into Canada, we take pictures, uncork champagne, hug, toast, and hurry on our way. Once we're out of the mountains, in Vancouver, we'll really celebrate by taking a cruise ship through the San Juan Islands to Seattle.

The first thing the ranger at Canada's Manning Provincial Park tells us is that we must travel one hundred miles down the road to let the officials know we're in the country. But we're leaving tomorrow! Then we learn that the last bus of the day heading for Vancouver arrives in five minutes at the bus stop down the road. And the cruise ship leaves on its last voyage of the season tomorrow! We must be on that bus!

We race down the road. The bus is sitting there, waiting to pull away. We stash our packs beneath the bus. The door opens. We climb the step and stare down the dim aisle. There are faces— empty, staring faces. They look at us but see nothing. We look back. We still ride on the crest of a world where feelings run deep and perceptions are always vivid.

We sit up front so we can see where we're going. While waiting to pull out, the driver starts to chatter. At first, we like his friendliness. But then, suddenly, his tone of voice changes and the words that come out of his mouth are memorized phrases

Todd and Cindy at Monument 78

from the Bible. He says them so quickly that we are in shock. He repeats, "Do you believe? Do you believe? Do you believe?"

Do I believe in what? I say to myself. Believe that the weather has a will of its own and the sun will finally come out? Believe in people that give their all, like Milt Kenny, and Ron and Mary Ann? Believe in my husband and love and sacrifice and dedication? Believe in horse angels and that God will take care of us? Believe that dreams really do come true?

It's more than Todd and I can take. We stagger through the narrow aisle and look for other seats.

People's arms and legs hang out in the aisle. Their heads droop with drowsiness and boredom. The only vacant seats are back in the smoking section. The air is so thick and stale that we can scarcely breathe.

Above the idling drone of the diesel, we hear hacking smokers' coughs. We slide into empty seats in the back. No pines. No breeze. The air is dead and motionless. Our legs, which carried us through eternity, are now cramped and constrained by the seat in front of us. Our bodies are confined but our spirits still soar. The passion, the wildness recoils and resists. There is a sudden surge, a rumble of the engine. The bus shakes and begins to roll forward. Our eyes meet and well with tears.

> *What they had done, what they had seen, heard, felt,*
> *feared—the places, the sounds, the colors, the cold, the*
> *darkness, the emptiness, the bleakness, the beauty. Till they*
> *died this stream of memory would set them apart, if*
> *imperceptibly to anyone but themselves, from everyone else.*
> —Bernard DeVoto

Epilogue

Todd and I are now in the midst of another adventure, an immobile journey. We're building a log home entirely by ourselves, using raw trees. We attended log-building school in northern Minnesota, where we learned the Scandinavian scribed-fit method of log construction, which uses only hand tools and chain saws.

We're doing all our own block work, brick work, electrical, plumbing, and septic tank work. It will all take a few years but we've stopped asking, "Is it all worth it?" Just as we did on the trail when times were rough. The trail taught us that dreams are worth it. Life is empty otherwise.

As we build, the lessons of the trail give us strength. While we were hiking, we tried not to dwell on the entire hike, the thousands of miles before us, the far-fetched goal of reaching Canada.

Instead, we took each day as it came. Now, we're applying that same attitude to our building. Take care of today. Figure out how to move that six-foot log now. Not the 32-footer that will come later.

What I was afraid of when I left for California that second year—when I looked into my father's eyes—came true upon our return. When I saw him again, I immediately told Todd, "He doesn't look good. He looks old and tired." We soon discovered that he had cancer; he died six months later. The trail helped me with that too. Living so close to the natural world helped me understand the life cycles of all living things, that we are directly connected to the earth and one another, and that death is an important and precious part of our existence. On the trail we had to do without our loved ones. We had to learn to rely on ourselves much of the time. We also learned to handle stress, difficulties, dangers. Life wasn't easy out there, so when life isn't easy here, back home, we can cope much better.

While we build our home, we are caretaking a National Park property right on the Appalachian Trail in Pennsylvania. One of our barns has been converted into an overnight shelter for Through-hikers. In this way, we are still in the mainstream of long-distance hiking and have a little of the hikers' spirit and energy touch our lives.

Todd is ready to start his own woodworking shop, designing and making furniture. I'm making paintings. And when the last log is lifted we will be ready to make babies.

Other books from The Mountaineers include:

TWO WHEELS & A TAXI: A Slightly Daft Adventure in the Andes, by Virginia Urrutia. A freewheeling exploration of Ecuador, by a 70-year-old grandmother on a bicycle, with her "support vehicle" — a local taxi driver-cum-guide, occasional translator and bodyguard.

KEEP IT MOVING: Baja by Canoe, by Valerie Fons. A compelling story of personal growth and partnership during a 2,411-mile journey around the Baja Peninsula by canoe.

MILES FROM NOWHERE: A Round-the-World Bicycle Adventure, by Barbara Savage. Best-selling account of the Savages' 2-year, 23,000-mile, 25-country tour as heard on NPR's "Radio Reader."

ON TOP OF THE WORLD: Five Women Explorers in Tibet, by Luree Miller. Adventures of Nina Mazuchelli, Annie Taylor, Isabella Bird Bishop, Fanny Bullock Workman and Alexandra David-Neel, each an explorer in Tibet in the late 1800s.

For illustrated catalog of more than 100 outdoor titles, call toll-free 1-800-553-4453 or write:

The Mountaineers • Books
306 Second Avenue West
Seattle WA 98119